The PLO and Palestine
Abdallah Frangi

The PLO and Palestine

Abdallah Frangi

Translated by Paul Knight

Zed Books Ltd., 57 Caledonian Road, London N1 9BU.

The PLO and Palestine was originally published under the
title *PLO und Palastina: Vergangenheit und Gegenwart* by
R.G. Fischer Verlag, Frankfurt, West Germany, in 1982.
All rights reserved.

First published in English, from an authorized translation
of the German language edition, by Zed Books Ltd.,
57 Caledonian Road, London N1 9BU in 1983.

Copyright © R.G. Fischer Verlag, Frankfurt, West Germany,
1982
Translation Copyright © Zed Books Ltd., 1983

Typeset by Wayside Graphics
Cover design by Jacque Solomons
Printed by The Pitman Press, Bath

British Library Cataloguing in Publication Data

Frangi, Abdallah
   The PLO and Palestine.
   1. Palestine Liberation Organisation—History
   I. Title   II. PLO und Palastina. *English*
   322.4'2'095694   DS119.7

   ISBN 0-86232-194-8
   ISBN 0-86232-195-6 Pbk

U.S. Distributor
Biblio Distribution Center, 81 Adams Drive, Totowa,
New Jersey 07512.

Contents

Preface	i
1. Palestine Before the Hebrews	1
Canaan and Its Original Inhabitants	1
The Hebrews: A Race of Conquerors Is Born	6
2. Israel	8
The Phase of Conquest	8
Canaan under Solomon: The Decline of the Hebrew Empire	10
Judaea and Israel: The End of Judaic Rule	11
3. The New Conquerors: What Became of the Israelites?	14
The Romans: The Rise of Christianity	14
The Attitude of the Jews and the Palestinians to Palestine: A Historical Appreciation	15
4. Islam	18
Palestine: A New Situation Emerges	18
The Islamic World: Muslims, Jews and Christians	20
The Crusaders and Palestine	21
5. Palestine under Ottoman Rule	23
Fiscal and Administrative Structures	23
The Palestinian Economy	26
The Decline of the Ottoman Empire and European Colonial Policy in the Arab Region	26
The Problem of the Holy Places	28
6. Zionism	29
7. Zionism and the European Great Powers: The Disastrous Results of British Diplomatic Tricks	35
British Promises to the Arabs	37
Anglo-French Arrangements (The Sykes-Picot Agreement)	39

The Balfour Declaration	41
More British Promises to the Arabs	43
The Peace Conference and the Fate of Palestine	44
The Mandate Regime and the League of Nations Pact in International Law	47
8. Palestine under the British Mandate	**50**
The Situation in Palestine at the Beginning of the Mandate	50
The Extension of Zionist Power in Palestine	51
The Struggle for Palestine: Confrontation	56
The Second World War: The Zionists and the Persecution of Jews	64
1945–47: The USA Supports Zionism; Palestine: The Decision Is Made	69
9. The Palestine Question and the United Nations	**74**
10. Jewish Terror up to the Founding of Israel	**81**
11. The Predetermined Defeat of the Palestinians	**85**
12. The Palestinian Exodus	**89**
The State of Israel after Its Founding	89
Flight and Expulsion	91
13. Palestinian Resistance	**94**
The Palestinians Go Underground	94
The Founding of the PLO	99
Al-Fatah and the Founding of the PLO	101
The Beginning of the Armed Struggle	102
14. The Arab Defeat of 1967	**104**
The June War	104
The Second Expulsion	106
Palestinian Resistance and the Arab Defeat of 1967	107
15. The Battle of Karameh: The Turning Point in Palestinian Resistance	**110**
16. Power Changes Hands in the PLO	**113**
17. The Civil War in Jordan	**115**
The Causes of the Conflict in Jordan	115
The Palestinian Resistance Movement Is Expelled from Jordan	117
The Causes of Defeat	118
Reflections on Terror and Resistance	119

18. **Palestinian Resistance Reorganized in the Mountains of Lebanon** — 123
    The Lebanese Civil War, 1975–76 — 127
19. **The October War** — 131
    'An Eye for an Eye, a Tooth for a Tooth' — 131
    The Fourth Middle East War — 133
    The PLO in the Fourth Middle East War — 135
    A New Weapon: Oil — 136
    Political Effects of the October War — 137
20. **International Recognition of the PLO** — 139
    Recognition by the Non-Aligned Countries — 139
    The Ten-Point Programme — 140
    The Arab Summit Conference in Rabat — 142
    Yasser Arafat at the United Nations — 143
    The Palestine Liberation Organization (PLO) — 145
21. **Europe and the Arab World** — 158
    The PLO and the European-Arab Dialogue — 162
22. **Camp David: A Blind Alley** — 165
23. **Occupation or Liberation? Israel in the West Bank and Gaza** — 172
24. **Palestinian Resistance in the Occupied Territories** — 183
25. **Israel's Ideas on Peace** — 190
26. **Israel Invades Lebanon** — 197
    Israel's Longest War against the Palestinians — 197
    The PLO Leaves Beirut — 210
27. **Palestine: Confrontation or Peace?** — 216
28. **The Massacre of Sabra and Shatila** — 222
29. **The 16th Palestinian National Council** — 241
    A Guide to Further Reading — 254

Charts
1. Structure of the PLO — 146
2. Structure of the PLO — 147
3. Structure of the PLO — 148
4. Structure of the PLO — 149
5. The Palestinian People — 150

Maps

1.	The Egyptian Empire in Antiquity	3
2.	The Kingdom of West Africa in Antiquity	5
3.	Palestine Under Hebrew Occupation	12
4.	Turkish Administrative Districts in Greater Syria	24
5.	The Division of the Middle East by the Sykes-Picot Agreement	36
6.	Boundaries of the Arab Empire Awarded to Sherif Hussein in the McMahon Plan	38
7.	The World Zionist Organization Plan for the Versailles Peace Conference (1919)	40
8.	Palestine Under the British Mandate	46
9.	The Beginning of the Establishment of Israeli Settlements in Palestine	53
10.	The UN Partition of Palestine	77
11.	Jewish Settlements, Planned Jewish State and Remainder of the British Mandate	83
12.	Settlement Blocks Mark the Land the Israeli Labour Party Plans to Keep	195

Preface

Over the years, in lectures and discussions and in talks with journalists and politicians I have frequently been asked about the history of the PLO and the history of Palestine.

One of the most common and important questions concerned the recognition of Israel by the PLO and the Palestinians. Another issue often raised was, could resistance and the use of terror be justified or not? Why, I was often asked, did the Arab states not provide a home for the Palestinians? Why did the Palestinians not integrate into other Arab countries? What political solutions did the PLO and the Palestinians accept or aspire to? How could a compromise or peace be achieved?

I have long been preoccupied by these questions and it was the wish to answer them which finally prompted me to write this book.

The Palestinian conflict has been in the forefront of international politics for decades and has often kept the world in suspense – in religious, political and historical terms.

The confrontation between the Israelis and the Palestinians in Lebanon in the summer of 1982 claimed the attention of the world for several weeks and led to intensive debates in the United Nations General Assembly and Security Council.

Since 1947, when it decided to partition Palestine, the United Nations has been constantly involved with the Palestinian problem.

Even under the British mandate, Palestine was the subject of debates at the League of Nations. Disputes, riots and rebellions have been rife in Palestine since the 1920s and 1930s, when Palestine became the goal of thousands of European Jewish immigrants; confrontation has continued up to the present. But only today, after more than three decades, has the conflict been resolved into its original elements. The Israeli invasion in the summer of 1982 was the longest war against the Palestinians and the Arab world in Israel's history, and the first in which the Palestinians fought without the support of the other Arab states. The PLO survived this war – even without Arab support. Today the confrontation is between Israel and Palestine – as the war in Lebanon emphatically underlined.

This fact was extremely displeasing to Israeli politicians. Since 1948 they had ignored the Palestinian problem and presented the conflict as one between Israel and the Arab world, totally bypassing the Palestinians; but the essence of the problem cannot simply be ignored. Even after the withdrawal of the fedayeen from Beirut the question remains: where do the Palestinians go now? This question has assumed an even greater urgency since the end of the war.

The Palestinians are again being dispersed: to Syria and Jordan, to Tunisia and Yemen, Iraq and Sudan. But the route back to Palestine remains barred, and this reveals the nature of the tragedy of the Palestinian people since expulsion first began.

In 1948, the Palestinians were dispersed to the four corners of the world. Israel believed then that it could solve the Palestinian problem by violence. In 1982, Israel once again resorted to force; but the fedayeen withdrawal from Beirut was no exodus – the fedayeen were not defeated. With their kalashnikovs in their hands and giving the victory sign, they left Beirut in convoy past wildly cheering crowds and to the sound of gun salutes. Military resistance had brought about a political victory.

After the war, President Mitterrand of France said: 'The PLO is the only Palestinian military organization I know which has the right to fight.' Austrian Chancellor Bruno Kreisky, a mediator in the Middle East conflict for many years, said:

> The tragedy of the battle of Beirut is that the PLO at war has found a degree of recognition which it was refused when it was pursuing peaceable goals. Today, everyone is talking about Arafat and the PLO – they know that they have to negotiate with them.

Kreisky's attitude to Israel was absolutely plain:

> I want nothing more to do with this Israel . . . . I am no longer somewhere in the middle. I have taken sides – taken sides with the persecuted and the oppressed – in accordance with my socialist principles.

Various other European states issued statements to the effect that the solution in Lebanon did not represent a solution of the Palestinian problem as such.

Even US Secretary of State George Shultz – while carefully avoiding the term 'self-determination' – said that 'the most important point is that the Palestinian people should have a voice to determine the conditions in which it should be governed'.

The world was finally forced to realize that there can be no peace in the Middle East without the participation of the Palestinians and without recognition of their national rights. The Palestinian problem cannot be solved by military means – as the three decades of confrontation since the foundation of Israel have shown.

In a conversation with Ben-Gurion, the late Nahum Goldmann said:

You know what the Talmud says: 'The worst thing about a sin is that it brings other sins with it.' And so the worst thing about a war is that it brings other wars in its wake. So for decades we have had wars and no peace.

I hope this book will contribute to a better understanding of the history and aspirations of the Palestinian people. I hope, too, that just and lasting peace will come to that part of the world. It was this hope which largely prompted the writing of this book.

Abdallah Frangi

1. Palestine Before the Hebrews

Canaan and its Original Inhabitants

The people of the Mediterranean

The founders of the Jewish State in Palestine argued that they were, after all, merely returning to the 'land of their fathers', to the Promised Land. The idea of the 'Promised Land' is inextricably bound up with the Jewish belief that they are the 'Chosen People' to whom God promised the land of Palestine more than 3,400 years ago. Here, however, we are not concerned with religious convictions. We simply wish to examine the idea of the 'land of their fathers' in legal and in historical terms. The question is: *whose* ancestors were the original inhabitants of Palestine?

As early as 4,000 years before Christ, Palestine was a land coveted by conquerors; geographically it occupied an extremely favourable position – at the crossroads of all the major civilizations of the ancient world. The caravans of the Mediterranean countries passed through, and in the Pharaonic era Egypt did a thriving trade with Sumeria, Akkad, Assyria and Babylon via Palestine. (These were the four great civilizations which developed in Mesopotamia – now Iraq – in the pre-Christian era.) Whoever ruled Palestine controlled the access to the Mediterranean through Asia and Arabia. More fertile, and blessed with a better climate than Egypt or the desert areas of Arabia, Palestine was bound to become the object of its neighbours' desires. Over thousands of years, the Sumerians, the Akkadians, the Assyrians, the Babylonians, the Hittites from the north, the Midianites from the south and the Philistines, constantly fought to gain control of this territory.

Biblical tradition has it that Adam, the first man, was created somewhere between the Mediterranean and the Red Sea. Be that as it may, there is no doubt that impressive and distinct cultures developed and flourished in this area – as historical and archaeological research has proved. It is also undisputed that this region was the cradle of the three great monotheistic religions. The sacred writings of Christianity, Judaism and of Islam, therefore, provide important information about the original history of this land.

The oldest known version of monotheism was that practised by the

Egyptian king, Echnaton. The oldest religion to worship one god instead of many gods and idols as was the common practice in the ancient world is the Jewish religion. From a historical and sociological point of view, the Old Testament provides valuable material on political developments in Palestine at this time. The findings of historians and the Bible provide the historical sources in this book, although of course controversial facts are examined in the light of the results of empirical research.

The first book of Moses, chapter 1, says that: 'In the beginning, God created heaven and earth.' By chapter 5, God is already disappointed with mankind. His creation, a nomad, by the name of Noah, is also disappointed with mankind. Noah originally migrated from the Arabian peninsula to settle in Ur in Chaldaea (north west Mesopotamia, now Iraq) some time between 7000 and 5000 BC. Like all the nomads who migrated from the Arab regions, Noah was a Semite. Strictly speaking, originally all the Arab tribes were Semites, including all Jews whose descendants never left Palestine and still live in Palestine today – as opposed to Jews who migrated to Palestine.

In Chaldaea, where Noah's tribe lived, there was a flourishing urban culture, which Noah disliked and to which he could not accustom himself. He warns his people of an impending disaster, which soon occurs: Ur is flooded by the Euphrates. In the Bible, this flood is depicted as the Deluge or Great Flood, God's punishment for man's wickedness.* Noah and his family escape the flood and are saved, and according to the Bible, Noah then made a covenant with God. For those of the Jewish faith, this means that Noah's descendants are to be regarded as the chosen people.

Noah had three sons: Sem, Ham and Yapheth. Ham's descendants were called Hamites, Sem's descendants were called Semites. Later, all of Noah's descendants were given the name of one of his sons, as is still the practice in Arab countries today; this son was Sem, Noah's descendants were thus known as Semites. Noah disowned Ham, whose son, Canaan, then migrated to Palestine, which from then on was known as Canaan.

Canaan's sons founded the tribes of the Canaanites, the Amorites (later the Syrians) and the Samaritans. Canaan's brother, Mizraim, founded the tribes of the Anamites and the Philistines, who were later to become a great seafaring race. The descendants of Canaan's brother Kush founded the Semitic dynasties of Akkad, Assur and Niniveh. Thus originated the great civilizations of Assyria and Babylon. Only the

---

*The legend of the Great Flood originally came from the Sumerians, who believed that the regular floods which afflicted their land were punishments from God. Like the modern Iraqis, the Sumerians built dykes and canals to regulate the waters of the Euphrates. The great flood of Sumerian legend may have occurred in the Stone Age, though it is more probable that the legend refers to the natural disaster which led to the formation of the Dead Sea and the Jordan valley.

Palestine Before the Hebrews

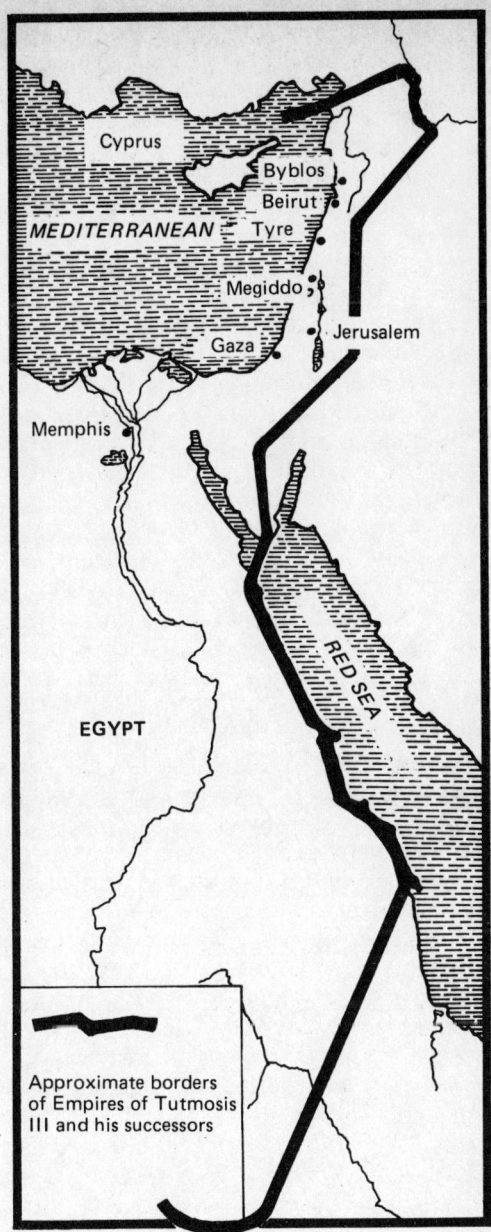

The Egyptian Empire in Antiquity

descendants of Canaan remained in Palestine and over the years they mixed with other nomadic races who passed through Palestine.

Historians still disagree about the precise dates of these events. It is, however, generally accepted that the land of Canaan was inhabited as early as 7000 BC and that the Canaanites settled there in the late Stone Age. Archaeologists today work on the assumption that Palestine was first settled before the late Stone Age. Early Stone Age finds indicate that the region was inhabited by Neanderthal man, and the Bible also proves that the Canaanites lived there in the late Stone Age. It seems that they first settled in towns, for example in Saida and Gaza, in Sichem (today's Nablus), Meggido, Jericho, Beersheba, Akka and Jerusalem. Rudimentary knives and forks have been found near Beersheba. The Canaanites' houses were made of clay and had flat roofs, as they do today. They were usually grouped around a watering place; the towns, often protected by imposing walls, contained castles and temples. Even at this early stage, the people were beginning to practise agriculture and cattle raising, as finds of ploughs, for example, have proved. Roads and other permanent installations testify to the fact that the original population was for a long period undisturbed in its possession of the land. Viniculture was first practised there probably around 4000 BC. The Hebrews later made rich findings there[1] and spoke of a huge population − all of which indicates that the Canaanites had reached an advanced stage of development. The Canaanites worshipped Baal, a powerful, choleric god. Egyptian reliefs of this period give an idea of what Canaanite towns of this period looked like.

For the period between 2000 and 1000 BC, historians have only a few inscriptions in the proto-Canaanite language to go on. It was here that the alphabetic script was invented but it was not perfected until around the 10th Century BC. However, in Syria, where the Akkadian cuneiform script was used, valuable material has been found on the political and social structure prevalent in Canaan at that time. It indicates, for example, that Canaanite society was organized in estates and that a system of guilds existed. Archaeological finds have shown that the Canaanites carried on a thriving trade with their neighbours. The Canaanites were working copper around 4000 BC; and 1,000 years later they were working bronze. The land was first conquered by the Egyptian Pharaohs around 2800 BC. Individual finds indicate, however, that Egyptian influence first began to make itself felt in Palestine even before 3000 BC. The first period of Egyptian rule lasted 350 years, and the Egyptians later reoccupied Palestine. The political upheavals of the time led to major ethnographic changes. Non-Semitic tribes such as the Hurrites increasingly gained influence and a cultural symbiosis with the original Semitic population soon took place. The Canaanite language and religion, however, continued to dominate. The Egyptians remained in Palestine − with some interruptions − until the 12th Century BC. Meanwhile the Hittites (in 1490 BC), the Amorites and the Philistines attempted to oust the

Palestine Before the Hebrews

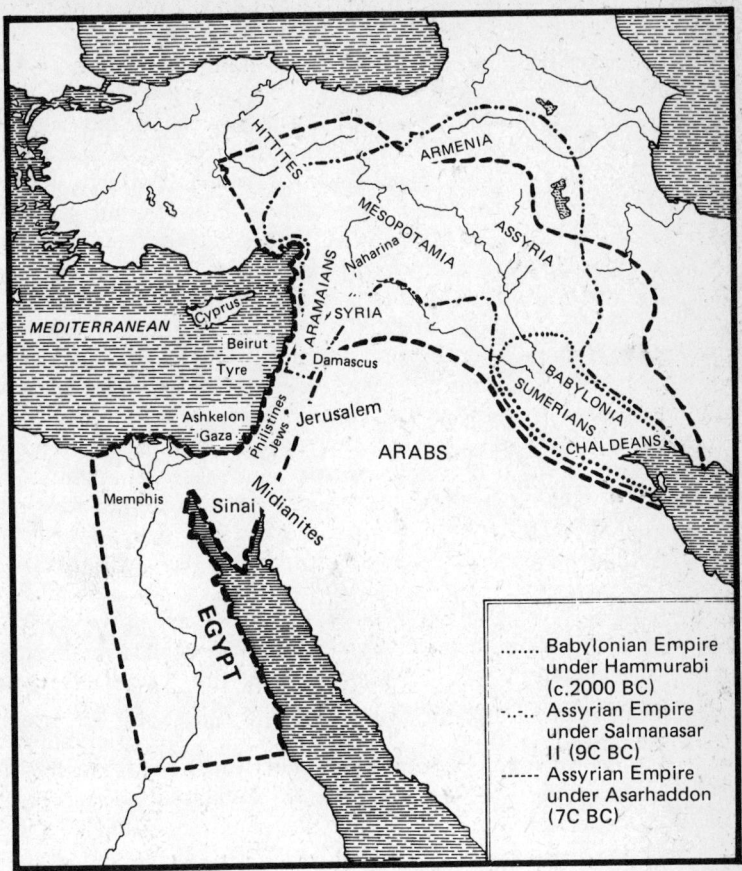

The Kingdom of West Asia in Antiquity

Egyptians and gain control of Palestine for themselves. The Canaanites, too, rebelled on several occasions against the occupying Egyptian forces. Driven out by the Egyptians, the Philistines settled in the coastal strips. Culturally, the Philistines were completely absorbed by the Canaanite civilization, but they gave the land the name which it bears today (Philistin = Palestine).

So much for the history of one branch of Noah's family, the branch which settled in Palestine. But what became of Sem's descendants? Let us return to Chaldaea and take up their story from there.

The Hebrews: A Race of Conquerors is Born

One of Sem's descendants was Abraham, the first great patriarch mentioned in the Bible. While the descendants of Sem mixed with non-Semitic tribes, Abraham was convinced that he was one of God's elect. Like the rest of his tribe, he lived in Ur in Mesopotamia. The Bible says that God appeared to Abraham and promised to give his descendants the land of Canaan. Probably some time between the 20th and the 19th Century BC, Abraham migrated to Canaan and settled in Sichem (today's Nablus). At the same time, many Semitic Bedouins from the Arabian steppe pushed forward into Palestine. But the inhabitants of the country distrusted this 'man from the other bank', whom they called an 'Ibrim', from which the modern word 'Hebrew' is derived. The Hebrews are, therefore, Semites from Mesopotamia. Their dream was to conquer the land of Canaan. Abraham constantly quarrelled with the Canaanites. He migrated to Beersheba and then to Egypt. He had a son named Ismail by his Egyptian maid and a son named Isaac by his wife from Chaldaea. Abraham's brother Nahor stayed in Mesopotamia; his descendants were the Aramaeans, whose language Jesus spoke. Lot, the son of Abraham's brother Nahor, founded the tribes of the Moabites and Ammonites. Abraham himself moved back to Hebron in Canaan, firmly believing that God would give that land to his descendants. However, Abraham showed no willingness whatever to integrate into Canaan society. In the Bible he constantly referred to a 'foreign land'. He forbade his son Isaac to marry a Canaanite woman. Abba Eban, in his book *This Is My People*, says that even at that time the Hebrews of Mesopotamia had been strongly influenced by the Sumerians, the Babylonians and the Akkadians. Isaac married an Aramaean wife, but lived in peace with the people of Canaan. He, too, had a sense of divine mission. His son Esau twice married Hurrite women. Isaac's son Jacob, however, felt it was his duty to continue the 'covenant with God'. His descendants would later conquer Canaan. God appeared to him, too, and repeated His promise. Jacob later called himself 'Israel'. His son Judah married a Canaanite; Jacob's son Joseph was sold as a slave to merchants who took him to Egypt, where he won the favour of the Pharaoh, married an Egyptian woman and became rich and powerful. When famine broke out in Palestine, Joseph brought his brothers to Egypt. The 12 brothers then founded the 12 tribes of Israel.

From c.1400 BC, under the next Pharaoh – historians think this was probably Rameses II – the Hebrews were oppressed. It is said that the Hyscites – rivals with the Egyptians for control of Palestine – formed an alliance with the tribe of Abraham and that they used the Hebrews to help them in their efforts to dominate Canaan. (This is a familiar tactic throughout history. One need only look at recent examples of major powers intervening in regional conflicts and gaining influence in the region by supporting one party or another.) This might also explain why the Pharaohs enslaved the Hebrews: to ensure that they retained power in Palestine.

The Bible tells the rest of the story. Moses, a Hebrew of the tribe of Israel, believed that it was his mission to fulfil the divine prophecy. He organized the flight from Egypt and led the Israelites into Canaan, the 'Promised Land'. God appeared to Moses and said:

> And I am come down to deliver them out of the hand of the Egyptians and to bring them up out of that land unto a good land and a large, unto a land flowing with milk and honey; unto the place of the Canaanites and the Hittites, and the Amorites and the Perizzites, and the Hivites and the Jebusites . . .[2]

This fertile land was Palestine, which was inhabited by the numerous tribes mentioned in the Bible. The Hebrews now set about conquering this land.

Notes

1. Moses IV, 13:33; V, 2:10.
2. Moses II, 3:8.

2. Israel

The Phase of Conquest

> 'When the Lord thy God has destroyed the peoples whose land the Lord, thy God will give you, that thou mayst live there and dwell in their towns and houses . . .'[1]

While the 12 tribes of Israel led by Moses were fleeing from Egypt, the Philistines and the Egyptians were at war in Canaan. After their defeat, the Philistines settled in the coastal strips in Palestine, especially in the towns of Gaza, Ashdod, Ascalon, Gath and Etron. The Egyptians left them in peace, hoping that the Philistines would further Egyptian interests by preventing uprisings by the Canaanites. After Rameses III, the Egyptian regime in Canaan collapsed. But new conquerors were now waiting to replace the Egyptians as the occupying force in Canaan.

The Hebrew tribes probably reached Canaan around the end of the 13th Century BC. For generations, they had lived as nomads in the Sinai desert.[2] Apart from the Bible, there are very few historical sources on this period in the desert: compared with the great historical events of this period, the activities of 12 nomadic tribes who spent a few generations roaming about the desert are not of great interest. In contrast with the civilizations of Sumeria, Akkad, Babylon and Egypt, there is little of note to be said about the culture of these nomads. The historical dimension is provided only by the Bible, which describes in detail the 'divine mission' which these tribes are to accomplish:

> And I will send my fear before thee, and will destroy all the people to whom thou shalt come, and I will make all thine enemies turn their backs unto thee.
>
> And I will send hornets before thee, which shall drive out the Hivite, the Canaanite and the Hittite from before thee.
>
> I will not drive them out . . . in one year; lest the land become desolate, and the beast of the field multiply against thee.
>
> By little and little I will drive them out from before thee, until thou be increased, and inherit the land.

> And I will set thy bounds from the Red Sea even unto the sea of the Philistines and from the desert unto the river: for I will deliver the inhabitants of the land into your hand; and thou shalt drive them out before thee.
>
> Thou shalt make no covenant with them, nor with their gods.
>
> They shall not dwell in thy land, lest they make thee sin against me: for if thou serve their gods, it will surely be a snare unto thee.[3]

Looked at coolly and without religious glorification, this means that the Hebrews wished to conquer a foreign land. And they did so. They began with raids and attacks on Canaanite farmers, and followed with campaigns of conquest against the tribes there. The Hebrews came up against 450 fortified villages in the Negev in the south, so they crossed the Jordan. Their spy network played an important part in the success of their operations. First they conquered Jericho, then Nablus and then Jerusalem.* The Hebrews, led by the conqueror Joshua, destroyed the flourishing urban culture they found in Canaan. They drove out or massacred the indigenous population and then settled, mainly in the fertile valleys in the north and in the mountains. Canaan was at that time an alliance of city states. The Hebrews were not able to take immediate control of the entire country. They were unable to occupy numerous areas, including the coastal strip, which remained in the hands of the Philistines. In the course of the next century, the Hebrews came increasingly under Philistine rule. The Philistines were now the Hebrews' bitterest enemies. The Bible tells the story of this enmity in the Book of Judges, especially in chapter 16. The judges are, in the biblical sense, 'saviours' who saved the Hebrew tribes in their hour of need. The best-known story is that of Samson, who lived among the Philistines in Gaza and was constantly attempting to conquer them. He fell in love with Delilah, who persuaded him to reveal the secret of his prodigious strength and then betrayed it to the Philistines. The Philistines took Samson prisoner. When he was brought before the ruler of the Philistines, he pulled down the pillars of the temple, burying himself and the entire court of the Philistines beneath the ruins.

Other tribes and towns, notably the town of Meggido near the coast, resisted the Hebrews for generations. The Israelites had great difficulty in conquering the valleys because, as the Bible recounts, the valley dwellers had wagons and weapons of iron. At various times, the Israelites had to fight against the king of Mesopotamia, then against the Moabites, then a Canaanite king, the Midianites and the Amorites and again against the Philistines.[4] The Hebrew leader Saul died on the battlefield fighting against the Philistines. Towards the end of the second millennium BC, Aramaean tribes pushed into Palestine and their language replaced Babylonian. These Aramaeans also fought against the Hebrews. Saul's

---

*Jerusalem was originally called Jebus, after a king of the Jebusites, a tribe which lived there.

successor, David, once a Philistine vassal, now united all the Hebrew-occupied areas of Canaan under his control. He defeated the Egyptians, who were then occupying Jerusalem, and founded the first Hebrew empire around 1000 BC.

Canaan under Solomon: The Decline of the Hebrew Empire

David ruled this newly-founded empire for 40 years – from 1010 to 970 BC. His son, King Solomon (970–930 BC), completed the process of unification. Under these two kings, the Israelites gradually settled the land. Under Solomon, the situation worsened. The clashes with the Aramaeans increased and intensified. But it was not only enemies from without who threatened the new rulers of Canaan. Problems arose in Canaan itself – the problems which always arise when a people is ruled by a foreign occupying force. Moreover, under Solomon many Hebrews relapsed into paganism. Numerous uprisings occurred. The Edom region (Negev desert) broke away from the empire, as did Damascus. On the other hand, Hebrew culture flourished under Solomon. The Hebrews had originally been nomadic tribes and bands of robbers. They lived in tents, until the Canaanites taught them how to build houses of brick and stone.

The Phoenicians, who then ruled the territory which is now Lebanon, helped to build and supplied the wood for the temple of Solomon. From the Phoenicians, the Hebrews also learnt how to work metal. The Hebrews never had an independent culture of their own. They owed their cultural development and refinement solely to their contact with the mixed culture of Canaan, which at that time was extremely cosmopolitan. However, greater Israel was not destined to survive for long. Solomon ruled for 33 years, and his death marked the end of the dream of greater Israel. The empire disintegrated, partly on account of internal disputes among the Hebrew tribes. According to biblical tradition, the collapse of the empire was a punishment from God, a sign of his anger at their electing kings. This does not sound very convincing, seeing that God was supposed to have promised them this great empire in the first place. At all events, the Bible gives a detailed account of the struggles among the Hebrews. According to the Book of Judges, the Hebrew tribes were constantly being attacked and driven out by indigenous tribes. 'But the children of Israel did evil in the sight of the Lord. And the Lord raised up Eglon, the king of the Moabites, and made him strong against them.'[5] Abraham's successors were never able to conquer the Promised Land definitively.

Judaea and Israel: The End of Judaic Rule

As a result of the collapse of greater Israel, ten tribes settled in the north of the country and called it the kingdom of Israel; the other two tribes founded the kingdom of Judaea in the south. From the names of these two kingdoms are derived the words 'Jews' and 'Israelites', denoting those who practise the Jewish faith. What were the frontiers of the Jewish sphere of influence?

Looking at the map, we see Judaea in the south and Israel in the north. The Mediterranean strip was ruled by the Philistines and, further north, in what is now the coast of Lebanon, the Phoenicians ruled. West of the Jordan, to the south lived the Moabites and the Ammonites, further north lived the tribes of Gilead and Mannasse. The area north of the Jordan was ruled by the Aramaeans and the Negev desert by the Edomites. The Sinai desert came within the Midianites' sphere of influence. The tribes on the west bank of the Jordan were at times attacked and their land occupied by Hebrew tribes, but the occupation was short-lived; the Aramaeans also occupied Hebrew territory at times. The internal disputes between Hebrew tribes which continued after division often invited and facilitated intervention by other powers. Egypt and Damascus then took the opportunity to support one or other of the disputing parties as part of their struggle for mastery in the region. Judaea and Israel both paid tribute to Damascus at different times. There could be no independent kingdoms with safe frontiers anywhere from the Nile to the Euphrates. Indeed, such frontiers never existed between Judaea and Israel at any time from the beginning of the Hebrew occupation.

The internal struggles were caused largely by the social situation in Hebrew-occupied Canaan. The two kingdoms were Jewish in character and the indigenous population had to pay tribute to the Hebrew rulers. In both Judaea and Israel, a Hebrew aristocracy ruled over the indigenous population. But the structure of this indigenous population remained intact, if only because the Hebrew aristocrats avoided any contact with them.

By the 8th Century BC, the Hebrew tribes were so weak that foreign powers seized the opportunity to end their occupation of Canaan. In the north were the powerful Assyrians, who had overthrown the Babylonians and now ruled Babylon, and had pushed forward to the Mediterranean around 1160 BC. By the 8th Century BC, they controlled what is now Iraq and parts of present-day Syria. In 722 BC, the Assyrians attacked Israel. They destroyed the power of the ten tribes of Israel and took them in captivity to Babylon, where in the course of time the majority of them were assimilated with the local population.

Thanks to its separate status, Judaea managed to avoid the same fate as Israel; it paid tribute to the Assyrians, who then left – for the time being. But in 586 BC, the Assyrian King Nebuchadnezzar II conquered the kingdom of Judaea. The temple of Jerusalem, symbol of Hebrew

The PLO and Palestine

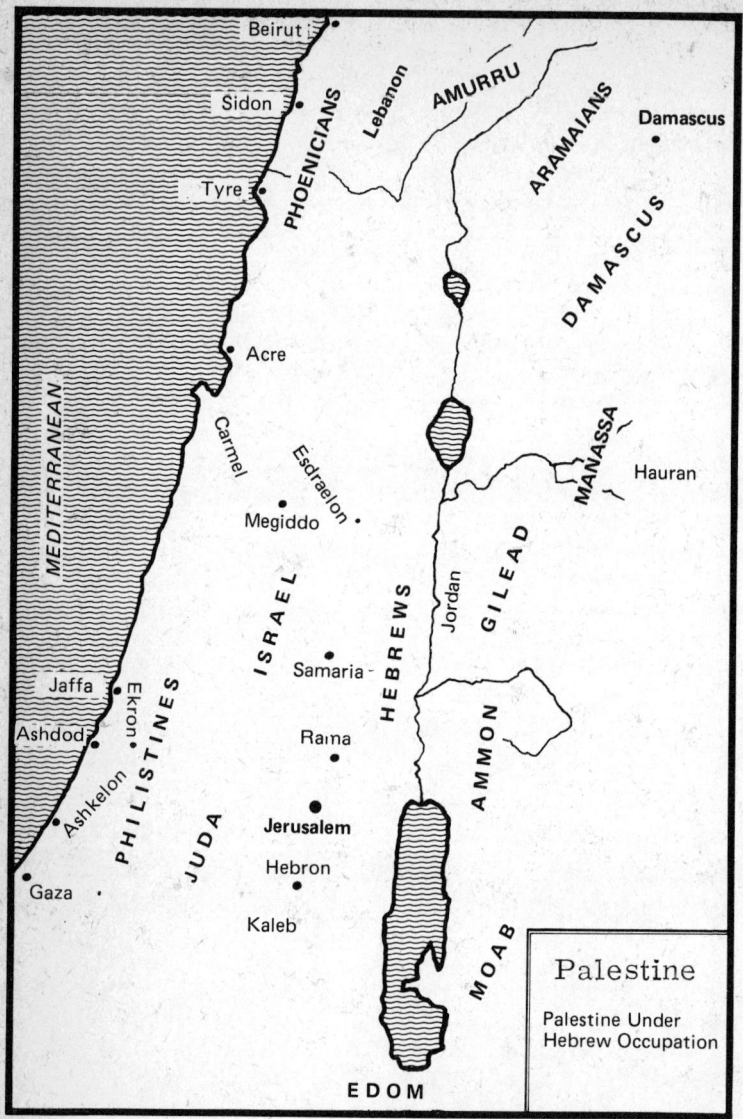

power, was destroyed and the Hebrew occupation of Palestine ended as violently as it had begun. The power of the Hebrews, which began in 1000 BC with unification under David, came to an end in 586 BC, when the Assyrians conquered Jerusalem. The Palestinians were rid of one conqueror; but the next one had already arrived in their land.

Notes

1. Moses V, 19:1.
2. Fischer, *Weltgeschichte Vol. III; Die Altorientalischen Reiche II* (Fischer Taschenbuchverlag, 1974), p. 205.
3. Exodus, 23:5, 27–33.
4. Judges.
5. Ibid., 3:12.

3. The New Conquerors: What Became of the Israelites?

The Romans: The Rise of Christianity

In the next centuries, one conqueror followed hard on the heels of another in Palestine. In 538 BC, less than 50 years after the Assyrian conquest, the Persians under Cyrus II occupied Babylon and Palestine. The Persians allowed the Hebrews to return from Babylon to Palestine and rebuild their temple in Jerusalem. But only a few took up this offer, most of them having settled in Babylon. Persian rule ended in 334 BC, when Alexander the Great conquered Palestine. Palestine was under Greek occupation when a Hebrew uprising occurred, in about 150 BC. For a brief interval the Hebrews now ruled part of the country. Then, in 63 BC, the Roman General Pompey conquered Palestine and occupied Jerusalem. Palestine became a Roman province. At this time, about half the Hebrews lived in Palestine, the rest being scattered about the Middle East. A large Jewish community was now established in Babylon. In Palestine itself, the Jews remained divided by internal quarrels. Those who returned from exile in Babylon accused Jews in Samaria – the Samaritans who had stayed in the country – of mixing with other races. The Samaritans replied that the Babylonian Jews had renounced their faith because they now spoke Aramaic, the language of the Babylonians, instead of Hebrew. In fact, the Hebrew language virtually died out during the period of Roman rule in Palestine.

For the Hebrews and other peoples of Palestine, the period of Roman rule was one of suffering. There were numerous uprisings, all suppressed. Lack of unity and solidarity among the people of Palestine frustrated all attempts to shake off Roman rule. The Pharisees and scribes collaborated with the Roman occupiers; the aristocracy, the high priests, could only maintain their privileges by obedience to the Romans.

This was the situation in Palestine when a man of Hebrew descent by the name of Jesus stepped on to the stage of history. Jesus spoke Aramaic. His ancestors, like Abraham, probably came from Mesopotamia. He tried to unite Palestinian society and attacked the corruption which had led to the decline of the Mosaic faith. This was the first attempt to unite all the tribes and especially the poorer classes. The fact that he spoke

Aramaic must be interpreted as emphasizing his distance from the Hebrew ruling class, which collaborated with the Romans. Jesus attempted to establish belief in God on new foundations. He refused to recognize any power but that of God – not even that of the Romans. This cost him his life. Some sections of the population now dissociated themselves from him, and the High Priest Caiphas betrayed him to the Romans. Jesus died on the cross, as did all rebels at that time.

This was the beginning of the Christian era. The faith proclaimed by Jesus spread, replacing the religion of Abraham in the region. New uprisings in Palestine followed, and Jerusalem was again destroyed in AD 132. Soon the Hebrews were again a minority in the land. Most of them were concentrated in and around Galilee. Others were absorbed into other nations, becoming assimilated or Christianized. The majority of them now lived in the Mediterranean area: in Babylon, Egypt, Syria, Asia Minor, Greece and Rome. But there were many foreign converts to the Jewish faith; even in Rome, many people were converted to Judaism. In Palestine, the Christian faith went from strength to strength. Soon resistance by Palestinian converts to Christianity petered out, probably because St. Paul preached that the faithful should submit to worldly powers.[1]

By AD 300 the Jews were a spent force, intellectually and politically, in Palestine. The Babylonian Jews became the spearhead of Judaism and economic difficulties led many Jews to emigrate from Palestine. Many historians have come to the conclusion that the Jews at this period were neither annihilated nor persecuted.[2] The first difficulties did not come until the Roman-Byzantine era.

The Attitude of the Jews and the Palestinians to Palestine: A Historical Appreciation

Despite the turbulent history of the land of Palestine and the frequent foreign occupations, there has been a fundamental, uninterrupted continuity in the original population of the country. Wars and occupations could not drive the descendants of the Canaanites, the Amorites, the Jebusites and the Philistines from the land. Of the 12 tribes of Israel which conquered the country, only two remained after the period of exile in Babylon; the others were gradually assimilated in Babylon. Those who returned to Palestine mixed with the original Palestinian population or left the country later, during the Roman occupation. Even before Christ, only a few remained true to the Mosaic faith, an élite consisting of scribes and aristocrats. This can be clearly established by a careful reading of the New Testament version of Jesus's life and by a study of the social conditions prevailing at the time. Jesus evidently wished to reform the old faith and unite the whole people in the Christian faith. There can be no doubt that Jesus tried to end the rivalries between the Hebrew tribes and between the Hebrews and the rest of the population.

The Jewish community was soon dispersed, the majority emigrating to Mediterranean or Arab countries. Their State had been of short duration. The Hebrews had been merely one occupying force among many. The Palestinians, on the other hand, remained in the country for thousands of years.

The few Jews who remained in Palestine kept their religion and are the only Israelis who can rightfully call themselves the descendants of Abraham *and* Palestinians. But what about the others? Does a common faith constitute sufficient grounds for a community to be called a 'race'? This question must be left to historians. But the claim that all members of the Jewish race are descendants of Abraham and therefore have a right to Palestine is untenable. If biblical tradition is to be believed, many Palestinians were descendants of Abraham – including many who were not Hebrews. Abraham, it must be emphasized, did not come from Palestine and the Hebrew community in Palestine was dispersed. But quite apart from this, we have to consider the Jews throughout the world from an ethnographic viewpoint. According to Raoul Roy, only 10% of all the Jews in the world are Semites. The rest are either a mixture of Semitic and other races or else are converts to Judaism.

To give one example: in 740 AD, the king of the Casars, and his princes and subjects were converted to Judaism. Asiatic Jews who were originally Semites have mixed with other races over the centuries. It is impossible for Jews from Ethiopia, Poland, Russia, China, Spain or Yemen to describe themselves with any justification as members of a single race.

However, the diaspora or dispersion of Jews to many parts of the world did not destroy their connection with Palestine. The corner-stone of this connection was the Jewish faith. And the ghetto life into which Jews were forced by the professional restrictions imposed on them only served to intensify this special relationship. Their connection with Palestine was, and for centuries remained, religious. It was an attachment in no way different from that of an Indonesian Muslim to Mecca or of an Irish Catholic to Bethlehem or Rome.

None the less, this religion, the Jewish faith, was to suffice to found a political and ideological movement: Zionism.

The ghettoization and persecution of Jews in Europe helped to bring about the founding of the Zionist movement and, indeed, was an important factor in its success in 1948. Zionism sowed the seeds which were to lead to a repetition of a historical confrontation: the descendants of the Canaanites now faced the descendants of the Hebrew conquerors: Palestinians against Zionists.

Notes

1. See Raoul Roy, *Jésus, Guerrier de l'indépendance* (Montreal, 1975), pp. 369–71.
2. Avi-Yonah Baron, *Geschichte der Juden im Zeitalter des Talmuds, in den Tagen von Rom und Byzanz III* (1962), p. 76.

4. Islam

Palestine: A New Situation Emerges

By the end of Byzantine rule, the population structure of Palestine was extremely complex as there had been considerable interbreeding. But the already existent Arab character of Palestine was further reinforced by the Islamic conquest. Even before the conquest, many of the inhabitants of Palestine had come from the Arabian peninsula and now another wave of Arab immigrants flooded into the land. These immigrants came into the country during the Islamic campaigns and were inspired by their faith in the prophet Muhammad, who was born c.AD 570 in Mecca. Muhammad converted the entire Arabian peninsula to belief in one God. But the implications of his teachings went far beyond religion. Islam was to influence the overall political structure of the Arab world and to transform the destiny of nations as far apart as India and Spain. In 633, Muhammad's followers conquered the Persian empire and in 634 they reached Palestine, where the population welcomed them as liberators. The Palestinian population whole-heartedly supported and believed in Islam.

The reasons for this lie in the country's social and ethnic structure. The Palestinian population had, from the earliest times, been Arab, though at this time there were still a few Jews living in the country. Most Arabs had been converted to Christianity. The population was therefore predominantly monotheistic. Under Roman and Byzantine rule, they had all – without exception – been oppressed. The excesses of the Roman emperors – including the Christian convert Constantine – have been historically documented. As the numerous uprisings under Roman rule indicate, the population longed to shake off the Roman tyrants.

Economic factors also played a part. The Palestinians had always traded with the Arabian peninsula. The social structure, too, made Palestine a fertile soil for the realization of the Islamic dream: the establishment of a centrally-ruled Arab-Islamic empire. In Muhammad's day, states as now defined in international law were unknown in the Arab world. Only Egypt under the Pharaohs could claim to be a centralized State, but when Pharaonic rule ended, the centralized system soon crumbled with it. This Pharaonic past, however, helps to explain why Egyptian nationalism has always, right up to the present day, insisted on its special position in the Islamic world.

In south Arabia, however, except in the settled urban and agricultural communities of Yemen, authority was in the hands of the tribes and families: the blood relationship was decisive, and every tribe had its own laws. In north Arabia, including Palestine, the people had long ceased to be nomadic. The majority lived in towns and agricultural communities. There had never been a fixed state structure: the Roman division of the land into provinces had not succeeded in destroying the tribal structures. The Hebrew conquerors had also had a tribal structure, and these tribes ruled only briefly over areas which were ill-defined and constantly changing. Monotheism, the numerous foreign occupations and the fact that the population was settled meant that the bonds between the various tribes were much closer than in south Arabia. In addition, there were legal and administrative structures which partially replaced the limited tribal system.

All these factors meant that it was easy to persuade the Palestinians to embrace the ideas of the Islamic-Arab nation. Palestine's integration into the Arab and Islamic empire meant that the old tribal structures were gradually effaced. Palestinian society was soon thoroughly Arab and Islamic in character. And for the first time a genuine Arab community arose in Palestine. For political and religious purposes it was part of the greater Islamic community but, none the less, it had its own autonomous administrative structure. Of course Palestine was not an independent State in the modern sense. Such states did not exist in the Islamic era, as Islam aspired to supra-national unity in its sphere of influence.

However, Palestine was regarded as an entity under Islam. This is illustrated by the fact that the name of Palestine is one of the few which Islam did not erase from the Arabic language. In those days, Palestine included parts of Syria and stretched from south Lebanon to the Sinai. Furthermore, Palestine occupied a place of honour in the Islamic community – for according to tradition it was in Jerusalem that Muhammad ascended into heaven. In 660, Muawiya was crowned caliph in Jerusalem. The famous Caliph Suleiman, who was very popular in Palestine, made Ramallah his residence. Caliph Abdel Malik ordered the famous Umar Mosque to be built on the site of the temple in Jerusalem. The Christians offered Caliph Umar the right to pray in their church, but he refused on the grounds that he did not wish to imply disrespect for the holy places of the Christians. Palestine was now as important for the Islamic community as Mecca and Medina and it has remained so, for these and other reasons, until the present day.

Under the Umayyads, the first dynasty of caliphs, socio-economic structures in Palestine developed rapidly. The caliphs reformed and vastly improved the age-old system of irrigation, and this in turn led to more intensive and productive agriculture.

The Islamic World: Muslims, Jews and Christians

At its height, Islamic influence extended over the entire Arab world and indeed much further: from Asia Minor to India, from North Africa to Spain and southern France. The residence of the Umayyads was Damascus, and it was from there that the first caliphs organized the first great state structure founded on a community of believers. A central government was set up which appointed independent governments for all the regions of the empire. A council of scholars interpreted the laws. From 750, the Abbasid dynasty ruled from its headquarters in Baghdad.

It was under these two dynasties that the Arab world attained its greatest cultural achievements. But subsequently the Arabs continued to contribute to the development of European culture; Europe also benefited from the achievements of Islam. To give a few examples: it was under Islam that the first attempts were made to write a systematic history of the world. The Arabs translated, and made their own important additions to, classical Greek and Indian works. It was through the Arabs that the principles of algebra, grammar and logarithms reached Europe; the Arabs also made crucial discoveries in the fields of medicine (Avicenna laid the foundations of modern surgery), philology, architecture, astronomy and astrology. They translated the works of Plato, Aristotle, Euclid and Hippocrates. In the caliphate of Cordoba in Andalusia, where the first caliph began his reign in 756, 27 free schools were founded. Islam, during its 800-year rule in Andalusia, not only bequeathed the region magnificent works of architecture but also substantially improved its economic structures.

How were non-Muslims treated in the Islamic empire? Andalusia provides an excellent example of the tolerance shown to religious minorities, particularly in the late period of Islam. Christians and, especially, Jews benefited from this tolerance. Jews played an extremely active part in the intellectual life of this period. They even gained prominence in politics under the Umayyads. When Abdel Rahman III ruled Andalusia, a Jewish doctor was minister of finance. In Granada a Jew held the post of vizier – roughly equivalent to prime minister – for 40 years; another Jew was a famous poet.

In Palestine, the Jewish community was politically and economically insignificant at this time. In south Arabia, on the other hand, the Jews had gained great influence and wealth. Even before Islam, a number of Arab princes had been converted to Judaism. In Baghdad and Damascus, Jewish influence increased under Islamic rule, and Christians and Jews were treated with tolerance in the courts of the caliph. Indeed Christians and Jews were highly esteemed not only as artists, merchants and goldsmiths but also as political advisers. Perhaps the most famous of these is the Christian Ibn al Mansur. Christians and Jews, moreover, played an important part in bringing Arab culture to the West. It was only under Turkish rule that this tolerance of Christians and Jews gradually ceased.

A surprisingly large number of modern Arab names are Jewish in origin: for example, Ibrahim, Musa, Youssef, etc. Under Islam, Jews not only retained their names, but many Arabs also took Jewish names.

Towards the end of Arab-Islamic rule in particular, tolerance was increasingly shown to non-Arab peoples such as Turks and Persians who had been converted to Islam. And in fact this was to prove the downfall of Arab Islam, because the Turks, who had begun as palace guards and then gradually assumed increasingly important military functions, took over power in 847. By now the emphasis in the Arab-Islamic empire had shifted to the Islamic element. Their universal all-embracing concept of an Islamic empire enabled the Arabs to integrate many foreign races into their community – but finally they were forced to hand over power to other races. Arab primacy in the Islamic empire came to an end. The Ottoman Turks who took over from them had long been Islamized, however, and their rule continued to be based on Islam. Thus the Islamic character of the Arab world, including Palestine, has not only endured but has intensified and deepened its influence steadily until the present day.

The Crusaders and Palestine

The unifying force of Islam posed a threat to the Christian West. The end of Byzantine rule meant that Europe had lost its influence in the Arab world. The Middle East had always been a vital bridgehead for Europe, to ensure political and economic access to Asia. This was why the Greeks and the Romans had colonized the region. Palestine, in particular, had always been the first and prime target of all European conquerors and therefore also the first victim of intrigues for political power in the region. The Palestinians would continue to suffer in this respect for many centuries.

No wonder, then, that the Europeans tried to exploit the havoc caused by the weakness of the Arab caliphs and the seizure of power by the Ottoman sultans. The Franks attacked Palestine not to rid the holy places of 'infidels' (these 'infidels' were monotheistic) but to protect their own interests. In 1099 the Franks captured Jerusalem. The Arab world now reunited in an effort to save Jerusalem. Sultan Salah al-Din (Saladin) liberated Jerusalem from the Franks in 1187 and also drove them out of Akko and Ascalon. Many centuries later, Lessing was to make Saladin a central figure in his play *Nathan the Wise*, which presents a magnificent plea for religious tolerance among Christians, Muslims and Jews.

Salah al-Din gave yet another fine example of the religious and political tolerance of Arab Islam. To save the city of Jerusalem from the destruction attendant on a violent assault, he offered the citizens freedom and a safe conduct if they would surrender. The crusaders overrode the wishes of the townspeople and rejected the offer. But even when he captured the city, Saladin showed magnanimity, allowing the citizens to buy their freedom. Seven thousand poor townspeople were freed at the Sultan's command in return for a token sum from Henry II's treasury. The Christian Patriarch, however, contrary to what had been agreed, tried to make away with church treasures, gold, monstrances and other precious objects. The Saracen emirs pressed Saladin to arrest him but Saladin allowed him to escape. So an Islamic Sultan taught a Christian Patriarch of Jerusalem the meaning of mercy and magnanimity. Under Saladin's successors, the crusaders occupied a part of Palestinian territory for ten years before they were finally driven out of the Middle East.

During the crusades, Jews and Muslims fought side by side against the Franks. The Jews had experienced Christian intolerance in the Byzantine era; this also prompted them to fight with the Islamic troops against the Christians in Andalusia. When Granada was captured by the Christians, the Jews suffered the same fate as the Muslims: they were persecuted, killed, expelled from Spain or forcibly converted to Christianity.

Between 1255 and 1260, another power tried to subjugate the Arab world: the Mongols, whose murdering and marauding troops achieved a grim notoriety under their leader Genghis Khan. A Turkish Mameluke dynasty ruled in Egypt at this time. In 1260 the Mamelukes, aided by the Syrians and the Palestinians, defeated the Mongols in the decisive battle of Nablus. In doing so, they incidentally saved Christian Europe by preventing the Mongols from pressing further north and destroying the European civilizations.

The victory of Islamic troops over the crusaders marked the end of the third attempt by Europeans to gain control of the Middle East. But there was still a long way to go before Europe began to revise its political attitude to the Middle East.

5. Palestine Under Ottoman Rule

When the Arab-Islamic empire collapsed, various Turkish dynasties fought for control of the former Arab caliphates. Finally, in 1517, power fell into the hands of the Turkish Ottomans. Only in Egypt did the Turkish Mamelukes manage to gain the upper hand. Egypt paid tribute to the Ottoman rulers but none the less its rulers retained their independence from the Ottoman empire over the next centuries.

For Palestine, the first phase of Ottoman rule, up to the 18th Century, had highly beneficial results. Palestine was now incorporated into a large, stable and well-governed empire. Safe from invaders, the country now prospered. Agriculture in particular went through a phase of considerable prosperity and development.

In the 16th Century, the Ottomans established a precise and complex system of administration and taxation in the areas under their control. *Daftars* – written documents on the system of taxation in the Ottoman empire – give a precise picture of the economic and demographic situation in Palestine at that time. The following information has been taken from these registers.

Fiscal and Administrative Structures

The Ottoman empire was divided into large administrative regions, which in turn were subdivided. The largest unit was the *vilayet*: Palestine and Syria together formed the *vilayet* Al-Shaam. Each *vilayet* was subdivided into *livas*. Palestinian territory was divided into the *livas* of Safad, Nablus, Kuds (Jerusalem) and Gaza. These *livas* were in turn subdivided into *nahiyas*, smaller administrative units. Many towns had large numbers of *nahiyas* attached to them: the *liva* of Jerusalem, for example, had 184 nearby villages attached to it; and from 1533 to 1539, Nablus had 276 *nahiyas*. The *livas* were roughly equivalent to provinces and their capital cities were known as *mir livas*. The divisions were primarily fiscal and administrative and were often dictated by natural frontiers.

There were many forms of taxation: local and regional taxes, taxes on various goods and services, for example on water-mills, vineyards, and

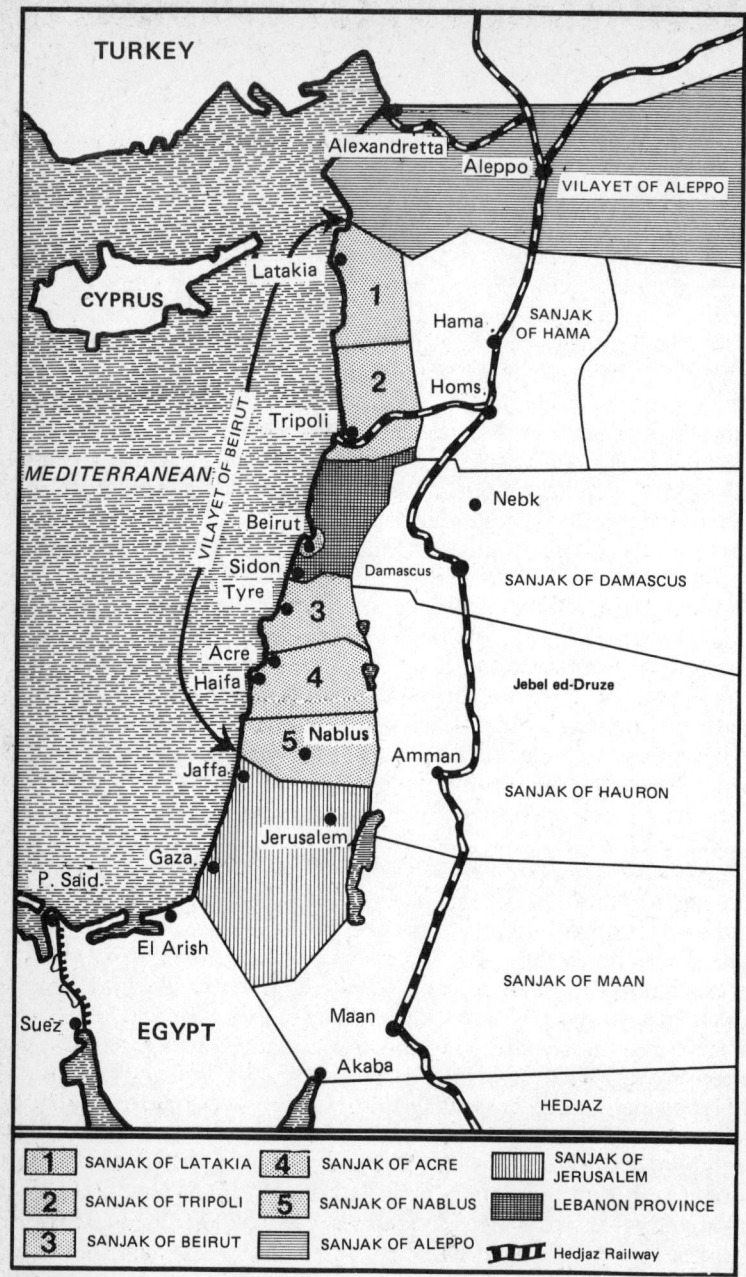

Turkish Administrative Districts in Greater Syria

orange and olive groves. There were also religious taxes. The chief cities of Palestine were much the same as they are today: Jerusalem, Nablus, Safad, Gaza, Beersheba, Tibnin, Ramallah, Jaffa and Lod. These were major trading centres and ports with thriving economic activity. Each agricultural settlement was registered in detail and each village had its legal statute. All families, unmarried men, clans, tribes and religious communities are precisely documented in the Turkish registers. These registers are incontrovertible evidence that even at that time Palestine was a densely populated country with constitutional structures. Classification of the inhabitants was so thorough that it even included their state of health. The lame, the blind and the dumb were registered as such.

For the purposes of religious taxation, distinctions were drawn between the various Islamic communities, and the Christians, Jews and Samaritans. It is interesting to examine the distribution of the Jewish population in Palestine in the 16th Century. The *daftars* provide exact information on the percentage of Jews living in the main Palestinian cities. One astonishing fact revealed by the *daftars* is that there were hardly any Jews living in Jerusalem. The largest Jewish community, comprising 904 Jewish families and 93 unmarried men, lived in Safad. In Gaza there were 73 Jewish families and no unmarried men; in Nablus there were 15 families and no unmarried men. Eleven families lived in Hebron, but there were none at all in Ramallah. There were only eight villages in Galilee inhabited by Jews. It is noteworthy that very few Jews lived in places of religious importance to them. The Jews in Palestine came from Andalusia, Sardinia, Germany and even from the East European countries. The majority of Spanish and Portuguese Jews had sought refuge in Palestine after the Inquisition. Under Ottoman rule, Jews were treated with great tolerance. A work in which the Turkish *daftars* are translated and commented on, includes the following quotation: the fact that the Jewish communities always retained the name of their country of origin 'shows that the Jewish population was not homogeneous . . . this practice was probably adopted by the Jewish population itself.'[1]

The Turkish registers also classify Jews according to whether they were residents, travellers or guests. Of course the Jews had no common language. They spoke the language of their country of origin. The various Jewish communities kept strictly to themselves. This applies to Spanish as much as to Moroccan or Yemenite Jews.

The population of Palestine in the 16th Century was 206,290. In the south, including Gaza, 18% of the population lived in towns. The most densely populated areas were the mountains around Jerusalem and Nablus, Galilee and the Gaza strip. It was unusual for one Palestinian village to be more than three kilometres away from the next.

Another important fact: less than a quarter of the total population was nomadic. Furthermore, all the large towns in the *vilayet* of Damascus – excepting Damascus itself – were on Palestinian territory.

A number of villages had disappeared by the 19th Century, but the towns and some other villages grew. The entire Ottoman empire suffered a demographic catastrophe in the 19th Century. Large tracts of land were depopulated. But 'this depopulation obviously did not occur in Palestine and the surrounding area'.[2] Palestine was spared the fate of Anatolia in what is now Turkey.

When, in the 19th Century, Ottoman military power waned, more and more *livas* in Palestine became autonomous.

The Palestinian Economy

Trade, handicrafts and agriculture were the main pillars of the Palestinian economy. The most important agricultural products were wheat, barley, rice, beans, olives and olive oil, wine, almonds, fruit and vegetables, sesame and cotton. Fishing was also an important activity on the coast. In addition, cattle were raised in the agricultural areas; the most important species were water buffaloes, goats and sheep.

The main trading centres were Safad, Akko, Kafr Kanna, Nablus, Qaqun, Lod, Jerusalem, Ramallah, Majdal, Hebron and Gaza. All these towns still exist. Gaza, the major trading centre, also benefited from its fertile hinterland. Arts and crafts, leather work and textile production flourished, mainly in Gaza, Nablus, Ramallah and Hebron.

Two major sources of currency and tax revenue in Palestine were the ports and resting places. The most important port was Jaffa, followed by Akko, Haifa and Gaza. The resting places were the contemporary equivalents of the service areas on motorways today. They were located on the country's major roads, such as the Via Maris, a major supra-regional road running parallel to the sea from Cairo to Damascus. This was one of the most important trade routes in the Middle East. Trading was carried on at all resting places and tolls were collected for the use of the roads.

Social services were provided by the religious foundations, which ran schools and charitable organizations. They even financed religious and cultural institutions in Egypt and what is now Saudi Arabia. From the cultural and scientific point of view, Ottoman rule contributed little to Palestine. The Ottomans were content to study or imitate Arab and Persian works.

The Decline of the Ottoman Empire and European Colonial Policy in the Arab Region

> I maintain that we are the first race on earth, and the more of the earth we inhabit, the better for the human race . . .[3]

Towards the end of the 18th Century, the idea of the nation-state was taken up enthusiastically throughout Europe. Nationalism, the extreme form of the sense of nationhood, soon led to the conviction that this or that nation was superior to others, and therefore ought to subjugate them and bestow on them the 'benefits' of its own life-style or attitudes. The European nations with this political philosophy now set about trying to conquer parts of Africa and Asia. At the same time, the Ottoman empire began to decline. Turkish troops lost the territories they had conquered in Europe and Russia. All the major European powers hoped to take over from the Ottomans in the Middle East.

In France, Napoleon came to power following the breakdown of revolutionary Jacobin rule. He defeated Prussia, Austria and Italy. Once the Napoleonic army had been driven from its soil, Russia left the anti-Napoleonic alliance. Napoleon had been unable to defeat England and after the French fleet had been destroyed in the Mediterranean, England became the major European maritime power. In 1798, Napoleon set out on his Egyptian expedition, his aim being to destroy England's position in the Mediterranean and sever its connection with India. The Ottomans intervened and fought against Napoleon. The English Admiral Nelson destroyed Napoleon's transport fleet and cut off his connections to Europe. In Europe, England had also established a powerful alliance against Napoleon. Under intense pressure from so many sides, Napoleon was forced to abandon his project and left Egypt in 1799.

The Ottomans now seized this opportunity to oust the Mameluke dynasty in Egypt. In 1799, after his abortive Egyptian expedition, Napoleon entered Palestine. Under the leadership of Djesar Pasha, the Palestinian people put up heroic resistance. In the 19th Century, Syria, with Palestine under Djesar Pasha, enjoyed virtually autonomous government. Soon, however, the declining Ottomans and the Mameluke rulers began a power struggle for the Turkish empire. In 1832, the Palestinians, led by the Egyptian Mameluke ruler Ibrahim Pasha, fought against the Ottomans. The Egyptian Pashas now came to power. This marked the beginning of a brief period of prosperity in Palestine. It was soon followed, though, by a new wave of repression and the Palestinian leaders now sought help from the Ottoman rulers in Istanbul. In 1834, peasant uprisings occurred in the mountains of Hebron and Nablus. In 1840, the Palestinians fought on the side of the Ottomans in the struggle against Egyptian rule. The joint forces of Turkey, England and the Russian empire besieged Akko in their efforts to drive Ibrahim Pasha out of Egypt. They finally succeeded.

The Europeans thus gained a foothold in the Middle East towards the end of the 19th Century. France, already a colonial power in North Africa, now attempted to extend its protectorate to the Middle East and thus came into conflict with other European powers pursuing similar goals. The European powers took any and every problem as a pretext for intervention in the Middle East. One example follows.

The Problem of the Holy Places

The Europeans used this problem as a pretext to gain control of the Middle East. Control over access to the holy places in Palestine, therefore, became a subject of dispute between European countries. The real issue, and the real object of their interest, was to take possession of the largest possible share of the crumbling Ottoman empire. From then until the beginning of the First World War, the entire Arab world became the scene of European power intrigues. England, France, Germany, Italy, Austria-Hungary and Russia attempted to play one Arab people off against another, supporting one national group one moment and another the next. In Lebanon, the English stirred up the Druses against the Christians, who in turn were supported by the French. In Egypt, the English bought Suez Canal shares. In 1878, there were English and French members in the Egyptian cabinet. Soon England established a protectorate in Egypt. The Turkish Ottoman empire became financially and militarily bankrupt.

The European powers could not reach any agreement on the Middle East before 1914. England was particularly interested in Palestine, for one reason, because it would provide a favourable overland connection with England's Indian colonies. France, already influential in Lebanon, wished to extend its influence to Palestine. And a German religious community, the Templars, settled in Palestine towards the end of the 19th Century and fervently set about trying to convert the population to Christianity. England and France, however, were now making prodigious diplomatic efforts to wrest territorial concessions from the Turks. They competed for contracts to build railways, which would guarantee their spheres of influence. Russia set itself up as the protector of Palestinian Jews and encouraged Russian Jews to emigrate to Palestine as a means of increasing its influence there. The Turks, fearing serious problems between the nationalities, attempted unsuccessfully to prevent this. By 1914, there were 80,000 Jews in Palestine, half of them of Russian origin. After 1914, most of them became Turkish citizens.

England, too, was eagerly seeking a community whose interests it could 'protect' in the Middle East and who would at the same time pave its way to power in the region. And it found this community in the shape of the Zionist movement in Europe. This movement was to help England wrest Palestine from the Ottoman empire and incorporate it into the British sphere of influence.

Notes

1. *Erlanger Geographische Arbeiten. Special Volume II* – Wolf-Dieter Hütteroth/Kamal Abdulfattah, *Historical Geography of Palestine, Transjordan and Southern Syria in the Late 16th Century* (Erlanger, 1977).
2. *Erlanger Arbeiten*, p. 58.
3. Cecil Rhodes, British colonist of Africa.

6. Zionism

Towards the end of the 19th Century, anti-Semitism intensified, and Jews suffered increasingly from its effects. A number of Jewish leaders, especially in East Europe, now tried to reply to and counter anti-Semitism. In 1882, Leo Pinsker wrote a pamphlet entitled 'The Self-Emancipation of the Jews'. In it he argued that Jews throughout the world had always been forced to work in finance and trade; as a result, they had lost the respect of the working population, whose involvement in the production process gave them stronger ties with the land. He proposed that the Jews should take their destiny in their own hands, colonize land and cultivate the earth. In 1884, he founded the 'Friends of Zion' and shortly afterwards the first Zionists emigrated from Romania to Palestine.

The situation in Palestine at the time was chaotic. The Turkish authorities had lost their power and no one was really in control. The European powers were competing between themselves for power and influence in the region.

The first Jewish settlers lived in harmony with the Arab population. Ben-Gurion wrote: 'They offered their Arab neighbours help, and they in turn repaid like with like. The Arabs lent Jews seed and cattle wherever necessary.'[1] Most of the financial support for these settlements came from the French banker Edmond de Rothschild.

Rothschild and other Zionist leaders were also prepared to establish settlements in other countries. They were not yet seeking to establish a Jewish State. Whereas the first Jewish settlers in Palestine were anxious to live on good terms with their Arab neighbours, European Zionism took a different, more radical direction.

By the end of the 19th Century, European Jews were split into two main camps: the advocates of assimilation on the one hand, the Zionists on the other. Both sides sought, in different ways, to solve the Jewish question. The advocates of assimilation wanted Jews to be completely integrated into the societies in which they lived – except of course that they wished to retain their religious rites and customs. And in fact at the close of the 19th Century, many Jews in West Europe were integrated. In East Europe, on the other hand, assimilation was minimal, as the pogroms against the Jews in Russia in 1881 grimly illustrated. Even in West

Europe, many Jews still felt that they faced discrimination, in spite of assimilation. In fact, anti-Semitic excesses were frequent. In Germany, for example, Treitschke wrote: 'The Jews are our misfortune.' Perhaps the most spectacular manifestation of anti-Semitism in West Europe occurred in France, in the Dreyfus affair. Dreyfus, a Jew and an officer in the French army, was accused of betraying military secrets and imprisoned for years, although he was obviously innocent. The emotions whipped up by the affair led to many outbursts of hatred against Jews.

Many advocates of assimilation, especially among the lower classes, hoped that Marxism would provide the solution. They argued that anti-Semitism was merely a manifestation of capitalism, and that it would disappear of itself in a classless society. Until 1918, this was the view held by many Russian Jews, who had pinned their hopes on the Russian revolution of 1917. Even after the murder of their leaders in 1918, many Russian Jews remained true to Marxism. Others emigrated to the United States (more than 4.9 million by 1939).

While many Jews saw socialism as their salvation, some pseudo-Marxists condemned the Jews as exploiters. The bourgeoisie also rejected the Jews, regarding them as dangerous rivals in business and finance. All this confirmed the Zionists' arguments and strengthened their position. They now put forward the view that assimilation could never succeed or that, if it did, it would lead to a loss of Jewish identity. But what was this identity?

For the Zionists, this identity meant belonging to a race. Convinced Zionists attempted to prove this claim with arguments which were extraordinarily similar to those of the anti-Semites. They talked of the 'otherness of Jewry', of the 'moral, spiritual and intellectual superiority which derives from the fact that the Jewish race has a special vitamin in it'.[2]

With arguments such as these, the Zionists played into the hands of the anti-Semites, intensifying their hostility towards Jews as a whole. But there were differences of opinion even among Zionists. One group, whose main spokesman was Israel Zangwill, wanted autonomous status for Jews on some territory, no matter where. His slogan was 'A land without people for a people without land.' At this point, the views and role of the Viennese journalist, Theodor Herzl, should be examined.

In 1895, Herzl wrote his best-known book, *The Jewish State*. Herzl is considered the founder of modern Zionism. It was under his chairmanship that the first Zionist Congress was held, in Basle in 1897. Herzl rejected assimilation. His arguments were shaped by the spirit of the age in which people were beginning to classify races into superior and inferior types. Herzl believed that assimilation could only be achieved by mixed marriages. But this, Herzl argued, would mean that Jews would increase their economic power, and this in turn would intensify hatred of them. The Jews themselves would lose their 'racial purity'. He accused rich assimilated Jews of exploiting their poorer fellows. These arguments show how uninterested wealthy Jews were in Zionism. Indeed wealthy

Jews were even accused of being 'Jewish anti-Semites'. Herzl therefore proposed that all Jews should combine their efforts and establish a State of their own. The ideal territory for this project would be Palestine because of the Jews' religious ties with this land, but he did not exclude other areas. He rightly assumed that anti-Semitism would help him to realize his dream. He proposed the colonization of Palestine. For this purpose, he proposed to set up a 'Jewish company' which would be responsible for the 'acquisition of land'. By this, he meant the purchase of Palestinian territory. The function of the Jewish company would be to subsidize the purchase of land and oversee its development and cultivation. The company would also explain the advantages of the scheme to the leaders of the European states and try to gain their support for it. The money was to come from rich assimilated Jews who did not intend to migrate to Palestine themselves and could thus avoid criticism from Zionists. The first settlers in Palestine were to be poor Jews who had nothing to lose by going there. Their task was to cultivate the land and thus create more favourable conditions which would then attract wealthier settlers and intellectuals. Herzl simply threw all the principles of modern international law overboard: for him it was not the right to a territory but a race's struggle for existence which led to the foundation of a State.

Herzl knew that another people was already living in Palestine. He was quite convinced that the Jewish settlers could only benefit the Arab population. Just like the colonial powers of the time, he regarded non-European peoples as mere uncivilized natives over whom one had a natural right to rule. He overlooked the problems which Jewish settlement in Palestine would inevitably bring, to the extent that he could even write in *The Jewish State*:

> It is fitting that there should also be people of a different faith and a different nationality among us. We will grant them protection and equality before the law. The new Jewish state must be founded respectably. We have to think of our future reputation in the world.

Herzl obviously could not, or did not wish to, imagine that the Zionists would later used armed force to drive the Palestinian people from their own land. He did not resort to the arguments which Zionists were to come up with later: namely that by taking over power in Palestine they were fulfilling a divine promise. There is no place for divine promises in international law. As Wagner writes: 'Divine promises, expulsion, a continuing inner bond to Palestine among Jews: none of these constitutes a legal claim to Palestine.'[3]

Theodor Herzl did not foresee the later development of Zionism and probably would not have approved of the course events took. He later visited Palestine with the Zionist Max Nordau. When Nordau pointed out that the country was densely populated, Herzl is said to have exclaimed:

'But we are committing an injustice!' The Jewish writer Werblonsky describes this as 'moral myopia'.[4] In his novel *Altneuland*, Herzl imagined that Arabs and Jews would live together like brothers in Palestine.

The Basle Programme was formulated at the Zionist Congress chaired by Herzl in 1897. It reads as follows:

> The aim of Zionism is the establishment of a constitutionally guaranteed home for the Jewish people in Palestine. The Congress proposes the following measures as a means of achieving this goal: 1) to support the settlement of Palestine by Jewish farmers, craftsmen and traders; 2) to organize and bring together all Jews by appropriate local and general assemblies according to the laws of the land; 3) to strengthen Jewish national feeling and national consciousness; 4) to take preparatory steps with a view to gaining government permission for measures necessary to attain the goal of Zionism.[5]

It is also worth observing here that Herzl proposed Argentina, Uganda, Cyprus and Sinai as potential Jewish homelands. It must be remembered that Zionism was born in the age of nationalism and colonialism. Thus the fathers of Zionism merely embodied the ideas of their time. The national element was decisive. Both anti-Semites and Zionists attached the greatest importance to 'national character' and 'racial characteristics'. Many colonial powers at first knew virtually nothing about the people of the countries they had conquered and colonized. And when they encountered 'natives', they justified their own presence in the country by arguing that they would bring the colonized people civilization and affluence. All states wanted to possess colonies and to prove their 'racial superiority'. Why should the Zionists be different?

Herzl's dream took place in a political vacuum. He did not even consider the possibility of Arab resistance in Palestine. Nahum Goldmann wrote later in his memoirs: 'One of the greatest errors of Zionism was that it did not take sufficient account of the Arab aspect when the Jewish State was being founded.'

After Herzl's death, the Zionists regarded Palestine as the only possible goal of Jewish settlement. There were still differences of opinion among the Zionist leaders. Some, for example, only wished for autonomy and regarded the settlement of Palestine as a philanthropic enterprise. The majority of American Jews – whose children and grandchildren make donations to Israel today – held this view. Others, notably Martin Buber, regarded Palestine as an intellectual and cultural centre of Judaism. Orthodox Jews categorically rejected the Jewish State on the grounds that only the Messiah could lead the Jews back to the 'Promised Land'. Weizmann, however, succeeded in reconciling all these conflicting views under the general heading of nationalism. It was easy enough, given the pressure of anti-Semitism, to inspire all Zionists with enthusiasm for a common goal.

There was one question, though, which remained controversial: that of 'Jewish work'. The Jewish writer Achad Ha'ams, for example, rejected the Jewish State because he realized that it could only be viable if work continued to be done by the Arab masses – though this would be under the leadership of a Jewish élite.[6]

And Smilansky, who was later to settle in Palestine, warned the Jews there: 'The Jewish people must realize that Jewish capitalists cannot secure the land for their people without Jewish work.'[7]

These statements indicate a conflict which was bound to arise for Jewish Marxists. Many Zionists believed in socialism and wished to establish a socialist society in Palestine. Yet Zionism strove to achieve a *pure* Jewish national State, which would inevitably oppress and exploit the original Palestinian people because, in a purely Jewish state, they would be excluded from all economic and political co-determination. Socialist Jews could not reconcile the relegation of the Arab population to the status of a working class without rights with their own political ideas. This situation could only lead to exploitation of the Arabs. To prevent this – but also to avoid having to share power – the 'Jewish work' slogan was coined. This meant that all work in the new Jewish State would be done by Jews. Theoretically, this meant that no Arabs would be exploited by Jews. But in fact this solution was bound to lead to the evil it was trying to avoid. To exclude the Arabs from the process of construction was, in practical terms, to deprive them of any chance of survival in their own country.

The scene was thus set for a tragedy which would inexorably lead to the expulsion or the annihilation of the Palestinian population. The most extreme conclusions were drawn by the radical Zionist leader Jabotinsky, whose most famous pupil is none other than Menachem Begin. Jabotinsky called for the establishment of a great Jewish State which would include the east bank of the Jordan and extend, as the Bible promised, from the Mediterranean to the Euphrates. For Jabotinsky and his supporters, the military question had clear priority: the task was to fight the Arab population and to prevent any agreement or reconciliation with them. This Zionist faction later founded the Herut party, of which Begin is a member.

Such was the philosophy that has determined the political direction of Israel until the present day. The contradiction between socialism and Zionism – indeed the fact that the two are irreconcilable – was obscured for as long as possible. Long after the founding of the Jewish State, young people from East and West were still being encouraged to immigrate to the Jewish State – on the spurious grounds that they could realize their socialist dreams there. It was a long time before this myth was destroyed and it became clear that the foundations of Zionism lay in colonialism with all its ugly manifestations.

Notes

1. David Ben-Gurion, *Israel. Die Geschichte eines Staates* (Frankfurt, 1973), p. 61.
2. Ibid., pp. 13, 18.
3. Heinz Wagner, *The Arab-Israeli Conflict in International Law* (Berlin, 1971), p. 60.
4. Israel and Eretz Israel, in *Les Temps Modernes*, No. 253b, 1967, 'Le conflit israelo-arabe', pp. 371ff.
5. Wagner, op. cit., p. 35.
6. Ben-Gurion, op. cit., p. 65.
7. Ibid., p. 66.

7. Zionism and the Great European Powers: The Disastrous Results of British Diplomatic Tricks

At the time when Herzl was attempting to make Palestine a 'Jewish State', the 'non-Jewish' community in Palestine constituted 92% of the population. In 1898, Theodor Herzl was still counting on the support of the German Kaiser for the Zionist plans. He tried to tempt the Germans by playing on their colonial ambitions. Herzl pursued a similar line with the Turkish sultan, as the Ottoman empire at this time inclined towards Germany. 'The sovereignty of the Sublime Porte (Ottoman empire) and a German Protectorate would probably provide the appropriate legal foundation (for the Zionist plans).'[1] But Germany was unable to play its part, either because of political weakness or because it did not wish to provoke the friendly sultan, who was after all ruler of Palestine. Kaiser Wilhelm met Herzl frequently and they both travelled to Palestine. However, Germany was forced to reject the Zionists' proposal.

Turkey, for its part, had no intention of risking further racial trouble in an empire already plagued by racial differences – even though Herzl promised in his *Jewish State* that: 'If his majesty the Sultan would give us Palestine, we would be only too glad to restore Turkey's finances to a state of health.'[2]

The Zionists now turned to the British, who in the period before the First World War were looking for a way to extend their influence in the Middle East to Palestine. The Zionists offered their services: they promised to support England's claims to Palestine if the English would allow them to settle Palestine under a British protectorate.

The Zionists hoped that British protection would facilitate the settlement of Palestine and they promised Britain the gratitude and support of Jews throughout the world. Herbert Samuel, a British Zionist, wrote in 1914: 'The freeing of the Holy Places of Christendom . . . would further increase the esteem this policy would enjoy among the British people.' The Zionists were not above using this popular and hoary argument – used to justify any foreign intervention – to win British support for their aims.

The PLO and Palestine

The Division of the Middle East by the Sykes-Picot Agreement

British Promises to the Arabs

In 1914, the Ottoman empire entered the war on the German side. So the British had to defeat the Turks before they could gain control of the Ottoman empire. The Zionists could not help them here, but others could – in particular the Arab population of the Ottoman empire, who wanted to get rid of their Turkish rulers once and for all. The Hejaz area – now part of Saudi Arabia – was one of the regions of the Ottoman empire to which the Turks attached particular importance. It included the holy cities of Mecca and Medina. The influence of the Ottoman government there was strong – as the people felt to their cost. Sharif Hussein, ruler of Mecca, declared his willingness to lead an Arab rebellion against the Turks. Before the First World War began, he asked Lord Kitchener, then British High Commissioner in Egypt, for British support in the Arab war of liberation. England's immediate reaction was negative, as it still had good relations with the Ottoman empire. But after the outbreak of war, the British saw the situation differently. The Turks were now the enemies of the Allies and the Allies were the enemies of the Germans. England realized that an Arab uprising would weaken the Turks; and a weakening of the Turks would help towards an Allied victory over Germany and the destruction of the Ottoman empire. A further advantage of a British-Arab alliance was that England could not be accused of waging an 'anti-Islamic' war in the Middle East.

On 14 July 1915, Sharif Hussein and Sir Henry McMahon, the new British High Commissioner in Egypt, first entered into correspondence. Hussein offered the British his help against the Turks. Nationalist Arab leaders had by now met in Damascus and produced the so-called Damascus protocol. They sent this document to Hussein. It contained the conditions that Hussein was later to make for his support of the British: the main condition was a commitment by the British to grant the Turkish-occupied areas independence at the end of the war. Between July 1915 and March 1916, there was a correspondence of ten letters between Hussein and McMahon on this subject. Hussein insisted that he should be recognized as caliph and that Saudi Arabia, Syria, Lebanon, Jordan, Iraq and Palestine should become independent. He further demanded guarantees that the Allies would respect these British promises after the war. McMahon accepted the first condition. As for independence, he attempted to leave the question open. But the Arabs insisted and finally McMahon wrote to Hussein: 'The districts of Messina and Alexandretta and parts of Syria west of the towns of Damascus, Homs, Hama and Aleppo cannot be described as purely Arab and must therefore be excluded from consideration. With this restriction and without prejudice to existing agreements with Arab princes we accept the frontiers of this region.'[3]

The reference to the parts of Syria west of the towns of Damascus, Homs, Hama and Aleppo was crucial for Palestine. As we know, Palestine under Turkish rule was part of the *vilayet* of Al-Shaam. Palestine, however,

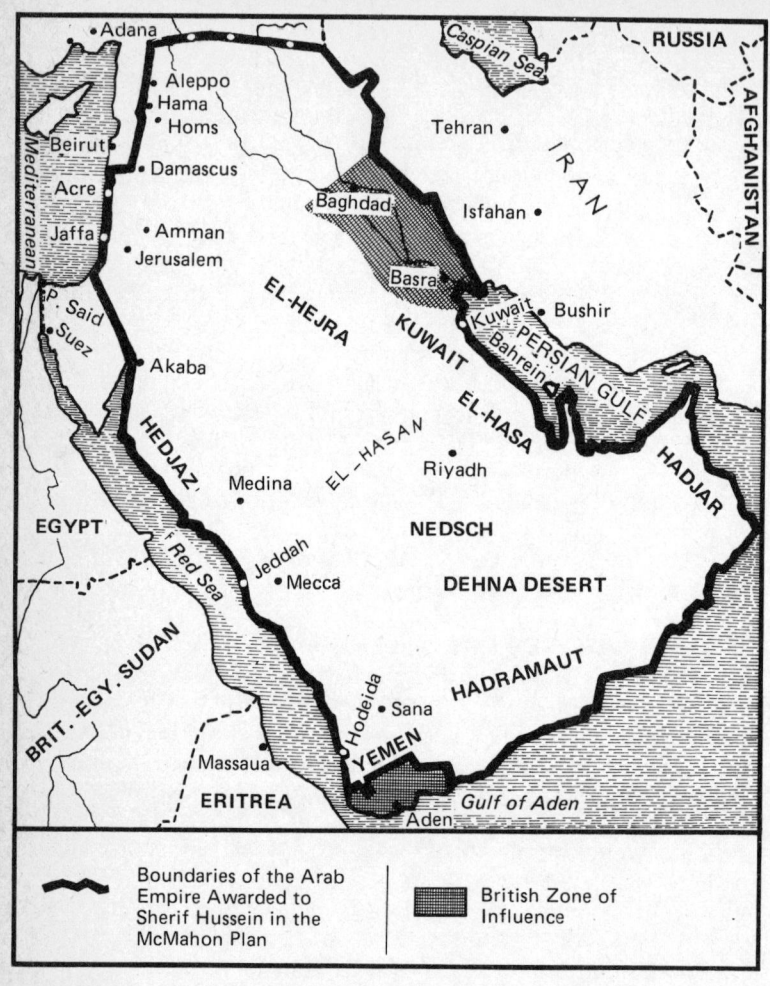

Boundaries of the Arab Empire Awarded to Sherif Hussein in the McMahon Plan

British Zone of Influence

is not to the west of the four towns mentioned above, but much further to the south. The exclusion area mentioned by the British was quite clearly Lebanon. In fact, McMahon referred to the need to respect French interests in his letter: Lebanon was part of the French sphere of influence. Hussein, otherwise satisfied with the British assurances, was prepared to wait till the end of the war for this region.

On 15 June 1916, the Arab rebellion against the Turks began. The troops of Hussein and his son Feisal captured the strategically important town of Aqaba on 6 July 1916. This enabled the British troops to cross the Suez canal and push on into Sinai.

Among those fighting with the Arabs was T. E. Lawrence, later to be glorified as the hero of a novel and to receive the epithet 'Lawrence of Arabia'. Lawrence's brotherly love of the Arabs is a gross exaggeration, for his first loyalty was to the British secret service and he was acting solely for British interests. Arab troops attacked enemy supply lines and the front along the Hejaz railway between Medina and Damascus. Liddell-Hart, military historian of the Allies in the First World War, wrote:

> In the crucial weeks while Allenby's stroke was being prepared and during its delivery, nearly half of the Turkish forces south of Damascus were distracted by the Arab forces . . . What the absence of these forces meant to the success of Allenby's stroke, it is easy to see. Nor did the Arab operation end when it had opened the way. For in the issue, it was the Arabs who almost entirely wiped out the Fourth Army, the still intact forces that might have barred the way to final victory. The wear and tear, the bodily and mental strain on men and material applied by the Arabs . . . prepared the way that produced their (the Turks) defeat.[4]

The Arabs therefore fought on the Allied side, wholly trusting the British assurances. They played a crucial part in the victory over the Turks and thus in the final victory over the Central Powers. But they did not know what was being planned at the same time in the chancelleries of England and France. The plans being concocted there were difficult to reconcile with the assurances given to the Arabs. The British wanted to defeat the Turks, but their object was to grab their share of the crumbling empire's Middle Eastern region. And the independence of the Arab regions conflicted with their goals. Regardless of their promises to the Arabs, the British now sought a way of consolidating their power in the Middle East after the war.

Anglo-French Arrangements (The Sykes-Picot Agreement)

The other Western powers were, of course, reluctant to allow the British to gobble up the entire Middle East cake. A complex game of secret diplomacy now developed in which each power strove to consolidate or extend its power in the Middle East. In a secret correspondence of October 1916, England, Russia and France divided the Middle East and Palestine into spheres of influence. The Sykes-Picot agreement (named after the British Foreign Secretary and the French ambassador in Great Britain) envisaged the following arrangements for Palestine.

The northern half of the region, to the west of the Jordan, was to be internationalized and brought under joint British, French and Russian control, with the exception of an enclave around the northern ports of

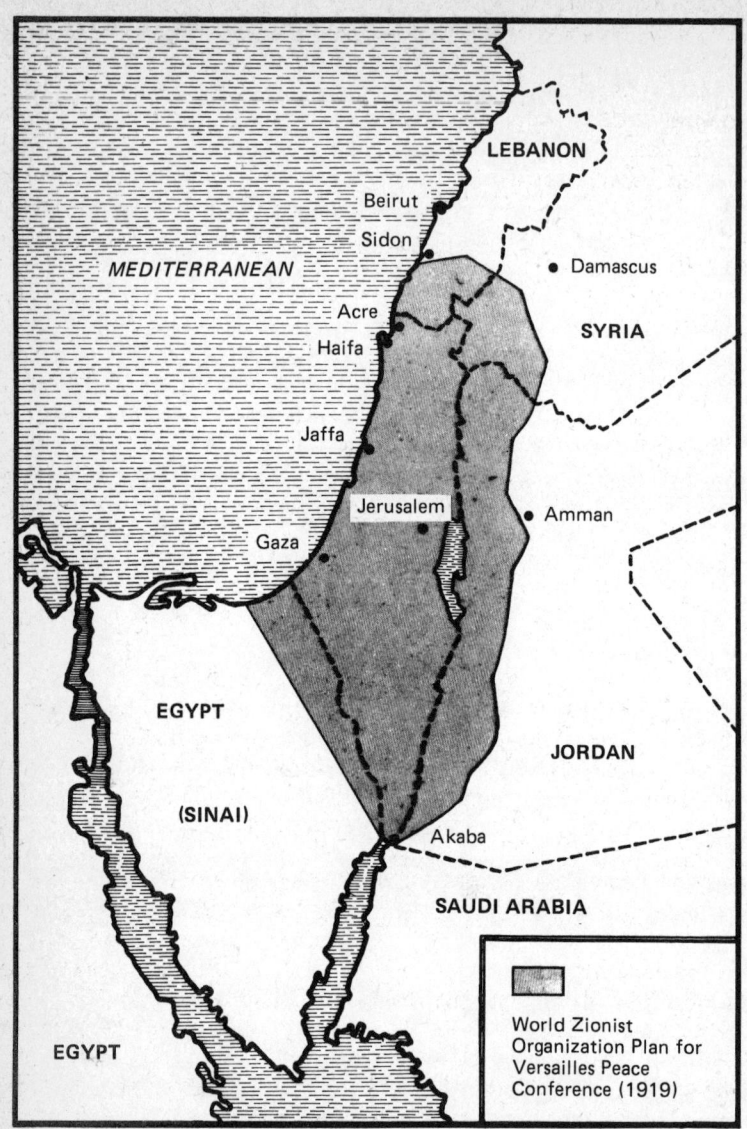

Akko and Haifa, which would be under British control. The southern part of the country – including Rafah, Beersheba and the Negev desert – was to be a British protectorate. The British were to retain extensive powers in the international zone. And in the newly-created zones, the Jews were to be granted political, religious and constitutional equality.

This last-mentioned guarantee did not go far enough for the Zionists. But they knew that the British were seeking control over the international zone. They also knew that after the war the Arabs could be of no further use to the British. But they, the Zionists, could.

However, for the time being the British had to show consideration for the Arabs, who had got wind of the Sykes-Picot agreement. After the Russian revolution of 1917, the Bolshevik government published the agreement. The Turks now hastened to make the contents of this agreement known throughout the Arab world. Hussein asked the British government for clarification. The reply: 'It's all Turkish war propaganda.'[5]

But this did not allay Arab suspicions. The Sykes-Picot agreement was now common knowledge and word also got out about a further British declaration which not only contradicted the British-Arab agreements but also posed a further threat to Arab hopes of independence.

The Balfour Declaration

Ever since the first calls for the founding of a Jewish State, the Zionists had been busy trying to convince Jews throughout the world that they belonged to one race. They fell back on the biblical promises, which they interpreted to mean that all Jews would one day return to Palestine to found a State of their own. The Zionist movement also tried to set itself up as the mouthpiece of Jews throughout the world. Anti-Zionist Jews were subjected to pressure, regardless of their ties to their home countries. With considerable diplomatic skill, the Zionists pursued their efforts to gain Allied support for their plans. At the beginning of the war, the Allies were in great difficulty and hoped that the Americans would enter the war on their side. A number of Zionists played an important part in persuading President Wilson to intervene on the Allied side. These Zionists were assured of England's gratitude.

England hoped to win over Russian Jews as allies against the revolution of 1917. A Jewish State in Palestine would guarantee British influence in the country and prevent possible Arab resistance to British domination. Furthermore, a Jewish State in a Palestine under British protectorate would provide a guarantee of British domination. The old principle of 'divide and rule' was again to come into its own. Britain had to assume that after the war the Arabs would demand that it fulfil its assurances and would resist its claims to domination. But if they could be kept busy fighting Zionist immigrants, Britain would stay out of the conflict and reap its benefits.

In 1916, Lloyd George became Prime Minister and Arthur Balfour Foreign Secretary in Great Britain. Balfour had long been a sympathizer with the Zionist cause and had played a prominent part in the colonization of South Africa. He believed in racial inequality and was convinced that some races were completely incapable of fighting for their rights. Balfour was on good terms with Weizmann, the most influential Zionist leader of the time. Together with Sykes, Balfour now set about modifying the Sykes-Picot agreement in order to include the Zionist claims to Palestine. Such a modification of the agreement was justified – so the pro-Zionist argument ran – because the third party to the agreement, Russia, now had a new government which no longer felt bound by it. In the United States, the Zionist leader Brandeis sought the support of President Wilson. By November 1917, Lloyd George, Churchill, Balfour and Wilson had been completely won over to the Zionist cause and on 2 November 1917 Lord Balfour wrote the following letter to Lord Rothschild:

> His Majesty's Government views with favour the establishment in Palestine of a national home for the Jewish people, and will use their best endeavours to facilitate the achievement of this object, it being clearly understood that nothing shall be done which may prejudice the civil and religious rights of existing non-Jewish communities in Palestine, or the rights and political status enjoyed by Jews in any other country.

This meant that the Zionists had now received from the British a written guarantee that their claims to Palestine would be made good. In February 1918, France and Italy accepted the Balfour Declaration and in October 1918, President Wilson of the United States added his blessing.

This declaration did not mention a sovereign Jewish State in Palestine. But the Zionists none the less regarded it as a licence to pursue their efforts to that end. Balfour mentioned the rights of 'non-Jewish communities' – who constituted 92% of the population – so as not to alarm the Arab population.

Balfour's choice of words creates the impression that the Palestinian Arabs were a minority requiring protection. The declaration raised two major problems. Firstly, the declaration specifically mentioned the rights of Jews in other countries. At this time anti-Zionist Jews were alarmed that they would be discriminated against in their own countries if a Jewish State were established in Palestine. The leading spokesman of these anti-Zionists was an English Jew, Sir Edwin Montagu. The anti-Zionists believed that it was no good trying to combat the prejudices of European non-Jews by colonizing a foreign country and stirring up new resentment and prejudice among the local population. Subsequent events in Palestine were to prove them right. However, the Zionists now had the support of the Allies and no longer needed to worry about dissidents in their own ranks. The Jewish-American lawyer Rosenblatt wrote in 1919:

> Now that we have convinced the powerful governments of Great Britain, France and Italy and gained the support of the Pope and finally of the President of the United States, we feel that we have won our case in the eyes of the world and that it is completely futile to waste valuable energy trying to convert a negligibly small opposition . . .[6]

The great problem for the British lay in the alarm the Sykes-Picot agreement and the Balfour Declaration had caused among Arabs. The British now set about solving this problem – with a new set of diplomatic tricks.

More British Promises to the Arabs

The need to resolve their conflicting and contradictory commitments on Palestine brought the Allies to the negotiating table again towards the end of the war. At last negotiations were opened in January 1918 between Hussein – now King Hussein of Jordan – and Hogarth, director of the Arabian department on Allenby's general staff. Hussein categorically rejected the establishment of a Jewish State in Palestine. Hogarth replied that no such State was intended but that given the religious character of the land a 'special regime, approved by the world' would have to be established. Hogarth also reiterated that in no circumstances would the Jewish immigrants be allowed to interfere with the political and economic rights of the Arab population.

At the same time, Hogarth stressed the benefits that an influx of wealthy Jews would bring to the Arabs. Hussein replied that he did not oppose limited immigration as long as the Jews were not pursuing any political goals which would encroach on Arab sovereignty in Palestine.

Similar declarations were made by the British High Commissioner in Egypt to seven Arab nationalist spokesmen in June 1918. In November 1918, England and France promised the Arabs that they would restrict themselves to assisting the freely elected Arab governments. The Arabs, logically, interpreted this to mean that the Sykes-Picot agreement and the Balfour Declaration were annulled.

Up to this point, Great Britain had successfully defended its world political interests. It had reduced the French zone of influence in Palestine and established British ascendancy. The British replied to French objections by pointing out that they had offered the Zionists protection in all of Palestine. They also referred to their agreement with Hussein, which excluded any French spheres of influence in Palestine.

In their dealings with the Zionists, the British emphasized the promises they had made to the Arabs. And they countered the objections of Arab nationalists by stressing France's interests in the region.

By these means, the British managed to stall the Arabs for a while. In fact the Arabs were the victims of this policy, because they were the first obstacle to Great Britain's power interests. The British therefore allowed the French to establish a zone of influence in Lebanon and Syria. As for Palestine, the British now tried to reinterpret their promises to Hussein.

The Hussein-McMahon agreement was now subjected to two new interpretations, each of them decidedly curious. First, the British argued that the region excluded from the agreement included everything west of the *vilayet* of Damascus. The agreement, however, refers clearly to the areas west of the towns of Damascus, Homs, Hama and Aleppo. This evidently means the territory of what is now Lebanon. By using the term '*vilayet*', the British were trying to exclude Palestine, instead of Lebanon, from the agreement. But under Turkish rule, Palestine belonged to the Al-Shaam *vilayet* – i.e. to the *vilayet* of Syria, and not the *vilayet* of Damascus. Besides, the only region west of this *vilayet* was the Mediterranean Sea! The main 'inspiration' behind this interpretation was Churchill. Historians were later to speak of the '*vilayet Churchill*' or '*vilayet Fantasy*'.

Unabashed, the British changed tack and began talking about the regions 'west of the district of Damascus'. A district of Damascus had never in fact existed and furthermore Palestine, as any map will show, lies to the south and not to the west of Damascus. The original agreement named the four towns of Damascus, Homs, Hama and Aleppo. To the west of these towns lies Lebanon, which, because of its large Christian population, could not be described as 'purely Arab' and was therefore excluded from the agreement.

The Arabs now realized that their naivety and inexperience were making them an easy prey to dubious diplomatic manoeuvres. None the less, they hoped that they would be able to live in peace with the Jewish immigrants. Hussein's son Feisal met Weizmann several times and the two men agreed on a kind of peace treaty. Hussein repeated that he was willing to grant the Jews refuge in Palestine provided they recognized Arab sovereignty there and did not question the rights of the Arabs. Pro-Zionist politicians later attempted to interpret Hussein's assurances as an acceptance of the Jewish State. But at this time neither Hussein nor the other Arab leaders realized that the British and the Zionists were working against Arab interests. Lacking contacts with Western chancelleries and inexperienced in European-style diplomacy, the Arabs took Western assurances at face value and walked into the trap that had been set for them. During the peace negotiations they quickly realized that they were going to be the losers in the division of the Ottoman empire.

The Peace Conference and the Fate of Palestine

After the war, a new balance of power was established in Europe. The victorious powers also advanced claims to the former Ottoman empire. The Zionists were present at all the important meetings of the Allies and exerted strong pressure on all the negotiating parties, especially on Wilson and Lloyd George. Their aim was to prevent Palestine from being internationalized – and this meant bringing it under British control. If France and Great Britain were to control the land jointly, the Arabs could seek the protection of France in the event of a struggle with the Zionists. Then, to maintain the *entente* with France, the British would be forced to drop their total support for the Zionists. Furthermore, the Zionists were aiming in the long term to gain sole control of the country. When the time came, it would be easier to get rid of the British alone than the French and the British together.

Unlike the Zionists, the Arabs were scarcely represented at the peace negotiations. King Feisal, who represented the Arab side, was advised by T. E. Lawrence – and Lawrence was working for British, not for Arab, interests.

On 2 July 1919, the General Syrian Congress, an assembly of national leaders from the entire Arab area, called for the complete independence of Greater Syria – which included Palestine – and rejected a European mandate. But France still pressed for a mandate for Syria and Lebanon. Great Britain backed this demand. In September 1919 the British pulled out of Damascus and the French marched in. Feisal tried to fight the French but was defeated.

In 1920, in Sèvres, a peace treaty was signed between Turkey and the Allies. The agreement brought the Arab region – except the Hejaz – under the mandate system. This division was finalized in Lausanne in 1922. The Allies had already settled this question in 1920 in San Remo, but Turkey did not then ratify the agreement. The Hejaz, according to the agreement, now became independent. Britain was granted a mandate for the territory comprising all of Palestine and what is now Jordan (which was thus separated from Greater Syria of which it was formerly a part). New borders were drawn up without Arab agreement. The Zionists still argue that the Palestinians were to establish their State in Jordan. In reality, the connection with Jordan has only existed since 1922 – thanks to an arbitrary act by the Allies. In 1928, the British themselves ended the connection by granting Jordan constitutional autonomy. In Palestine, other rules had applied from the beginning.

On 24 July 1922, the League of Nations approved the British mandate for Palestine. As the League of Nations statutes required that the population had to be consulted before government by mandate, Wilson sent the King-Crane Commission to the Middle East. England and France refused to take part in the commission: they were not in the least interested in the views of the Arab population. The results of the poll were clear: the Arabs did not want the mandate; they wanted independence. But if there had to be a transitional mandate, they said they would prefer the United States to be the mandatory power. They also rejected the Zionist plans. But no one bothered about the commission's findings. The British, the Zionists and the French spread the rumour that the results had been rigged.

The PLO and Palestine

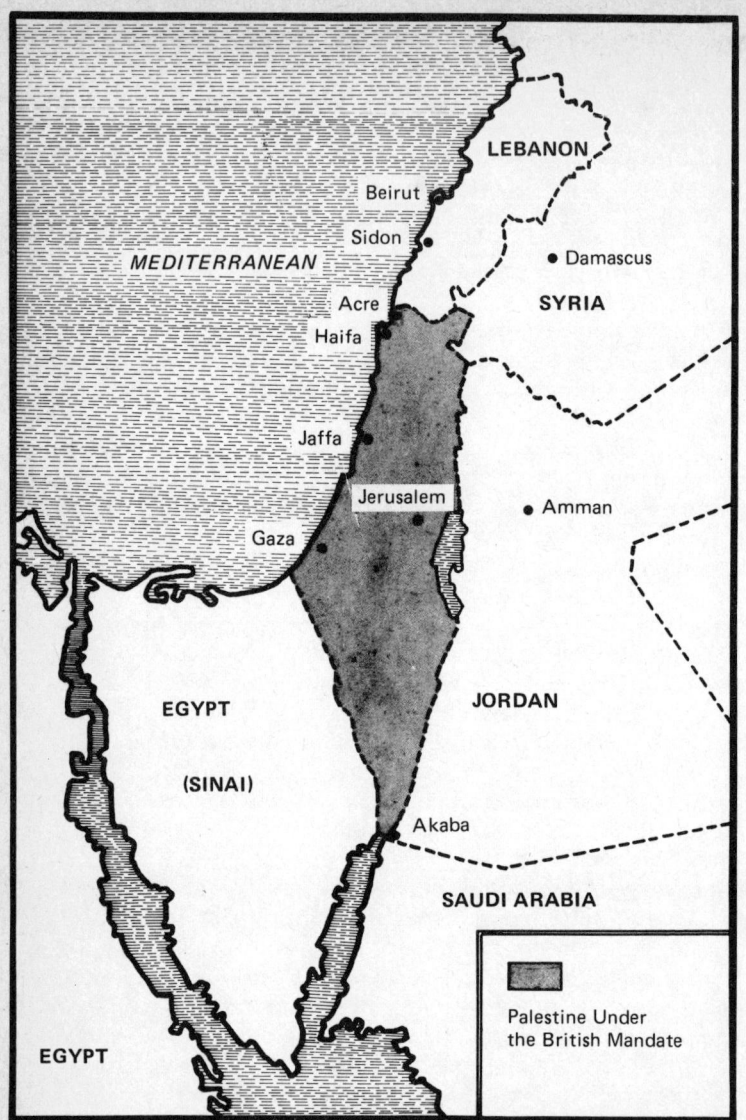

The Mandate Regime and the League of Nations Pact in International Law

To all appearances, the mandate system did not violate the statutes of the League of Nations. Article 22 of the League of Nations statutes says:

1. To those colonies and territories, which as a consequence of the late war have ceased to be under the sovereignty of the States which formerly governed them, and which are inhabited by peoples not yet able to stand by themselves under the strenuous conditions of the modern world, there should be applied the principle that the well-being and development of such peoples form a sacred trust of civilisation, and that securities for the performance of this trust should be embodied in this Covenant.

2. The best method of giving practical effect to this principle is that the tutelage of such peoples should be entrusted to advanced nations who, by reason of their resources, their experience, or their geographical position, can best undertake this responsibility, and who are willing to accept it, and that this tutelage should be exercised by them as Mandatories on behalf of the League.

3. The character of the Mandate must differ according to the stage of the development of the people, the geographical situation of the territory, its economic conditions and other similar circumstances.

4. Certain communities formerly belonging to the Turkish Empire have reached a stage of development where their existence as independent nations can be provisionally recognised subject to the rendering of administrative advice and assistance by a Mandatory until such time as they are able to stand alone. The wishes of these communities must be a principal consideration in the selection of the Mandatory.

5. Other peoples, especially those of Central Africa, are at such a stage that the Mandatory must be responsible for the administration of the territory under conditions which will guarantee freedom of conscience and religion, subject only to the maintenance of public order and morals, the prohibition of abuses such as the slave trade, the arms traffic and the liquor traffic, and the prevention of the establishment of fortifications or military and naval bases, and of military training of the natives for other than police purposes and the defence of territory, and will also secure equal opportunities for the trade and commerce of other Members of the League.

These principles fully conform to Article 22 of the League of Nations statutes. But other articles of the document conflict with the statutes – in particular Article 2, in which the Balfour Declaration is reproduced in full.

From the legal point of view, the Balfour Declaration must be regarded as null and void. In this declaration of 1917, England promised to hand over a country which it did not possess to a political group which had no right to it. Furthermore, the declaration was made in a private letter to Lord Rothschild, a private individual who represented no legally recognized community. The alleged purpose of the occupation of Palestine at that time was to drive out the Turks, not to dispose of the country at will.

Even assuming that Palestine was occupied in time of war and that the conventions of war could be cited, the preamble to Convention IV of the Hague Agreement would be applicable. This states that the population of an occupied region enjoys the protection of international law. And this in turn forbids an occupying power to alienate land to another power. This, however, is precisely what the Balfour Declaration did.

Quite apart from its nullity, the Balfour Declaration conflicts with important principles of the statutes of the League of Nations. Article 20 of the statutes says:

> 1. The Members of the League severally agree that this Covenant is accepted as abrogating all obligations or understandings *inter se* which are inconsistent with the terms thereof, and solemnly undertake that they will not hereafter enter into any engagements inconsistent with the terms thereof.

This principle ought to have been applied first and foremost to the Balfour Declaration. Instead it was merely written into the mandate document. The establishment of a national homeland for Jews in Palestine clearly violated the rights of the Arab population of the country – and England's duty was precisely to protect those rights. By including the Balfour Declaration in the mandate document, Britain committed itself to work against the interests of the Arabs, in favour of the Zionists. In a number of supplementary articles, Britain even committed itself to ensuring that the promises of the Zionists would be kept.

It must finally be noted that Article 22 of the League of Nations statutes required the Arab people to give their approval to the mandate. They did not do so. Legally, those clauses of the mandate document which conflicted with the Pact of the League of Nations must be regarded as null and void. This did not prevent Great Britain from being granted the mandate for Palestine.

International jurist Heinz Wagner has described the other measures of the Allies in the Middle East as 'like something out of a Gilbert and Sullivan opera'. Winston Churchill allocated the thrones in the Middle East: the throne of Jordan went to Emir Abdullah; to compensate for the loss of Syria, Feisal was given Iraq; with Hussein in Hejaz, the Hashemite dynasty now ruled Hejaz, Iraq and Jordan (then known as Transjordan). This region became independent in 1946. But the British wished to retain control of Palestine for as long as possible.

Despite the inclusion of the Balfour Declaration, the mandate document does not state that the Zionists could set up an independent Jewish State in Palestine. In 1920, Churchill wrote in a memorandum: 'The text of the Balfour Declaration does not state that all of Palestine should be transformed into a Jewish national homeland, it states that such a homeland should be established *in* Palestine. It never envisaged the disappearance or subjugation of the Arab population, its language and its traditions in Palestine.'

Notes

1. Theodor Herzl, *Der Judenstaat* (1895) p. 213, quoted in Richard Stevens, *Palastina Monographien No. 8* (Rastatt, 1976), p. 25.
2. Ibid., p. 213.
3. Heinz Wagner, *The Arab-Israeli Conflict in International Law* (Berlin, 1971), p. 107.
4. Joseph Jeffries, *Palestine: The Reality* (New York, 1939), pp. 234–5.
5. Wagner, op. cit., p. 122.
6. *Palastina Monographien No. 8*, p. 94.

8. Palestine under the British Mandate

The Situation in Palestine at the Beginning of the Mandate

> There has never been a Palestinian people . . . it is not true that there was a Palestinian people that felt that they were one race and that we came along and threw them out and took away their land. Such a people did not exist.[1]

At the beginning of the mandate, the total area of Palestine, including inland waters, was 27,026 sq.km. In 1918, Palestine had a population of about 700,000, of whom 644,000 were Arabs (574,000 Muslims and 70,000 Christians) and 56,000 were Jews. In 1922, the total population was 757,182, of whom 590,000 were Muslims, 83,794 were Jews, 73,014 were Christians and 9,474 were members of other religions. So between 1918 and 1922 the number of Jews in Palestine had risen to over 12%. In 1918, total agricultural land in Palestine was 2,663,231 hectares, of which Jews owned about 2%.

During the British conquest of Palestine – the professed purpose of which was liberation from Turkish rule – the British had set up a military administration. In 1920 this was replaced by a civilian administration. When the League of Nations granted Great Britain the mandate for Palestine, it set up a mandate government. Now the statutes of the League of Nations stipulated that mandatory powers should only rule indirectly. And this was in fact the case with mandate governments in most Arab states. But in Palestine this statute was violated: there Great Britain ruled directly and the mandate government had full legislative, administrative and judicial competence.

Legislation was enacted through the 'ordinances' issued by the British High Commissioner. Laws could be passed in Palestine not only by the mandate government but also by the British government itself. The High Commissioner appointed by Great Britain was the head of the executive. He was assisted by an executive council and an advisory council.

By its own admission, Great Britain could not allow a process of democratization to take place in Palestine. It had included the Balfour

Declaration in the mandate document and had thereby committed itself to call for the founding of a 'Jewish national home'.[2] If Palestine with its overwhelming Arab majority had had democratic institutions, the Zionists' demands could never have been realized.

England now sent a considerable number of British Zionists to Palestine to ensure the implementation of the Balfour Declaration. Among them was Herbert Samuel, one of the master-minds of the Balfour Declaration. These officials promulgated the first immigration law as early as 1920. The law set an immigration quota of 16,500 Jews per annum.

The British mandate government passed a number of important laws on the division of land, and the registration and settlement of Jews. These laws were bound to sow discord between property owners and their tenants. The beneficiaries were to be the Zionists, as we shall see later.

The British also granted the Jews licences to exploit mineral resources and carry out infrastructural projects. Jewish firms increasingly took control of irrigation, electrification and the exploitation of the country's most important mineral resources.

All these measures taken by the British government served to implement the Balfour Declaration. But as already mentioned in the previous chapter, the mandate also imposed on Great Britain numerous obligations to the population of the mandated territory. The majority at this time was Arab (1922: 88%). A conflict was therefore bound to arise for the British government between the Balfour Declaration on the one hand and the obligations to the Palestinian population laid down in the mandate document, the statutes of the League of Nations and the British-Arab agreements on the other hand. This conflict was to worsen steadily till the end of the mandate, as Great Britain was never able to exorcize the evil spirits it had raised.

The Extension of Zionist Power in Palestine

The ultimate aim of the Zionists in Palestine was clear: to make Palestine into a Jewish State. The Balfour Declaration and its inclusion in the mandate document provided an excellent starting point for this aim. Officially, however, no mention of an independent State was made: the Jews were to have a 'homeland' in Palestine. The Zionists now proposed to gain as much as possible from and through the British until they were in a position to achieve their ends without British help.

On the diplomatic level, the Zionists tried to interpret British commitments to the 'national home' as strongly as possible in their favour. They also sought the support of Jews throughout the world and of the Western powers. On the practical level, they set about building up efficient organizations for the pursuit of two major objectives: to exercise maximum influence over the British mandate administration and policies, and to create structures which would later enable them to take over power in Palestine.

With financial backing from rich Jews and Zionists abroad and with the help of influential members of Western governments, the Zionists established numerous organizations inside and outside Palestine. As early as April 1918, when Palestine was still under military administration, the Zionist Commission in Palestine was founded. Its first leader was Weizmann.

This organization, like all Zionist organizations in Palestine, claimed to represent all the Jews in the world, as Zionist ideology stated that Palestine was to become the home of all Jews. This commission advised the military government on all questions connected with the 'Jewish national home'. A practice which was highly dubious in international law was thereby established: an organization claiming to represent people the majority of whom did not live in the country and were unlikely ever to do so became involved in the administration of that country. Understandably, there were conflicts between the British mandate government and the Zionist Commission, which insisted that the British should do everything in their power to establish the 'Jewish national home' immediately. The mandate document did, after all, commit the British to safeguard the well-being and the rights of the Arab population. In 1920, the British governor of Palestine wrote to the British government:

> On the other hand, the Zionist Commission accuses me and my officers of anti-Zionism. The situation is intolerable, and in justice to my officers and myself, must be fairly faced.
>
> It is manifestly impossible to please partisans who officially claim nothing more than a 'National Home' but in reality will be satisfied with nothing less than a Jewish state and all that it politically implies.[3]

The Zionist Commission would only grant the mandatory power the right to defend the country. It demanded sole competence in the administration of the country. At a Zionist congress in 1918, the Zionist Commission called for: the Jewish flag to be the official national flag; the country to be named 'Eretz Israel'; a military organization for the Jewish community and a large degree of control over decisions by the military government. All this at a time when the Jews constituted just 10% of Palestine's population! Zionist logic was based on the assumption that all the Jews in the world were potential future inhabitants of Israel. According to this logic, the Jews were in the majority and all political decisions were to be made in favour of this future Jewish majority.

The Zionist movement would have remained weak if it had not received substantial support at the international level. This support came from the world-wide Zionist Organization, which later was effectively absorbed into the Jewish Agency; one and the same person was usually the leader of both organizations. The Zionist Organization was founded in

Palestine under the British Mandate

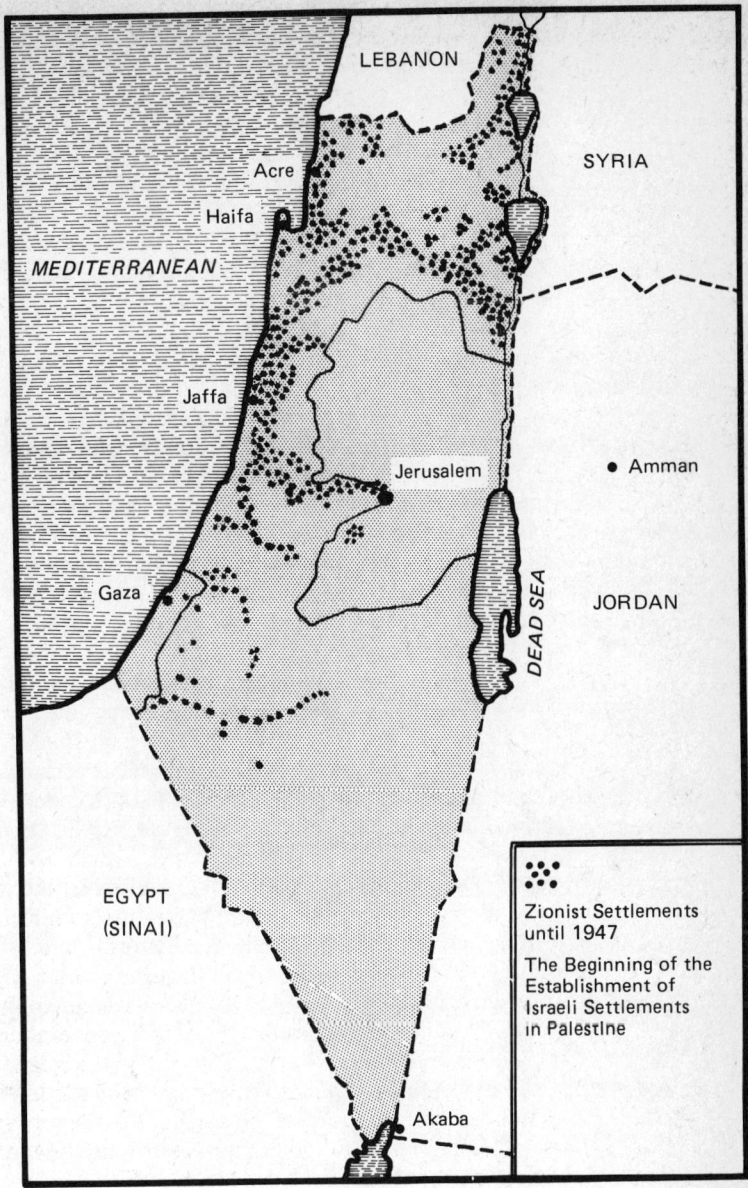

1897 in Basle and was divided into national associations, though it also included a number of special associations with different social, religious, national or political orientations. The differences, which still exist, between Jews throughout the world must be remembered: between Slav, Russian and Central European, and Spanish, Yemenite and Moroccan Jews; strictly orthodox Jews and Jews who called themselves socialist or nationalist. All these groups sent delegates to the regular congresses of the Zionist Organization. The unifying factor of all these groups was their common aim: the founding of a Jewish State. But in addition to this, they also pursued other supplementary goals, on which they differed. They also differed on the means of achieving these goals. Some wanted a socialist State, others wanted a theocratic State. The revisionists – extreme right-wingers led by Jabotinsky – even wanted all of Jordan to be incorporated into this State.

The supreme body of the Zionist Organization was the World Zionist Congress, which met every two years. In 1928, the executive of this organization was expanded and the Jewish Agency was formed. This meant that non-Zionist Jews were now also involved in the construction of the Jewish State. In fact the majority of Jews at that time wished to remain in their home countries and saw no reason for emigrating to Palestine. Pressured by the Zionists to help their co-religionists, they performed this duty by donating money or by propaganda and pressure on Western governments.

The Agency was to advise the Zionist Organization in Palestine and to assist it in the construction of the Jewish State. The Agency's supreme body was the Council. The Agency spearheaded the establishment of Jewish organizations and groups in Palestine. Although the Agency was officially a supranational organization, it soon developed into a second government in Palestine alongside the mandate government. The mandate government acquiesced in this arrangement and, furthermore, recognized the Zionist organizations. It granted the Agency a right of participation in the development but not in the administration of the country. A bizarre arrangement: for how can one contribute to the development of a country without administrative authority?

In reality it was the Jewish Agency which controlled immigration – legal and illegal – colonization, and settlement policy. Its offices in Europe, America and Palestine decided who was allowed to enter Palestine: primarily skilled craftsmen, agricultural workers, young, healthy people, intellectuals and wealthy Jews. In Palestine, the Agency set up a separate education and health system for the Jews. It also ran two funds to finance the Palestine project: *Keren Hajessod* and *Keren Kayamet Leisrael* (KKL). The KKL was responsible for the purchase of land and its allocation to Jewish settlers. *Keren Hajessod* provided funds for development, infrastructure and settlement. The KKL allocated land to Jews on the following conditions: the land purchased was to be regarded as the inalienable property of the Jewish race and could only be cultivated by Jews. It was never to be sold to Arabs. The purpose of these measures was to ensure that land bought by Jews remained in Jewish hands for ever. (For a further discussion of Jewish land acquisition in Palestine see the next section of this chapter.) The principle of 'Jewish labour' also applied: the result was that workers, farmers and tenants on land purchased by Jews became unemployed and were forced to leave that land. By this method, certain areas could be 'cleared of Palestinians' during the British mandate. This was the first method the Zionists applied to drive the Palestinians from their land.

Keren Hajessod was also funded from donations. Thanks to these two funds and with the aid of a number of banks such as the Jewish Colonial Bank, the Zionists gradually gained control of the country's economy. And with the licences they had acquired they soon dominated industry in Palestine.

Another key institution in the construction of the Jewish State was *Histadruth*. It was meant to be a trades union but in fact it was – and still is – the most important employer and entrepreneur in Palestine.

Histadruth ensured strict observance of the principle of 'Jewish labour'. It created most of the new jobs in Palestine – but only for Jews, with the result that increasingly large numbers of Palestinians became jobless. Wagner writes: 'One of the extraordinary follies of Jewish workers was that, in all seriousness, they regarded the ban on the employment of Arab workers as consistent with the class struggle.'[4]

Supporters of *Histadruth* in fact described themselves as socialists. They said that refusing work to Arabs was a means of preventing the exploitation of the Arab proletariat by Jewish entrepreneurs! This policy was bound to widen the gap between Palestinians and Jewish immigrants still further. A Jewish co-operative also ensured that Jews produced the goods they needed themselves and did not buy them from Arabs. This meant a permanent boycott of Arab products, which plunged Arab farmers into even worse crises and distress. The Jewish settlers also established kibbutzim or communities of settlers in areas which, though not very productive, were regarded as strategically important for the subsequent construction of the Jewish State. And of course only Jews were permitted to settle in the kibbutzim.

Finally, the right-wing Zionist leader Jabotinsky founded the Haganah, a Jewish underground army, in 1920.

All the institutions which the Zionists created at the beginning of the British mandate were designed to achieve Jewish political and economic power in all of Palestine. The Palestinian population was to be isolated, deprived of land and work, and finally forced to leave the country. Thus, any chance of agreement between the Palestinian and the Jewish populations was quite deliberately destroyed.

With their institutions thus consolidated, the Zionists were able to exert political pressure on Western governments. They concentrated their efforts on London and Geneva, the headquarters of the League of

Nations, and later on the United States. In London, Zionists were extremely influential at the beginning of the thirties. And in Geneva, where Great Britain was constantly called upon to justify its mandate policy before the League of Nations Mandate Commission, the Geneva office of the Jewish Agency succeeded in influencing almost all the members of the Commission. This was the background against which the struggle for Palestine began.

The Struggle for Palestine: Confrontation

The Palestinians now realized the extent of the danger posed by the Zionist movement. They tried to organize themselves politically. But the position from which they started was far less favourable than that of the Zionists. The country had long been ruled by the Ottomans and simply lacked structures which could have hastened and facilitated such organization. Arabs from Syria and Palestine did set up the General Syrian Congress in 1920, but as free elections were impossible under colonial rule, it consisted mainly of appointed dignitaries, the heads of influential families and intellectuals. The British, while actually preventing free and representative elections, at first refused to recognize the members of the congress on the grounds that they had not been freely elected! The other European states reacted in the same way. This meant that there were scarcely any Arab spokesmen who were recognized as such in the West. The British were pursuing a subtle tactic here: they appointed and dismissed leading Arab personalities and thus stirred up rivalry between leading Arab families. In 1918, for example, the mayor of Jerusalem was dismissed by the British for taking part in a nationalist demonstration. With tactics such as these, the mandatory power tried to prevent any consistent, co-ordinated approach by the Palestinians. While Zionists throughout the world were putting pressure on governments, the voices of the Palestinians fell on deaf ears. Furthermore, the Palestinians refused to found institutions which would have been controlled by the mandatory powers because they had always rejected the mandate system.

In Palestine, the Arabs organized themselves in the Supreme Muslim Council under the leadership of Hadj Amin El Husseini. But the authority of the council did not extend much beyond religious matters. In 1920, the Arab Executive, led by Musa Kasim Pasha, was founded at the first Palestinian-Arab Congress in Haifa. This date marks the beginning of the Palestinian national movement. The congress had been called by Christians and Muslims. Both communities, Christian and Muslim, decided on joint measures against Zionism and the British mandatory government. The delegates were representatives of both Christian and Muslim associations in Palestine.

The congress called on the British to hold free elections to a representative parliament. The British refused because this would have ruined the Zionists' plans.

Some months before, on Easter Sunday, the Palestinians had demonstrated against Zionist policies. The British then set up a Commission of Enquiry, which could do no more than record the fears and disappointment of the Arab population. The Palestinians complained to the Mandate Commission in Geneva, where they stressed the right of national self-determination. But the Commission said that it was not competent to question the mandate. It declared itself still convinced that Great Britain was capable of honouring its dual obligations.

The Zionists were now openly admitting their aims. In 1921, Dr Eder, a member of the Zionist Commission, insisted that only Jews should be allowed to carry arms in Palestine. In March 1921, there were serious outbreaks of violence in Palestine. There was fierce street fighting in Jaffa. 157 Palestinians were killed and 705 injured. On 3 July, the British government finally made a statement in which it quoted the Churchill memorandum (mentioned previously) with the object of calming the Palestinian population. But the statement also reaffirmed the Zionists' right to Palestine. At any rate, it did not prevent the continuing influx of Jewish immigrants.

In 1921, the mandatory government said that immigration quotas would be linked to the number of jobs available. But the Zionists, who now increasingly controlled the country's economic life, had no difficulty in proving that jobs existed.

In the 1920s, Palestinian resistance took on new, more powerful forms: strikes, mass demonstrations and limited operations emphasized the Palestinian people's rejection of the British mandate and of Jewish plans.

In 1922, the British tried to set up a joint administrative institution on which Jews, Christians and Muslims were represented. This body would have limited authority and the Arabs would have a majority of votes. But there would also be British civil servants on this legislative council. The Jews accepted the plan conditionally but the Arabs rejected it on the grounds that the Jews and pro-Zionist British officials together would have a *de facto* majority when decisions were taken. The legislative council could not be elected in 1923 because the Arabs boycotted the elections. The same year, the Arab Executive again rejected the establishment of a Jewish national home and demanded that the Palestinian people be given full power to run their own affairs.

In 1925, Christians and Muslims went on strike when Lord Balfour came to Jerusalem to open the university. Demonstrations against British pro-Zionist policy were also held in Damascus.

By 1927, these demonstrations had become so frequent that the British were using bombers to deter demonstrators. On 23 July 1927, the seventh Arab Congress sent the British High Commissioner a letter calling for a parliamentary government in Palestine.

In 1929, the Mufti of Jerusalem called for Arabs to be given political and economic equality with Jews and for restrictions to be placed on immigration. The same year there were further outbreaks of unrest. The Palestinians went on strike and Great Britain responded by increasing the penalties for resistance to the mandatory power. The Zionists took advantage of the unrest to increase their military strength. The British even helped them here by their intransigence towards Arab demands.

Finally, Great Britain imposed martial law in Palestine in 1929 and set up a new Commission of Enquiry. The result was the Shaw Report which blamed the 'national home' policy for the unrest. The Commission recommended that the British should review their immigration policies as the number of Jewish immigrants in 1925 and 1926 had been excessively high. The Commission also called for a review of Jewish acquisition of land. Shortly afterwards, another commission reported that the country's economic capacity for immigrants was exhausted. It added that there was not enough land to feed all the Arab families. Only improvements in farmers' standards of living and in methods of cultivation could create space for a further 20,000 immigrants. In 1930, the Passfield White Paper was published. It emphasized that the mandatory power attached equal importance to its obligations to the Zionists and to the Arabs. The report accepted the findings of both the previous commission reports and called for tighter controls on immigration. The British government justified this attitude as follows:

> These points are emphasized because claims have been made on behalf of the Jewish Agency to a position in regard to the general administration of the country which His Majesty's Government cannot but regard as going far beyond the clear intention of the Mandate.[5]

Although the Passfield White Paper stressed the rights of the Palestinians, the Palestinian response to it was far from enthusiastic. The British government still insisted that it could meet its obligations to the Palestinians and to the Zionists and still refused to see any incompatibility between the two. The Palestinians, however, had rejected the mandate system from the beginning precisely because they were aware of this incompatibility and because they feared that they would become its victims. It was clear even then that the mandatory government would never succeed in keeping Zionist ambitions in check. It must be acknowledged that some English politicians did not approve of the Zionist plans and foresaw their disastrous consequences. But their efforts were neutralized by intense Zionist pressure. This situation was underlined by Zionist reactions to the White Paper. Although they had hitherto only been able to realize their plans with British help, they now accused the British of being anti-Semites. Zionist pressure on the British Parliament was so intense that Prime Minister MacDonald issued a statement to calm Zionist rage.

The Arabs now found that although one commission after another acknowledged the justice of their cause, Zionist influence on Western politicians prevented any action on their behalf. Since 1920, the Palestinians had constantly been trying to bring pressure to bear at the political level. They had made representations to British Commissions of Enquiry, to the Mandate Commission in Geneva and to the British Parliament. Commissions which produced no results, constant Zionist pressure, and the loss of their land and of their economic means of survival forced the Palestinians to resort more and more frequently to strikes and mass demonstrations. They knew that the Zionists did not want a homeland, but all of Palestine as a Jewish State in which the Arabs would end up as an outlawed minority. England was proving increasingly incapable of resisting Zionist pressure. There were a number of Zionists in the British administrative apparatus. The Palestinians, on the other hand, had no means of co-ordinating their internal policies against the mandatory power. They also lacked the international contacts which might have enabled them to match the Zionist pressure on Western governments. The Zionists had a great advantage here: having originally come from Europe, they were thoroughly familiar with the centres of power there. The Zionist reactions to the Passfield White Paper provide clear evidence of this influence. In *Israel: The History of a State*, David Ben-Gurion describes what happened after the publication of the Passfield White Paper. The Mapai party which had been founded in 1930 sent Dov Hos to Ernest Bevin, a member of the British Labour party. Ben-Gurion writes:

> Hos's mission was a complete success. He and Bevin did not address one another as comrades but as brothers, and when Hos gave brother Bevin details of the White Paper Bevin promised to instruct his 'boys' to vote against the government if the White Paper was not withdrawn. Bevin went to MacDonald and threatened that his people would vote against him. The Prime Minister was alarmed. A cabinet commission chaired by Arthur Henderson, a pro-Zionist, was set up. Henderson 'interpreted' Passfield's White Paper, turning its meaning upside down. The MacDonald cabinet approved this interpretation and published it even before the congress in a letter to Weizmann.[6]

Such accounts make it easy enough to understand why the Palestinians did not trust the British and regarded them as allies of Zionism. The Arab political parties founded in Palestine during the 1930s therefore concentrated mainly on the struggle against the British as the mandatory power. They hoped that the end of the mandate would also mean the end of Jewish immigration.

The Zionists, on the other hand, concentrated on the acquisition of Palestinian land. Nor were they fussy about the methods they used. Land purchase was the first method. To a certain extent, the property laws of the time worked in their favour. In the Ottoman era, the notion of private property was nothing like as clearly defined as in Europe. To take the case of estates owned by the State: this property was not listed in the land register as belonging to any one individual or group of individuals. It was generally placed at the disposal of village communities, which in turn allocated it to farmers. These farmers were allowed to use the land as long as they cultivated it. Many families, indeed entire villages, lived on land which they had cultivated for centuries and to which they therefore had a right by customary law. In return, they had to pay a certain tax on their harvest to the Ottoman empire. During the reform of the Ottoman empire, the Turks introduced new laws on property. The dissatisfaction of the Arab population and economic considerations led them to extend the system of private property. They gave some Arab families the opportunity to use state property as a capital investment. These Arab families relieved the Turks of the tedious tasks of administration and tax gathering. It is a well-known fact that two or three influential families from other Arab countries acquired property in Palestine in this way, and so got their names on to the land registers as its owners. In fact, these families were only supposed to administer the property, but corruption at the end of the Ottoman empire was so rife that manoeuvres such as these were possible. These few families, who were effectively working on behalf of the Ottoman rulers, were cut off from their property after the Turkish defeat. These properties were now controlled by the British, who led the farmers to believe that they were no longer bound to the registered owners since Ottoman rule had come to an end. As these families could no longer make any profit from the land, they sold it to the Zionists, who then drove out the Palestinian farmers. The most typical example of this phenomenon is that of the Sursock family of Beirut. In 1872, this family got its name on the register as the owner of 18,000 hectares near Haifa. There were 22 villages in this area. The Sursock family had bought the right to administer it from the Turkish government. Sursock became the steward and tax gatherer and bought up the harvest. The farmers did not notice any change and did not complain. After 1918, the family was cut off from its property and sold the land to the Zionists.

This method of land acquisition was not very much used by the Zionists. By 1948, only 4% of Palestinian land had passed into Zionist hands in this way, because Palestinian farmers with small plots of land definitively refused to sell their land. The Zionists therefore set about acquiring more land by claiming property not registered as belonging to private individuals – i.e. land which the British had taken over from the Turks. The inhabitants of this land, who had cultivated it for generations but could produce no written evidence of ownership, were thus robbed of their land. The Bedouins were also unable to prove their claims to pasture land they had used for generations; they, too, lost their land. With British support, the Zionists now settled in these ares, driving out the villagers, tenants and Bedouins. This policy is still being pursued today in the Negev desert.

In spite of all this, the Zionists still owned only 5.4% of Palestinian land by 1945. As the Zionists could never grab all of Palestine by this method, they were obliged to resort to the final means – violence.

By the end of 1934, the number of Jewish immigrants in Palestine had risen from 175,000 (1931) to 250,000. *The Times* reported that there were as many illegal as legal immigrants in the country at that time. Palestinian discontent and militancy increased. To placate the Arab population, the British tried again in 1935 to establish a mixed executive council. Again the Arabs refused, knowing that they could always be outvoted by the Zionists and the British civil servants. The mandatory government made it clear to the Arabs that it would not permit a democratically elected government until the Arabs recognized the 'national home policy'.

The Zionists also rejected the British proposals. For them, an Arab majority on the legislative council meant the end of Jewish colonization of Palestine. They were convinced that the British would not use their veto against Arab decisions indefinitely. They therefore mobilized their influence in the British Parliament and at the permanent Mandate Commission, which finally rejected the plan.

In 1936, the Arab political parties again called for a democratic government, the end of Jewish immigration and a ban on the sale of land to Jews. In April, the Palestinian people proclaimed their support for these demands and called a general strike. There was fierce street fighting between Arabs and Jews in Jaffa, Tel Aviv and other towns. The Palestinian people now summoned up all their strength to resist the Zionist land purchase policy. They sold their valuables to buy weapons. They went on strike for six months, paralysing the country's economy. The British government reacted firmly to the strike: it supplied the police with tanks and tightened emergency measures. The number of arrests and house searches increased continually. The strikers were forced to pay heavy fines; anyone caught with a weapon faced the death penalty. The owners of houses from which rebels had sniped or shot at police and troops had their property confiscated. But this brutal repression only strengthened the Palestinian people's will to resist. The Palestinians rejected the establishment of British commissions of enquiry and negotiations with the mandatory government until Jewish immigration was stopped. The Jews by now constituted 30% of the population. The Arab parties reorganized themselves into the Arab Higher Committee in 1936. At the request of the kings of Saudi Arabia, Iraq and Jordan, the Committee, on 4 October 1936, called on the population to cease hostilities and end the strikes. The Zionists had meanwhile even managed to capitalize on the strike. The port of Jaffa had been closed as a result of the fighting and the British High Commissioner gave the Zionists permission to built a new port in Tel Aviv.

When the fighting stopped, the British set up yet another Commission of Enquiry, the Peel Commission. In its report, published in 1937, the British conceded for the first time that their dual obligations to Arabs and Zionists were incompatible and could not be fulfilled. If the mandate was to continue, Jewish land purchase would have to be restricted to certain areas. Immigration, it said, should no longer be regulated solely according to economic requirements; political aspects would also have to be taken into account. In the next five years, immigration would have to be limited to 12,000 people per year. (144,093 Jews immigrated to Palestine between 1932 and 1935.) The report said that unless the mandate were prolonged, Palestine would have to be partitioned. A Jewish State would have to be established in part of Palestine. Another area would be Arab territory and would be united with Jordan. The rest of Palestine would remain under British mandate. According to this plan, Jews, who then owned about 5.6% of the land, would get 40% of Palestinian territory, and the most fertile part at that! Forcible resettlement of the Arab population was also considered.

The British government agreed to the Commission's proposals and agreed to reduce the immigration quota to 8,000 for the next eight months. The Arab population objected violently to a partition of Palestine. Many Palestinians were now arrested or murdered, some by special Jewish troops trained by the British. Moshe Dayan was a member of this élite special unit.

Then two British civil servants were murdered. The mandatory government closed down the telephone network, occupied all strategic points in the country and disbanded the Arab Higher Committee. The Mufti of Jerusalem, El Husseini, was arrested but escaped and fled to Damascus. Most Arab leaders were deported. Military courts were set up in the place of civil courts. Palestinian resistance went on continuously until 1939.

Great Britain was now entrusted by the League of Nations with the task of the partition of Palestine. Official statistics for August 1937 show that the population of Palestine totalled 1,360,142, of whom 61.2% were Muslims, 29.6% Jews and 8.4% Christians.

The Zionists could not at first agree about the plan to partition Palestine. The official leadership (Weizmann and Ben-Gurion) was encouraged by the fact that a Jewish State, instead of a homeland, had been officially mentioned for the first time. They regarded this as a first step; they could always appropriate the rest of Palestine later. Right-wing radical leaders such as Jabotinsky regarded the plan as a betrayal of the final goal: the establishment of Greater Israel on both sides of the Jordan. American Jews were also against the plan. However, it was difficult for the Zionist movement to reject the plan. The seizure of power by Hitler in Germany forced the Zionists to avoid a confrontation with Great Britain at this point. The Zionists therefore criticized the plan but decided to accept it for the time being.

The British government now fixed the immigration quota for the period from 1 August 1937 to 31 March 1938 at 9,600. The Arabs still rejected the plans to partition Palestine, and so the British government sent the Woodhead Commission to Palestine. It presented a new plan but this soon went by the board. The British were now forced, for world political reasons, to take more account of Arab feeling. War with Germany was looming again and, as in 1914, every effort had to be made to prevent the Arabs from going over to England's enemies, Germany and Italy. This, however, was precisely what the Arabs now threatened to do. To prevent the opening of a third front and to maintain their influence in the Middle East, the British now called a conference in London. The imprisoned members of the Arab Committee were released for the occasion. Between July and September 1938, 604 Palestinians, 106 Jews and 28 Britons were killed in Palestine.

At the London conference in February 1939 the Palestinians called for independence for Palestine, and a halt to Jewish immigration and Jewish land acquisition. They guaranteed the Jewish minority protection, respect for their rights and their equality as citizens, and free access to the holy places of Judaism. The Zionists rejected this offer and accepted the plan of partition. The conference ended without agreement. On 17 March 1939, the British published a final White Paper by means of which they hoped to guarantee Arab neutrality at least in the war which now loomed. This document, known as the MacDonald White Paper, stated that Great Britain did not intend to make Palestine a Jewish State. Its aim, the paper declared, was for Palestine to become a sovereign, democratic State. It promised that only 75,000 Jews would be allowed to immigrate to Palestine by 1944, after which any further immigration would occur only with the approval of the Arab population. The proportion of Jews in the Palestinian population was not to exceed one third. And in certain zones the British High Commissioner would forbid the purchase of land by Jews.

Soon afterwards, alarmed at the high rate of illegal immigration, the mandatory government stopped immigration. Palestinian reactions to the White Paper were mixed. The Arab Higher Committee rejected it because it provided for Palestine to become independent only after ten years and by then Jews might form the majority of the population. The Mandate Commission of the League of Nations and pro-Zionist British politicians, such as Churchill, rejected the White Paper. The Zionists of course rejected it outright. From 1938 onwards, they stepped up illegal immigration, partly with the connivance of the French government which allowed Jews to enter Lebanon, from where they could easily enter Palestine. The Jewish Agency regarded the White Paper as illegal and promised to fight its proposals tooth and nail. In Palestine itself the Jews organized protest marches and demonstrations, shot British policemen, attacked Arabs and stoned Arab shops. But the official Zionist leadership was in an awkward position. With war looming, they could not fight against England. Ben-Gurion summed up his strategy at the Zionist Congress in Geneva in August 1939: 'We will fight with England against Hitler as if the White Paper did not exist and we will fight the White Paper as if there were no war.'[7] A few days later the war began.

The Second World War: The Zionists and the Persecution of Jews

One of the most important moves in the campaign against the White Paper was the transfer of the Zionist headquarters from London to Washington. The Zionists now counted mainly on the United States. They had successfully used the British to repress the Palestinians and to implement their plans, but they now realized that there was no more to be gained from the British. In the USA, on the other hand, Zionist influence was steadily increasing. Ben-Gurion wrote: 'America's entry into the war no longer left any doubt that the United States, not England, would be the decisive factor after the war.'[8]

The Zionists were now backing another horse – a strategy they had always employed and which always paid off. Before the First World War they had offered Germany and Turkey their aid against the British. In the First World War itself, they offered their support to further British ambitions in the Middle East. And now that Great Britain was about to lose its place in the forefront of world politics to the United States, the Zionists sought an alliance with the USA.

While Weizmann continued to cultivate contacts in London, Ben-Gurion travelled all over the United States drumming up the support of American Jews against the MacDonald White Paper. This double strategy enabled the Zionists to strengthen their support in the United States while at the same time maintaining good contacts with leading British pro-Zionists. The strategy culminated in the calling of a meeting of all Zionist organizations and parties at the Biltmore Hotel, New York, in May 1942. The delegates at this meeting, which was chaired by Ben-Gurion, called for:

> the gates of Palestine to be opened, the Jewish Agency to control immigration and to be given competence for all questions of the cultivation and development of the land. Palestine to become 'an independent Jewish commonwealth'.[9]

The term 'commonwealth' was cleverly chosen to conciliate the British. Now, for the first time, all Zionist groupings were officially demanding an end to the British mandate and the founding of a Jewish State in Palestine. Ben-Gurion now became leader of the Zionist movement, and won over the USA as the new protector and patron of the Zionists. At the same time, Zionist activities in Palestine were stepped up in conformity with the Zionist double strategy. As Ben-Gurion had recommended, the official leadership avoided any confrontation with Great Britain in the war years, yet at the same time Jewish underground organizations in Palestine itself became increasingly violent. Naturally the official leadership always denied responsibility for acts of violence. In fact the Zionists in Palestine itself had worked out an allocation of roles. In 1937, Irgun-Zwai-Leumi broke away from the Haganah. Irgun-Zwai-Leumi, a paramilitary organization, was led by a former Jabotinsky follower and allegedly regarded the Haganah as too moderate. Later Begin became leader of the Irgun. The Irgun's aim was to conduct a campaign of terror against the Arab population as well as the British. Later the 'Stern group' broke away from Irgun. This group wished to declare war on Great Britain, whereas the Irgun, officially at least, argued against formal hostilities against the British during the war.

Officially, the Haganah was a military organization which acted only on instructions from the Jewish Agency. Irgun and the Stern group, on the other hand, constituted the so-called uncontrollable elements who did not feel bound by the Jewish Agency's instructions. This meant that Irgun carried out acts which Haganah could not perform because of official Zionist policy. Acts which Irgun could not admit to were then attributed to the Stern group. As the Jewish Agency was allegedly in control of the Haganah only, the British could not blame the Agency for acts of terrorism in Palestine. None the less, it is well known that North American Zionists supported and financed such acts of terror, and Ben-Gurion, leader of the Agency, was also the undisputed leader of the US Zionists. All British reports at that time state that the Jewish Agency was working together with armed underground militias in Palestine.

The British have always claimed that in fact the Haganah, Irgun and the Stern group were working together – a view which is corroborated by the many weapon finds among the three groups in the war years.

The Haganah had begun arming itself in the twenties. By 1946, according to British reports, it had developed into a well-organized, illegal military organization consisting of three groups: a settlers' army of 40,000, a field army of 16,000 for mobile operations and an army proper (the Palmach) which in wartime totalled 6,000. The same British report said that the Stern group consisted of '200 to 300 dangerous fanatics' and that Irgun had from 3,000 to 5,000 members.[10]

The British found the first Zionist arms and ammunition caches as early as 1935. The weapons had been smuggled in from Belgium. During the Second World War, while the British were concentrating on the German threat, more and more weapons were bought and smuggled in. In 1939, 34 Jews in uniform were captured and arrested for carrying out military exercises with bombs and weapons. In the same year, 38 revisionists were caught in possession of arms and bombs. During a raid on a Jewish settlement in 1943, a munitions dump was discovered. In 1943, a considerable haul of weapons was stolen from military installations. The British authorities discovered that British soldiers working for the Haganah were involved. In fact, England partly had itself to blame for this development.

The British had accepted a proposal by Jewish military units that they should fight together against the Germans. The Jewish underground groups naturally took advantage of this opportunity to get hold of British weapons. During the war years, the Zionists also organized illegal immigration into Palestine. The persecution of Jews in Germany increased immigration to Palestine and furthered Zionist plans. The Jewish Agency adopted the most extraordinary methods here. A number of states, including the United States, refused several times to admit Jewish refugees from Germany. The Zionist organizations also bore responsibility for this by insisting that Palestine was the only land to which Jews should emigrate. So those who did not want to go to Palestine could not go anywhere else. The American President, Roosevelt, tried to persuade other countries to admit Jewish refugees during the war, but this plan failed because of Zionist resistance.[11]

The Zionists realized at a very early stage that they could benefit from anti-Semitism. When, for example, the first Jews fled from Tsarist pogroms and requested asylum in Great Britain, Theodor Herzl supported right-wing British politicians who objected to the Jews being granted asylum. Chamberlain also spoke out against the admission of Jews and thereby supported Herzl's plans. And Arthur Balfour, author of the declaration on a Jewish homeland in Palestine, made numerous fervent speeches which revealed him to be a fanatical anti-Semite.[12]

At the beginning of the Hitler regime in Germany, the Zionist newspaper *Jüdische Rundschau* was the only officially tolerated Jewish publication and managed to increase its circulation considerably – even though Jews were now being persecuted and driven out of public life. The Nazis helped the Zionists to force those Jews who were willing to assimilate into a corner. Eliahu Ben Elissar, the present Israeli ambassador in Egypt, wrote: 'It was the Zionists who declared their willingness to rid Germany of its Jews.'[13] In the same book, Ben Elissar describes the circumstances leading up to the Ha'avara agreement between the Nazis and the Zionist Organization. Non-Zionist Jews urged a trade boycott against the Nazis; at this, the Zionist leaders declared that a boycott of Germany would be 'completely un-Zionist'.[14] The Zionists had reached an agreement with the Nazis that wealthy Jews would be allowed to emigrate to Palestine. These Jews paid part of their fortunes to German traders who used the money to export German goods to Palestine. So while the rest of the world was boycotting German goods, Palestine was flooded with them. It was, however, a highly dubious practice to enable only wealthy Jews to emigrate to Palestine while leaving the poorer Jewish classes at the mercy of the Nazi terror. This agreement remained in force till the beginning of the Second World War, by which time there were scarcely any wealthy Jews left in Germany. At the beginning of the war, the Nazis supported illegal immigration into Palestine. In this way the Nazis could get rid of the Jews, confiscate their wealth and harm the British in Palestine – aims which suited Zionist purposes admirably. Pinhas Ginsberg, a Zionist delegate in Germany, describes the aid a Zionist representative was given by the Germans:

By the time the emissary reached the Zionist offices, excited officials told him that the Gestapo answer was waiting for him. He could stay. He could start work at once. He could even pick young Jewish pioneers who had been sent to concentration camps. He would not require to pass through the endless red tape of official channels. He could set up special training camps for the selected immigrants who would make the illegal run to Palestine through the British blockade . . . He had brought with him his long spoon; he was not worried that now he was about to sup with the devil. In fact he felt no little satisfaction as he read the Gestapo reply.[15]

The same authors also describe co-operation between Zionist leaders and Eichmann. It is interesting to note that the extreme right-wing revisionists only chose wealthy Jews for emigration, whereas other Zionists insisted on taking only young and healthy Jews. Eichmann helped them to carry out these plans, in return for which the Zionist Organization paid large sums to the Nazis. As Kimche says about the Zionist delegates in Germany: 'They had not come to Germany to save Jews. That was not their job.'[16]

When the Nazis began the systematic murder of Jews in 1941, the Zionists decided neither to support Jewish resistance in Europe, nor to attack the Nazis, nor to say anything about the mass liquidation of their fellow Jews. Their sole purpose was to save certain selected Jews as future settlers in Palestine. They were not interested in Jews who wished to stay in their home countries and fight the Nazis. Although the Zionists were very well organized, there is no record of Zionists leading or organizing Jewish resistance in Europe. Only left-wing groups and anti-racist organizations supported the Jews who were fighting in the ghettos. Reuben Ainzstein tells how the Nazis appointed a Zionist chief of the ghetto police in the Wilna ghetto.[17] He was responsible for the selection of Jews who were to be allowed to emigrate to Palestine – and on Nazi instructions he had the rest of the Jews murdered. Cases such as this became increasingly frequent. Zionist policies also frustrated the plans of non-Zionist Jews who were trying to organize resistance to save *all* Jews. When the Wilna ghetto was destroyed, the local Zionist leader saved 50 people, all members of the Zionist Hashomer Hatzair.

When non-Zionist Jews attempted to warn their co-religionists about collaboration between Zionists and Nazis, they were often delivered up into the hands of the Nazis by Zionists. The uprising in the Warsaw ghetto was crushed thanks partly to measures taken by Zionist ghetto leaders. Although the Zionists were fully aware of the fact and the extent of the mass murder of Jews, they did not even once call for resistance to the Nazis. They even rejected a British offer of help for Jewish resistance fighters.

After the war, a Jewish survivor from Germany accused the Zionist leader Kastner of collaboration with the Nazis. The subsequent trial in Israel showed that the Jewish Agency had obviously not passed on to the British Jewish requests that military action should be taken against concentration camps.

Kastner had signed an agreement with Eichmann by which 600 prominent Zionists were saved in return for the sacrifice of 800,000 Jews in Hungary. Kastner's accuser later told the court that 'Kastner's activities cost the lives of hundreds of thousands of Jews'.[18] But before Kastner could give any further evidence in a second trial about his collaboration with the Nazis, he was murdered by an agent of the Israeli government. And Adolf Eichmann was executed in Israel before he could give further evidence on this subject.

While Kastner was negotiating with the Nazi government, Rabbi Weissmandel wrote a letter to the Zionist movement describing the deportation and gassing of Jews in Auschwitz. He concluded his letter with these words: 'You are brutal, indeed you are murderers, because of your callous silence as you look on . . . you are sitting with your hands in your laps, although you could end or at least delay the killing of Jews . . . are you insane?'[19] Kastner, after the war, saved Kurt Becher, a murderer of Jews who was then in Nuremberg prison. Becher had been a former negotiating partner of Kastner's. When the Jewish negotiator Joel Brand was on the point of saving Hungarian Jews by promising Eichmann to deliver 10,000 lorries and other goods to the Nazis, the Zionists stepped in and scotched the deal. They told the British that Brand was an enemy the state; the Hungarian Jews were killed. Rabbi Weissmandel also tried to buy the freedom of Slovakian Jews for 50,000 Reichmarks, but as in many similar cases the Zionists refused to put up the money. In 1941, Irgun published a manifesto promising the Nazis their support in a number of areas. They approved of the Nazis' 'new order', because they too were striving to build a state which would be as Jewish as Germany was 'Aryan'. In Palestine, the Irgun or Haganah blew up a ship in the port of Haifa because it was carrying Jewish immigrants to Mauritius. 240 Jews were killed.[20] The British historian Faris Yahya has written a detailed account of these facts in his book *Zionist Relations with Nazi Germany*. Yahya, who grew up in Palestine, quotes a large number of sources in the appendix of his book. They prove the facts mentioned here beyond doubt.

The Zionists justify this strange collaboration by arguing that it saved Jews. However, if they had supported all Jews resisting Nazism instead of just an 'élite' predestined for immigration to Palestine, perhaps more Jews would have been saved. The Zionists certainly did not contribute to the struggle against national socialism. Yet they objected to the British immigration controls on the grounds that the Jews of the world had to be saved from persecution. In fact, this persecution provided them with new immigrants from Germany and the east of Europe who, before the war, had wanted to remain in their own countries. Palestine was the first to pay the price for the Nazi atrocities.

1945–47: The USA Supports Zionism; Palestine: The Decision Is Made

Before the war ended, the British government gave way to American pressure and allowed a further 20,000 Jews to emigrate to Palestine. The president of the United States at the time was Roosevelt. He died in 1945 and was succeeded by Truman. One of the first acts of his presidency was to write to Churchill stating that the 'American people' rejected the White Paper and the immigration restrictions it had recommended. The Zionists and their new-found protectors, the Americans, now exploited the persecution of the Jews as a means of presenting Palestine as the only possible place of refuge for the world's Jews. They also called for a rejection of the White Paper's proposals. By now, however, the war was as good as over. Furthermore, the United States authorities were reluctant to allow European Jews to immigrate to the United States. Robert Divine, a North American expert on immigration, has described the hostility of the US Congress and US lobbies towards those who survived Nazism.[21] Truman's commitment to Jewish immigration to Palestine was not based on compassion: it was a self-interested favour to the Zionists, who had no interest in Jews migrating to the United States. Truman destroyed any remaining sympathies the Arabs might have had for the United States when he told Arab diplomats: 'I am sorry, gentlemen, but I have to answer to the hundreds of thousands who want the Zionists to succeed. I have no hundreds of thousands of Arabs in my electorate.'[22]

The Zionists had now succeeded in exercising a decisive influence on United States politics – an influence they have retained until the present day. Support for the Zionists was presented as a moral obligation, when in fact it was a matter of tangible political interest.

Donations to the KKL and the *Keren Hajessod* rose dramatically in 1945.

Truman was now trying to influence the British government in favour of the Zionist cause. The newly-elected Labour government contained many pro-Zionists but was still pondering the best course of action in Palestine.

The Zionists wanted to act quickly, so as to capitalize on world sympathy at the fate of the Jews under Nazism.

In 1945, the Arab League was founded. Its statutes called for independence for the Palestinian people.

With American aid, specially trained Jews were smuggled into Palestine. With US protection, the Zionists could now afford openly to fight the British mandatory government and the Palestinian population. American support for Zionism partly accounts for the sluggish reaction of the British to the acts of Jewish terror groups.

The Zionists called for an administration in Palestine which accorded completely with the requirements and goals of the Jewish settlers. They openly declared that the Palestinian population should become a minority under Jewish control. The Jewish Agency called on the British to proclaim Palestine a Jewish State and demanded that Germany should pay reparations to the victims of Nazism. The Agency also passed a resolution accusing Great Britain of responsibility for the deaths of hundreds of thousands of European Jews – even though the Zionists had prevented Great Britain from settling Jewish refugees outside Palestine!

Soon after, Truman called on the British to allow a further 100,000 Jews to immigrate to Palestine. The General Secretary of the Arab League now declared that the Palestinians should take up armed struggle, at the same time insisting yet again that the Arabs were prepared to live on equal terms with the Jews in an independent Palestine. The British refused to allow a substantial increase in immigration quotas and so the Jewish underground movements stepped up their campaign of terror.

Between 1936 and 1939 Zionist terrorism had been directed mainly at Arab targets. In this period about 170 Palestinians were killed in Jewish attacks on markets, cafés and public transport. Double this number were injured. These figures do not include deaths and casualties incurred in street fighting. From 1944, Jewish terrorists concentrated their attacks on the British. Several attempts were made on the life of the British High Commissioner in 1944.

In November 1944, Lord Moyne, the British Resident Minister in the Middle East, was killed in Cairo. His murderers were arrested and said that they were members of the Stern gang, which then issued a statement that Lord Moyne had been acting against Zionist interests. Thereupon Winston Churchill, the most fervent supporter of the Zionists, declared:

> If our dreams for Zionism are to end in the smoke of assassins' pistols and our labours for its future are to produce a new set of gangsters worthy of Nazi Germany, many like myself will have to reconsider the position we have maintained so consistently and so long in the past. If there is to be any hope of a peaceful and successful future for Zionism, these wicked activities must cease; and those responsible for them must be destroyed, root and branch.[23]

It should be noted here that for decades Churchill had been attacking all the measures of the British government which he did not consider pro-Zionist enough.

From 1942, the incidence of Stern gang and Irgun attacks on British commissioners and police increased. By 1947, about 200 British officials had been killed in bomb attacks and other armed attacks. In 1946, Irgun took several British officials and judges hostage in an effort to force the release of imprisoned members of their organization. Two of the hostages were hanged, two others were attached to mines and blown to pieces. On top of this came maltreatment of hostages and prisoners and letter and parcel bombs which killed dozens of people.

In 1946, Irgun, working together with Haganah and the Jewish

Agency, blew up a wing of the King David Hotel in Jerusalem, headquarters of the civil administration of the British mandate government. The clerical staff included Jews as well as Palestinians. As the explosion occurred when the building was full, nearly 100 people were buried beneath the ruins.

Palestinian administrative centres were also attacked. Palestinian and British banks were favoured targets for attacks and robberies. Irgun and the Stern gang always claimed responsibility.

Attacks on public transport were a favourite Jewish terrorist tactic. Menachem Begin has described how he and the terrorists he led would allow the 'reconnaissance' locomotive to pass over mines but, as soon as the train followed, the mines were detonated.[24] In 1946 and 1947, more than 100 people were killed in attacks on railways, trains, railway stations and vehicles.

The sabotage of industrial installations was another Zionist speciality. In 1947, three oil pipelines, an oil storage depot and a refinery were blown up. From 1947, political developments in Palestine forced the terrorists to change their tactics: they directed more and more of their attacks against the Palestinian population.

In this period the British government responded to US and Zionist pressure by juggling with immigration quotas for Palestine, sometimes increasing, sometimes reducing them.

The British now tried to persuade the United States to take a share of the military and financial responsibility for Palestine. In Palestine itself, they tried to combat Jewish terrorism – but without success. In 1946, the Haganah could call on 75,000 men, all armed with modern weapons, many of them from the USA. Irgun comprised 5,000 to 6,000 men specializing in street fighting and sabotage. The Stern gang specialized in assassination and murder, as Prime Minister Attlee even told the House of Commons.[25]

The governments of the United States, Great Britain, France, Yugoslavia and Czechoslovakia paid $25 million to the victims of Nazism, most of which went straight into the coffers of Zionist organizations. In 1946, the British again proposed the partition of Palestine and again the Palestinians rejected the proposal. Churchill now for the first time considered handing over the Palestine mandate to the United Nations. The United States also called for the partition of Palestine and Truman renewed his demands for higher immigration quotas. In October 1946, Truman backed a Zionist proposal that in the event of partition, 75% of Palestine should be allocated to the Jews. At this point, the Zionists controlled less than 7.5% of Palestinian territory.

The Palestinian situation was becoming more and more precarious for Great Britain: the Zionists blamed the British for provoking the explosion of violence in Palestine; but the Jewish National Council in Palestine decided to stop co-operating with the British authority. In 1946, Goldmann, on behalf of the Jewish Agency, said he was ready to enter into negotiations on the partition of Palestine. But the Jewish Agency refused to take part in a conference on Palestine called by the British.

In 1945 and 1946 the Palestinians and the Arab states concentrated their efforts on bringing about independence for Palestine and preventing partition. They also tried – in vain – to stop Jewish immigration. In 1945 Palestine became an official member of the Arab League, which decided to boycott Jewish industry and goods.

The Council of the Arab Union founded in 1946 called for the disarmament of Jewish armed forces and terror organizations. It also adopted a number of economic and political measures to help the Palestinian population.

The Arabs from Palestine also refused to take part in the London conference on Palestine in 1946 because they rejected the partition of Palestine.

In January 1947, Irgun declared war on Great Britain and carried out 17 attacks in Tel Aviv. Great Britain responded by issuing an ultimatum to the Jewish Agency. Though the Palestinians did in fact take part in the London conference after all, it produced no results.

For the first time since the inception of its ill-starred Palestinian policy 30 years before, the British government now had to admit that it could not meet its obligations to either the Palestinians or the Zionists. In 1947 Great Britain handed over the Palestinian mandate – and responsibility for solving the country's problems – to the United Nations.

Notes

1. Golda Meir, *Sunday Times*, 15 June 1969.
2. Balfour Declaration, in Wagner, *The Arab-Israeli Conflict in International Law*, Berlin 1971, p. 110.
3. Neville Barbour, *Nisi Dominus*, London 1946, p. 97.
4. Wagner, op. cit., p. 250.
5. Cmd. 3692 – The Passfield White Paper, October 1930.
6. David Ben-Gurion, *Israel. Die Geschichte eines Staates*, Frankfurt 1973, p. 76.
7. Ibid., p. 85.
8. Ibid.
9. Wagner, op. cit., p. 189. See also: *Jewish Agency for Palestine*, Book of Documents submitted to the United Nations General Assembly (May 1947), p. 227.
10. Arnold Harttung, *Zeittafel zum Nahostkonflikt*, Berlin 1979, p. 31.
11. Morris Ernst, *So Far So Good*, New York 1948, pp. 170–7.
12. *Jewish Chronicle*, 23 December 1940.
13. Eliahu Ben Elissar, *La Diplomatie du IIIième Reich et Les Juifs*, Paris 1969, pp. 86–7.
14. Letter from Blumenfeld of the Zionist Organization to Bülow-Schwante, Nazi representative, 11 June 1934.

15. John and David Kimche, *The Secret Roads*, London 1954, pp. 15–6.
16. Ibid., pp. 30–1.
17. Ruben Ainzstein, *Jewish Resistance in Nazi-occupied Eastern Europe*, London 1974, p. 74.
18. Faris Yahya, *Zionist Relations with Nazi Germany*, Beirut 1978, p. 56.
19. Ibid., pp. 57–8.
20. J. Schechtmann, *The Jabotinsky Story I. Fighter and Prophet*, New York 1961, p. 483.
21. Robert Divine, *American Emigration Policy 1924–1952*, New Haven 1957, pp. 112–28.
22. Walid Khalidi, Das Palästina-Problem. Ursachen und Entwicklung, *Palästina-Monographien No. 6*, Rastatt/Baden 1972, p. 67.
23. A Survey of Palestine, 1945–46 in: Sami Hadawi, *Bitter Harvest*, New York 1979, p. 73.
24. Menachem Begin, *The Revolt. Story of the Irgun*, London 1951, p. 71.
25. See: Palestine. Supplementary Memorandum to UNSCOP, p. 58; Keesings Contemporary Archives, III (1939–40), IV (1941–2), V (1943–5), VI (1946–8); Begin, op. cit.

9. The Palestine Question and the United Nations

On 1 May 1947 the United Nations set up a UN Special Committee on Palestine (UNSCOP). At the same time it rejected an Arab resolution to end the mandate and declare independence for Palestine.

According to British government reports, there were 1,897,000 people living in Palestine in 1947, including 608,000 Jews.

The committee now listened to the views of Jewish and Palestinian representatives. When it completed its hearings, the committee reported to the United Nations General Assembly. UNSCOP presented its report on 3 September 1947. Seven of the 11 committee members came out in favour of the so-called majority plan, which envisaged the partition of Palestine into two independent states, with a special status for Jerusalem. The plan also proposed an economic union for the two states. Three committee members – India, Iran and Yugoslavia – argued that Palestine should become a federation, with a Jewish and an Arab region and Jerusalem as capital. The Zionists categorically rejected this latter plan, but they accepted the majority plan. At the same time, they exerted intense diplomatic pressure to ensure that the Jewish State would be as large as possible.

The Arab attitude was unchanged. They would not accept any partition of Palestine. The Palestinians organized strikes and demonstrations. The Arab Higher Committee refused to co-operate with UNSCOP, partly on the grounds that UNSCOP was trying to establish a connection between the persecution of the Jews by the Nazis and the need for the partition of Palestine. The Palestinians saw no reason why they should have to suffer the consequences of German anti-Semitism.

The UNSCOP proposals required a two-thirds majority in the General Assembly, which now set up a special committee. This in turn formed subcommittees, one of which looked into a joint Syrian-Iraqi-Saudi Arabian plan for an Arab-Palestinian State with guarantees for the Jewish minority.

However, this plan was rejected at the special committee stage by 29 votes to 14, with 14 abstentions. It was never presented to the General Assembly, where the only vote taken was on the partition of Palestine – a plan which had been drawn up without Arab participation. The Zionists took an active part in drawing up this plan and influenced all the committee members.

The Arab Higher Committee boycotted the committee's work because of the obvious pro-Zionist majority on the committee. The Arabs proposed that the question should be decided by the International Court of Justice at the Hague. In particular they wanted a court ruling on whether the United Nations had the right to partition Palestine without the consent of the people. A UN majority rejected this proposal and later also rejected a Lebanese mediation proposal. Finally, a majority in the General Assembly voted in favour of the partition plan (33 votes for, 13 against, 10 abstentions).

The countries voting for the plan were: Australia, Belgium, the White Russian SSR, Bolivia, Brazil, Canada, Costa Rica, Czechoslovakia, Denmark, the Dominican Republic, Ecuador, France, Guatemala, Haiti, Iceland, Liberia, Luxemburg, New Zealand, the Netherlands, Nicaragua, Norway, Panama, Paraguay, Peru, the Philippines, Poland, Sweden, the Soviet Union, South Africa, the Ukrainian SSR, Uruguay, USA, Venezuela.

The following countries voted against: Afghanistan, Egypt, Greece, India, Iraq, Iran, Yemen, Cuba, Lebanon, Pakistan, Saudi Arabia, Syria, Turkey.

The following countries abstained: Argentina, Ethiopia, Chile, China, El Salvador, Great Britain, Honduras, Yugoslavia, Colombia, Mexico.

The Arab states, the Arab League and the Arab Higher Committee rejected the decision to partition Palestine. They argued, rightly, that the UN could only make recommendations and could not pass binding resolutions. In particular, the United Nations did not and does not have the right to determine a country's fate without consulting the people of that country. And the statutes of the United Nations emphasize unequivocally the right to national independence. For these reasons the UN ought to have ended the mandate and allowed the Arab majority in Palestine to decide its future. But at the time of the vote, the largest bloc in the United Nations was that of the colonial states whose primary concern was to uphold their influence in their former colonies. These countries put their domestic-political interests higher than the moral principles of the United Nations' statutes. In the debates on partition, the USA now engaged in dubious manoeuvres. Itself subjected to intense Zionist pressure, it leaned heavily on smaller states to vote for partition. In every state of the USA, leading figures were called upon in letters, telegrams and public meetings to support the intervention plan. The Palestinian problem became an electoral issue; for the first time, the term 'Jewish vote' was used. The Jewish vote has played an important part in North American elections ever since and will continue to do so.

Truman at that time was backing Zionist interests for reasons of home policy. The US Department of State, for example, did not want the

Negev desert included in the future State of Israel, but Truman reacted to pressure from Weizmann by instructing the US delegation to the United Nations to insist on the inclusion of the Negev desert. Intense Zionist and American pressure on other states operated at several levels: both delegation members and governments of the states in question were subjected to this pressure. Pro-Zionist senators sent telegrams to the Philippine government; in Liberia, a US company, Firestone, exerted pressure on the government. The ugliest threat was that of the withdrawal of US aid to small states. The literature on this subject also proves that huge sums were paid in bribes.[1]

The Arab states could exert pressure in only two ways, by threatening to withdraw oil concessions and wage war on Israel. This latter threat was not taken seriously at the time.

The Arabs now became the target of a Zionist press campaign in the United States which attempted to put the Arabs on a par with anti-Semitic Nazis. The Arabs were also criticized for sitting on the fence during the war. This deliberately ignored the fact that the Arabs – and the Palestinians in particular – had no reason to be thankful to the British or the French, who had supported the Zionist movement in Palestine. The Second World War was not an Arab war.

Quite understandably, a number of Arabs tried to enlist German aid, in the hope that Germany would help them in their struggle against Great Britain. But 'it is understandable that the importance of these feeble attempts, the radio broadcasts, the exchange of visits, arms supplies and the presence of a few agents during the war has been over-rated by their opponents.'[2]

This is particularly true of Hadj Amin El Husseini who, after his persecution by the British, sought refuge first in Damascus and then in Berlin, where he requested German help in his efforts to prevent further Jewish immigration to Palestine. But, as we have seen, the Nazis to some extent supported this immigration. El Husseini was allowed to remain in Berlin, but was completely ignored by the Germans.

At the UN, the Palestinians argued that in 1945 Palestine had taken in more Jewish immigrants than all the other UN member states put together – those member states who made such fine moral speeches whenever the question of Jewish immigration to Palestine arose. The Pakistani delegate Zafrulla remarked that Australia, Canada and the USA, rich states with vast uncultivated areas, rejected Jewish immigration to their countries; that was their contribution to humanity. The Soviet Union also voted for the partition plan. Many Soviet Jews had emigrated to Palestine following the Tsarist pogroms, the Russian revolution and the persecution of East European Jews by the Nazis. The Soviet Union was hoping that the Jewish State would become part of a Soviet zone of influence in the Middle East. The Zionists encouraged the Soviet Union in this belief; especially as the majority of members of the Zionist movement called themselves 'socialist'.

The Palestine Question and the United Nations

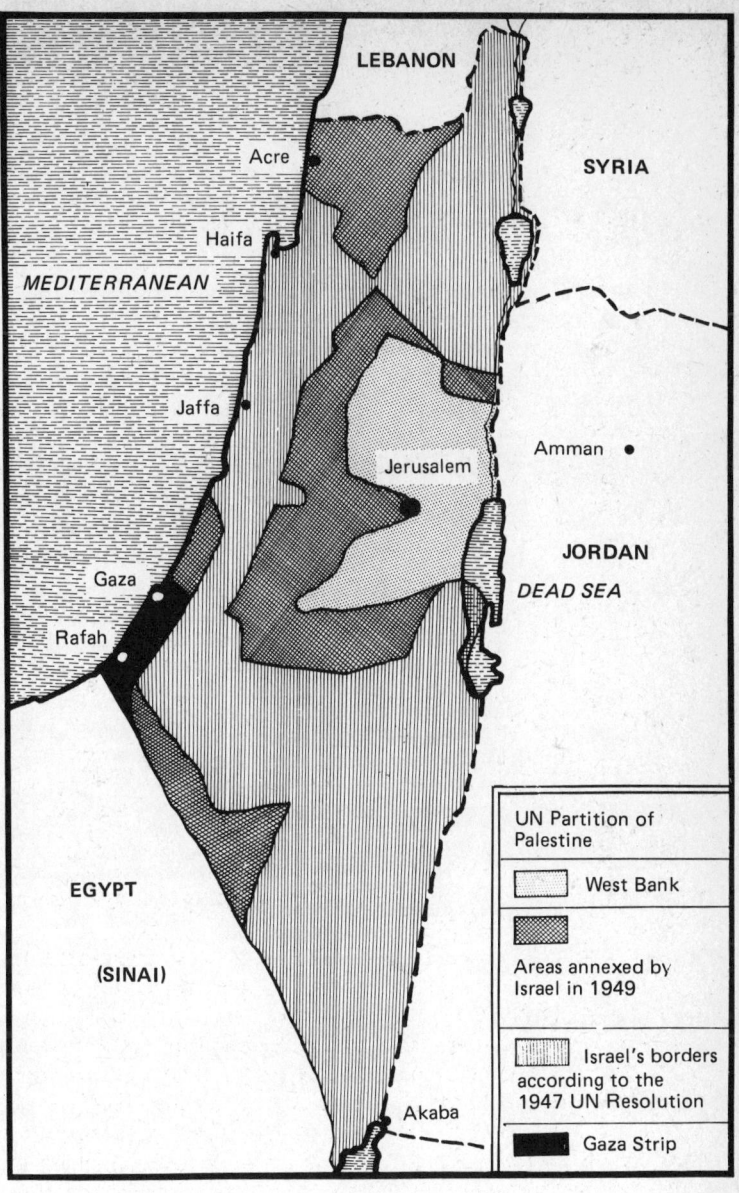

The majority plan had been accepted. Now it had to be implemented. The geographical realities of Palestine and the political and demographic structure of its population constituted the first difficulty. How could the country be divided in two when everywhere Jewish and Arab settlements were next to one another? The only possibility seemed to be to create a mosaic of enclaves and zones; and this, in the words of Herbert Samuel, former British High Commissioner in Palestine, would lead to the establishment of half a dozen Danzigs and Memels, several Saarlands and several Polish corridors.

Any transfer of the population would only have been possible by means of cruel violence. This was something which the United Nations clearly could not propose. Furthermore, the economic union recommended in the plan scarcely seemed viable, as the Arab State would have closer ties with the Arab world and the Jewish State would look more to the West.

This meant that the UN resolution could only have been implemented by military force. The UN clearly could do nothing of the kind and so the General Assembly attempted to persuade Great Britain to guarantee the implementation of the plan. Great Britain, however, was not prepared to take on this responsibility. It refused to co-operate in any plan that might involve fighting and announced that it was pulling its troops out of Palestine.

The UN therefore set up a commission comprising five member states. Its task was to take over, for a transitional period, the administration of Palestine. It was to have full administrative and executive powers. However, the United Nations had no authority to make this kind of intervention and Great Britain refused to co-operate with the commission. Furthermore, the commission had no military power to implement the resolution in Palestine. The British said that they would hand over power on 15 May 1948; and they did so in such a way that their departure soon came to be known as 'Operation Chaos'.

Nor could the United Nations Security Council take on responsibility for the implementation of the resolution, as its members had no authority to use force to implement a General Assembly recommendation. Even the United States finally accepted this view.

While the UN was slowly beginning to realize that the plan could only be implemented, if at all, by the use of force, the Zionists in Palestine had already begun to force through the partition plan by violence. Zionist violence, Palestinian counter-violence and the impotence of the Palestine Commission and the mandate government plunged the country into chaos.

In Palestine, the Arab Higher Committee called a general strike in December 1947 and stepped up its boycott of the Jews in Palestine. The Arab states declared that they would use military force to resist the partition plan but decided not to act while British troops were still stationed in Palestine.

On 5 January 1948 the Haganah attacked the Semiramis Hotel in Jerusalem, headquarters of two Palestinian youth organizations. Twenty Palestinians were killed. On the same day, the headquarters of the Arab National Committee was blown up and 60 people were killed.

The Arab Higher Committee decided to establish a national administration for all Palestine. The Jewish Agency and the Jewish National Council now also declared that they were forming a provisional government for the Jewish State. The Palestinians reacted by attacking Jewish settlements and besieging 1,500 Jews in the old part of Jerusalem.

Following the partition resolution, 42 Britons, 345 Palestinians and 333 Jews were killed.

The Palestine Commission now informed the United Nations that it was powerless to prevent these events, warning that there could be a catastrophe in Palestine after the British troops pulled out. Great Britain complained about the continuing influx of illegal Jewish immigrants to Palestine. The Bulgarian government, for example, allowed ships full of Jewish emigrants to leave the country's ports. Great Britain now made increasingly strenuous efforts to prevent the illegal transport of weapons to Palestine and the Arab states.

The Arab League now appointed the Grand Mufti of Jerusalem as a full member and placed the 'Palestinian Liberation Army' under the command of the Iraqi General Ismail Pasha. It said that this army would only intervene if an attempt were made to implement partition by force.

The Jewish Agency now stepped up its attacks on Great Britain, accusing it of helping the Palestinians to fight the partition plan. But the British had only one thing in mind: to get out of the country as quickly as possible and to hand over responsibility to the Palestine Commission on 15 May 1948. The Palestine Commission said that it was in no position to take on this responsibility. On 9 March 1948, the Jewish Agency gave the United Nations a list of the members of the provisional Jewish government – with the name of David Ben-Gurion top of the list.

On 14 March, the Yarmuk Brigade – Arab resistance fighters – set up their headquarters near Nablus.

In the meantime, the UN Security Council was again debating the Palestinian question. The Soviet Union insisted on the immediate implementation of the partition resolution. The USA, on the other hand, proposed a postponement of partition. It now wanted Palestine to become, temporarily, a United Nations trust territory. All Zionist organizations fiercely attacked this proposal. The Arab League, however, said that it was prepared to take over the trusteeship for the time being, to allow Jews blockaded in Cyprus to enter Palestine and to accept a democratic government for all Palestine with full rights for the Jews.

But Truman was forced to succumb to Zionist pressure. The Jewish Agency and the Jewish National Council said they would fight this plan and announced that the Jewish government would take office by 16 May.

Notes

1. R. P. Stevens, *American Zionism and US Foreign Policy 1942–47*, New York 1962.
2. Wagner, *The Arab-Israeli Conflict in International Law*, Berlin 1971, p. 204.

10. Jewish Terror up to the Founding of Israel

'You longed to be like the peoples of Europe who murdered you. Now you are like them.'[1]

The British had now started to withdraw their troops. The Jewish military and terror groups – Haganah, Irgun and the Stern gang – now joined forces. While the British were pulling out, the Jews intensified their attacks on the British and Palestinians.

The death toll had risen to 2,307 since the partition resolution. Fighting was especially fierce along the Tel Aviv to Jerusalem road and in the towns of Haifa and Jaffa. It would require another book to give an exhaustive list of all the terrorist attacks by Jewish underground groups in 1947 and 1948. I will confine myself here to mentioning the most important operations which paved the way for the takeover of the Palestinian population.

Between 13 December 1947 and 10 February 1948, 161 Palestinians were killed and 320 injured in Irgun, Stern and Haganah attacks on market-places and cafés. In the same period attacks by these organizations on Arab buses killed 15 Palestinians and injured 26. In 1948, the terror groups blew up several trains, killing 93 and wounding 161 Palestinians. They also attacked Arab hotels, houses and offices. The attacks on the Semiramis Hotel and the National Committee building have already been mentioned. In addition, Zionist groups blew up police stations, banks and many private houses. More than 200 people, many of them children, were buried beneath the rubble.

That these were not isolated acts but part of a concerted campaign of terror against the Arab population is proved by the organized attacks by Haganah, Irgun and the Stern gang against Palestinian villages and the civilian population. From 12 December 1947 to 20 April 1948, at least 17 Arab villages or towns were attacked. The method was always the same: the Jewish immigrants surrounded the villages and shot all the inhabitants or else blew their houses up with them inside. These attacks often occurred when the men were at work, so that the victims were mostly women and children. About 600 Palestinian civilians were killed in these attacks. Hundreds of houses were blown up and thousands of people injured.

Two notorious examples: on 30 December 1947 a Palmach group attacked the village of Bald al-Shaikh, killing 60 Palestinians. The attackers set fire to the houses and many women and children died in the flames.

On 9 April 1948, Irgun and Stern commandos attacked the village of Deir Yassin. After the massacre Red Cross workers found the bodies of 254 men, women and children.

In his book *The Palestinians*, Jonathan Dimbleby describes this massacre:

> Altogether 250 men, women and children had been butchered to death. The survivors, at the point of hysterical collapse from shock and grief, recorded their hideous experience for the British authorities: families had been lined up and shot down in a barrage of machine-gun fire; young girls raped; a pregnant mother was first slaughtered and then had her stomach cut open by her murderer with a butcher's knife; a girl who tried to remove the unborn child from the woman's womb was shot down. Some of the Irgun fighters slashed their victims to pieces with cutlasses.[2]

The Jewish underground organizations had no qualms about murdering either Jews or British. Jews and British had been killed in the bombing of the King David Hotel in Jerusalem on 22 July 1946. In the final months of the British mandate in Palestine, several British soldiers and officials were shot on the streets by members of Haganah, Irgun or Stern. Two such attacks occurred on 14 November and on 16 December 1947 in Jerusalem.

As the end of the British mandate drew near, the Zionists started attacking Arab towns in an effort to drive out the Arab population. Nathan Chofski, a Jewish pioneer in Palestine, has described this as follows:

> Many were driven out by armed force. Others were persuaded to leave by deception, lies and other false promises. One need only mention here the names of the towns of Jaffa, Lydda, Ramallah, Beersheba, Akko. There were countless others.[3]

Shortly after midnight on 22 April 1948, Jewish troops attacked Haifa and occupied houses and streets. Thirty Arabs were killed and 200 injured. The other inhabitants, panicking, evacuated their families to Akko. On the way to Akko, another 100 Palestinians were killed and 200 wounded. On 25 April, the Zionists bombarded Jaffa, dispersing the panic-stricken population in all directions. The Jewish troops blew up houses and apartments.

On 28 April, Jewish groups blew up Manshieh police station in Jaffa, bringing the entire traffic between Jaffa and Tel Aviv to a standstill.

On 12 April, the Zionist General Council formed a 37-man government

Jewish Terror up to the Founding of Israel

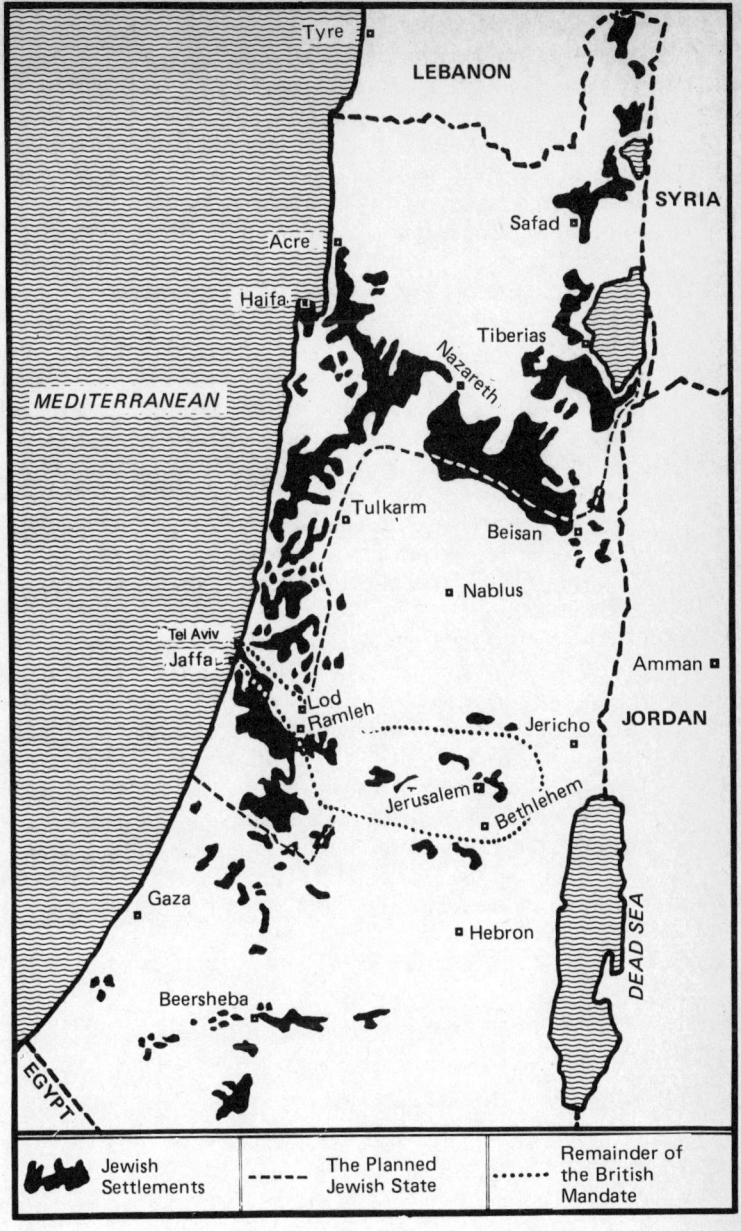

for the Jewish State.

On 19 April, the first British contingents left Palestine. The remaining British troops at first fought the Jewish troops who were attacking Jaffa.

On 30 April, Haganah launched a large-scale attack on Jerusalem. Yet on 8 May, Haganah promised the British High Commissioner that it would observe an armistice. This soon proved to be an empty promise. At midnight on 14 May 1948 the British mandate ended and on the same day the provisional Jewish government proclaimed the State of Israel.

By this time Haganah, Stern and Irgun had already executed their plans to attack and in some cases occupy several towns, including Haifa, Jaffa, Akko, Safad and Tiberias. They even attacked towns and villages which the UN partition plan had allocated to the Arab State.

When the British withdrawal was completed, the Arab states intervened to prevent further armed conquest of Palestine but by now the Israeli units were on the offensive. Not only were they better trained and equipped with modern weapons, but they were also numerically superior.

There were 20,000 armed men on the Arab side, including the Arab expeditionary force. As these units had no joint supreme command, their operations were isolated, uncoordinated and often ineffective.

Against this, the Israelis had at least 45,000 experienced troops and another 65,000 reservists.

At the end of the first Middle East war, the new State of Israel controlled 77.4% of the country. The UN partition plan had allocated them 56.4%. In 1949, Jews owned only 7.23% of the country's total area.

This first in a long series of Israeli military successes meant that Israel had not only ignored the UN partition resolution but had also shown – by refusing to allow Palestinian refugees to return – that it was not prepared to tolerate an Arab-Palestinian State in Palestine.

The victory brought Israel more land. But it did not bring peace. On the contrary, it laid the foundations for the confrontation that has continued until the present day.

Notes

1. Erich Fried, *Höre Israel*.
2. Jonathan Dimbleby, *The Palestinians*, London, 1979, p. 79.
3. *Jewish Newsletter*, New York, 9 February 1959.

11. The Predetermined Defeat of the Palestinians

The foundation of the State of Israel on 15 May 1948 sealed the defeat of the Palestinian nationalist movement. Palestinian resistance was indeed a lost cause from the beginning. Until 1920 the nationalist movement in Palestine was Greater Arab, part of the Greater Syrian movement for the liberation of the Arab world from European colonialism. The movement was led by the Syrian and Palestinian middle classes, i.e. by urban businessmen, artisans and owners of small businesses. When Great Britain took over the Palestine mandate, the Palestinian leadership had to concentrate on strictly nationalist goals. But the political situation in the Arab world was unfavourable. Other Arab states were either colonies or under British or French mandate and were therefore scarcely in a position to help the Palestinians in their struggle for independence. Even the few Arab states which had recently become independent were still under the influence of European great powers. In Egypt the British controlled the government and the Suez Canal; the Transjordanian army led by Glubb Pasha was under British control. The oil fields of the Arabian peninsula were controlled by the USA and Europe. Every national movement in these states was quickly suppressed. The nationalist elements in these countries who were fighting against European domination supported the Palestinian nationalist movement, but they were too weak to offer any effective help.

The Arab heads of state were constantly urged by the European powers to exert pressure on the Palestinian leadership. It could expect no help from the Arab states in its struggle. Fully aware of this, the British saw no reason whatsoever to consider the demands of the Palestinian leadership, which was isolated and without effective support in the Arab world. The Palestinian people's appeals to the British authorities, the British government, the League of Nations and the United Nations Commission were all in vain. This lack of political support weakened the nationalist movement in its political negotiations with the British. The Palestinian leadership remained isolated while the Zionist organizations exerted influence in all directions. The Jewish immigrants had, in many cases, originally come from Europe and had strong and influential supporters in the European bastions of power. In addition, the Zionists benefited from the compassion felt by the entire world for the victims of Nazi persecution. After the Nazi atrocities, the Zionists took advantage of the world's collective sense of guilt and reiterated that the only way it could compensate for its culpable passivity was by unconditional support for the aims of Zionism.

The chances of success for armed resistance to Jewish settlement and expropriation policies were slim. When settlement began, the Palestinians had accepted Jewish immigration without demur or alarm. The first settlers did not seek confrontation with the Arabs; the Palestinians did not at first realize the danger posed by increasing Jewish immigration. However, from 1920, the population began to feel the effects of Zionist policies. This was when the first demonstrations and strikes took place, when violence first broke out between the Palestinians on the one side and the British and the Jews on the other. In the first national uprising in May 1921, 47 Jews and 48 Arabs were killed, and 146 Jews and 73 Arabs were injured. The British mandate government's response to the Arab uprising was extremely severe. It proclaimed a state of emergency, introduced collective punishments, arrested Palestinians arbitrarily and banished several leaders without trial. At the same time, the British openly helped the Zionists. Jewish settlers were recruited into the British forces, trained and armed. After the British had crushed the uprising, a British Commission of Enquiry into its causes found that the violence had been triggered by anti-Zionist feeling – feeling created by forced Jewish immigration, Jewish land purchase, the expulsion of Palestinian farmers and Jewish claims to rule Palestine.

To calm the population, the British would always make apparent concessions after these uprisings: new enquiry reports and communiqués gave the false impression that the British were sympathetic towards Palestinian demands. These attempts at appeasement became less and less successful. In 1923 the entire Palestinian population boycotted the elections. In 1925 the vast majority of the population followed the national leadership's call for strikes in protest at Lord Balfour's visit to Palestine. All sections of the population resisted the Jewish land purchase policy, refusing to leave their land. They were forcibly expelled by Jewish settlers and the British mandate police. Peaceful coexistence between the Jewish settlers and the Arab population then became impossible. Zionist propaganda had persuaded the settlers that anti-Semitism was the motive behind the Arab population's reactions – and this propaganda achieved its aim, creating an atmosphere of deep hostility. Violence between Jews and Arabs now became the order of the day, each act forming a link in an unbroken chain. The most violent Arab uprising to date occurred in 1929. The Zionists, who often played on Jewish religious feelings, provoked counter-reactions among the Arabs. Soon Arab religious leaders also started whipping up religious feeling, which was often expressed over trivial issues such as prayers at the Wailing Wall. The real motives lay elsewhere: in the Palestinians' fear that they might lose their country.

They now united under the leadership of Hadj Amin El Husseini, but, without even the support of his weak Arab neighbours, he could not establish a disciplined organization able to come anywhere near challenging the Zionists. Furthermore, the Jewish settlers and underground armies were far better equipped. Virtually undisturbed by the British, the Zionists, legally or illegally, imported arms from Belgium or Czechoslovakia or simply helped themselves to British army stocks.

The Palestinians, on the other hand, had only a few old guns and rifles – and in most cases their wives had to sell their jewellery to pay for them.

From 1930, a group of young Palestinian intellectuals gained influence, founding patriotic clubs, improving the school system and spreading patriotic ideas. People were beginning to realize that armed struggle offered the only hope of success: this was reflected in the founding of new parties such as Istiqlal. Like all Third World liberation movements, these organizations fought for national sovereignty and against colonialism as manifested in the British government's support for Zionist settlement in Palestine.

The best-known Palestinian resistance leader in the 1930s was Sheikh Ezzedin Al-Qassam, who was very popular with the poor. He and the armed organizations he led made numerous attacks on Jewish settlements and British installations in the early thirties. In 1935 he was shot by the British during one of these attacks. This was the first militant resistance group to form spontaneously among the poorer population. This and other groups planned and carried out the general strike and the armed uprising of 1936.

The year 1936 saw fierce fighting between Arabs and Jews. The Arab population observed a general strike for six months. The armed organizations, supported by volunteers from Syria and Iraq, carried out acts of sabotage, bomb attacks and military attacks on Jewish settlements and British military installations. By 1935, the British had a total of 50,000 troops in Palestine to crush popular uprisings. The Arab population totalled 900,000 and they also had to fight against the armed Jewish underground organizations. The full force of British military power was concentrated against Palestinian resistance, as there was no sign of armed resistance in any British colony at the time.

As if their military inferiority were not enough, the Palestinian nationalist movement finally had to call off the strikes and attacks in 1936 at the request of the Arab heads of state. The British had exerted their influence on the Arab leaders and forced them to issue this appeal. When the British proposed the partition of Palestine in 1937, fighting again broke out. By 1938 the British had brought in more reinforcements. The same year they arrested a number of Palestinian leaders. In 1938, in the White Paper, the British made a number of apparent concessions to the Arabs, to prevent them from siding with the Germans in the coming war. By now, however, the defeat of the Palestinians was inevitable. The Zionists had won the support of the USA, from which they received even more weapons and military equipment. By now the British had eliminated the leaders of the Palestinian resistance movement. Official statistics show that by the end of 1939 more than 5,000 Palestinians had been killed – in military action, in the crushing of uprisings or by hanging.

By 1948, the Palestinians had lost their best fighters and leaders. The people in the towns and villages were exhausted and demoralized by the violence of Jewish terror groups and by British repression. Finally, world opinion was on the Zionists' side. The atrocities committed by the Nazis against the Jews blinded world opinion to the atrocities which the Zionists committed against the Palestinians. The settlement of Palestine, the expulsion of its original population and the foundation of the State of Israel were presented as the deliverance of the Jews.

12. The Palestinian Exodus

The State of Israel after its Founding

The founding of Israel had two direct consequences: it led to the first war between Israel and the Arab states and it created the problem of 900,000 Palestinian refugees.

The first phase after the founding of Israel was no different from the phase that preceded it. The Jewish underground and terror groups now formed the regular Israeli army and continued the war with the same means. The murder of the people of Deir Yassin had merely been a signal for what was to come.

After 15 May 1948, the Israeli army attacked countless defenceless Arab villages, blew up houses and entire villages and indiscriminately killed men, women and children. The survivors were driven out of the villages. News of these appalling massacres spread like wildfire and those who did not believe the reports were likely to become the next victims.

The Israelis' psychological warfare was based on shock tactics. Israeli radio was constantly calling on the Palestinians to flee 'to avoid a bloodbath'. Israeli army vehicles with loudspeakers drove through the streets of towns and villages pointing out escape routes. This happened, for example, at 5.15 on 15 May 1948 in Jerusalem and on 21 April just before the attack on Haifa. But rumours and radio reports were not the only reasons for panic and headlong flight. The Israeli army deliberately and systematically destroyed villages and drove out their inhabitants. This happened not only during the first Middle East war in districts such as El Ghazel and Jabba or villages such as Anan and Kafr Bar'am. Even after the war, Zionist violence was continually and cruelly directed against Palestinians under Israeli control. The massacres and atrocities committed in Arab towns and villages such as Igrith (December 1951), Al-Tirah (July 1953), Abu Ghosh (September 1953), Akko (June 1956) and Kafr Kassem (October 1956) are perhaps the most notorious but by no means the only examples of this wave of Israeli violence. To take the example of Kafr Kassem:

On the eve of its attack on Egypt in 1956, the Israeli army imposed a curfew in the village of Kafr Kassem, which was located on the ceasefire line but within Israeli-occupied territory. At 16.30 on 29 October 1956 Israeli border police units reached the village and told the mayor that a curfew would be imposed from 17.00 of the same day and that anyone found outside his house after this time would be shot. Many villagers were still working in the fields or outside the village and there was no way of informing them that the curfew had been imposed. When they returned, unsuspecting, at 17.00 hours they were shot at the village gates. That evening, 51 people were killed and 13 wounded. Among the dead were 12 women and girls, ten boys aged between 14 and 17 and seven boys aged between 8 and 13.

From 1948 to 1956, Israel not only attacked towns and villages directly under its control, but also launched military attacks on neighbouring areas. Israel was condemned for such actions by the United Nations Security Council in 1951, 1953, 1955 and 1956.[1]

One of the attacks for which Israel was condemned was that on the village of Qibya on the West Bank on 14 and 15 October 1953. Half a battalion of Israeli soldiers blew up 41 houses and a school and cold-bloodedly murdered 42 men, women and children. Even before the founding of Israel, the Israelis had adopted the tactic of bombing crowds of refugees to hasten their departure. In August 1954 the Israelis attacked the UNWRA refugee camp at Bureij in the Gaza strip, killing 20 and injuring 62 people.

Yitzhak Rabin, former Chief of Staff and later Prime Minister of Israel, summed up this policy with brutal clarity: 'By razing villages to the ground and driving out the inhabitants we will ensure that there are no villages left for the Arabs to return to.'[2]

These tactics nipped resistance in the bud and reduced the Palestinian population to helplessness.

The murder of the UN mediator Count Folke Bernadotte by members of the Stern gang on 17 September 1948 was a particularly odious crime. Bernadotte was killed because of his strict neutrality and his efforts to help Palestinian refugees to return to their towns and villages. He was merely implementing a UN resolution to this effect. The Israeli government was criticized by the UN Security Council in October 1948 for blocking investigations into this murder.

These are just a few examples. They have been mentioned not for superficial propagandist reasons but to show how the State of Israel set about the first phase of its consolidation. The Israeli motto was: the end justifies the means.

Right up to the present day, world opinion has taken little or no note of the atrocities Israel committed at that time. It would not and could not believe that the Jews, who had the whole-hearted sympathy of the entire world after their dreadful experiences under Nazism, could perpetrate such cruelties on another people. The Israelis themselves sowed the seeds of armed resistance in the hearts of the Palestinians at this time. Many acts by the Palestinians which world opinion would later condemn as terrorism can be better understood in the light of this historical background.

Flight and Expulsion

> We came to this land which was inhabited by Arabs and established a Hebrew, i.e. a Jewish State . . . Jewish villages were built where Arab villages had once stood. You do not even know the names of these villages and I do not blame you, because the geography books with their names no longer exist – and the villages no longer exist.[3]

The Palestinians had seen their villages destroyed, they had been forced to flee with nothing but what they could carry. Often enough, this meant only their children. Yet they took with them something else as a token of their determination to return: the keys to the doors of their houses. These keys can still be seen hanging above the doors of small houses in refugee camps in Jordan, Syria and Lebanon, bearing silent but eloquent witness to the expulsion from and longing for Palestine.

From spring 1948 to spring 1949, streams of refugees left the country, with the Israeli army behind them and an uncertain future before them. Families would often walk on at night and hide from Israeli attacks by day. Children wept because they were hungry, their fathers remained silent and despondent, their mothers were too helpless and weak, too numbed by horror to comfort their children. They slept under trees and behind bushes till they came to a country which provided refuge against this first persecution. The tents they were given provided scant protection against the wind, the rain and the cold of winter. Their starvation rations did nothing to dispel their inner despair and deep sense of humiliation. They were a nation in exile. 900,000 individuals shared this collective fate – forgotten by the world, humiliated, insulted, despairing, silent.

> The first refugees were forced to live in fields; others lived in mosques, churches, monasteries, schools and abandoned buildings. In June 1950, 29.3% of refugees recognized by UNWRA were housed in camps; this estimate rose to 38.6% by June 1957 and went on rising slightly. Since 1956, tents in the 56 UNWRA camps have been replaced by emergency accommodation. In June 1958 there were no more than 4,900 tents. Accommodation in the camps consisted of huts with clay walls, a mixture of dirt and straw covered with tent canvas and – in the more modern camps – buildings made of cement and concrete with corrugated iron roofs. Seven to nine people have to live in this accommodation, which consists of only one room. Often they have to sleep on the floor. There is no water and no electricity.[4]

The refugees' plight was one of poverty and bitter hardship. Those who received UNWRA aid were better off than the rest. On account of the UNWRA definition of a 'refugee', 48% of Palestinians received nothing at all. It is no exaggeration to say that UNWRA rations were not enough to live on but just too much to die on. In *Le Monde Diplomatique*, Michelene Paulet gave the following description of UNWRA rations:

> Less than $18 per year per head in the form of flour, rice, pulses, sugar, oil and dates; this is the magnificent food ration which guarantees everyone 1,500 calories in summer and 1,600 calories in winter; 5 litres of fuel per year; one blanket for three people per year.[5]

Inadequate food supplies inevitably led to disease. Children's bodies were covered in sores. Their hair fell out or went white. Tuberculosis was rife.

The host countries, themselves underdeveloped and unable to provide jobs for their own people, simply could not cope with hundreds of thousands of refugees. The Palestinians themselves did not wish to assimilate in the host countries. Agreements between UNWRA and the Arab host countries could not be reached because of objections by the Palestinian refugees. Knowing that they were the victims of injustice, they insisted that they wanted to return to their country.

Twice, in 1948 and 1953, the UN passed long resolutions on the right of the Palestinians either to return home or to receive compensation. But Israel refused to recognize these resolutions. Faced by Israeli obduracy, Palestinian villagers from time to time crossed the ceasefire line in order to 'steal' what they rightfully owned. A former Israeli now living in the USA wrote in the *New York Times* of 2 January 1953 that five to seven of these 'infiltrators' were shot every week as part of 'military routine'. The *New York Times* estimated the number of those killed in 1952 at 394, with 227 injured and 2,595 imprisoned. Those who returned were also punished by the Egyptian and Jordanian authorities – in accordance with UN resolutions. Israel's main concern was to maintain its control of the conquered and occupied areas. Israel justified this by pleading the requirements of 'national security'. And the world believed Israel; it knew nothing about the fate that had befallen an entire people, about the Palestinian tragedy.

A nation without a land, a people without a country, the Palestinians were condemned to vegetate in camps. Within sight, across the border, were their houses and fields, to which they were forbidden to return.

The Palestinians in the camps had no passports, no work and no future. Those who remained in Palestine were subjected to degrading and scandalous discrimination. Palestinian identity in Israel was being crushed.

The violent expulsion and uprooting of the Palestinian people by the new State of Israel, the theft of their homes and the refusal to allow them to return – all this contained the seeds of a new confrontation. A new generation was growing up in the camps, the generation of resistance.

Year after year, the Palestinians in the camps went on hoping to return to their homes. But the hopes they had pinned on UN resolutions proved vain. Israel humiliated the United Nations, and the world made the

Palestinians pay for its humiliation.

In the loneliness and obscurity of huts and tents, the Palestinians learnt new laws of survival. They learnt to rely on themselves and take their fate into their own hands. The queues for UNWRA rations disappeared. The Palestinians sought work, throughout the world. They knew that the only chance was education. They wanted their children to be able to cope better with the future, to study and not to have to rely on others. Groups were formed in the camps and courses were started, even though the teachers themselves often had no school-leaving certificates or training. Small schools were set up. Mosques and churches were soon crammed with students and pupils studying hard, even at night, by the light of oil lamps. Illiteracy soon disappeared.

But no real change in their situation could be expected in the near future. The radio report for which they had waited so long in their tents and huts, telling them that they could return to their homes, did not come. But they were no longer resigned and hopeless.

The Palestinians had begun to take their fate into their own hands. A new chapter now began: resistance.

Notes

1. See: *Die VN-Resolutionen zum Nahostkonflikt* (Berlin, 1978), pp. 112 ff.
2. Quoted in: D. Lapierre and Larry Collins, *Ô Jérusalem* (Paris, 1978), p. 258.
3. Moshe Dayan, in a speech to students at the Technical University in Haifa, reported in *Ha'aretz*, 4 April 1969.
4. Nathan Weinstock, *Das Ende Israels* (Berlin, 1975), p. 225.
5. June 1960, p. 10.

13. Palestinian Resistance

The Palestinians Go Underground

On 4 and 5 April 1956, the Israelis bombarded the centre of Gaza with 120mm mortars, killing 56 men, women and children and injuring 103. This was a challenge to which the new Egyptian revolutionary government under Gamal Abdul Nasser had to respond. Mustafa Hafez, an Egyptian army officer, recruited Palestinian volunteers to help him avenge this crime. Hafez and his fedayeen conducted a brilliant military operation. Using the Gaza strip as its base, this unit carried out operations in Israeli-occupied Palestine, penetrating as far as the West Bank and finally withdrawing to Cairo via Amman. Israel's 'security' was in danger and it was quick to respond. On 13 July 1956 Mustafa Hafez was killed by a letter bomb. The following day Salah Mustafa, the Egyptian military attaché and Hafez's contact in Amman, was killed by the same method.

Israel even used these guerrilla activities as a pretext for joining the Anglo-French war against Egypt and for occupying the Gaza strip shortly after. The fedayeen unit was disbanded before the arrival of the UN forces made guerrilla strikes impossible. The campaign had, however, taught the Palestinian resistance movement an important lesson. It proved that even a small military unit could be effective; but it also demonstrated that without independent Palestinian leadership and without political goals the military struggle was doomed to failure.

The way back to Palestine was still barred but the determination to return remained. Palestinian resistance now began.

The expulsion of the Palestinians, their dispersal among various Arab countries and in the tents of the refugee camps plus the wide-ranging controls to which they were subjected by Arab host governments meant that this nascent resistance took a number of different forms. Their common goal was to find ways of liberating their country. Many Palestinians, for example, now joined the Ba'ath party led by Michel Aflaq. This party, whose main strongholds were in Syria and Iraq, advocated Arab unity as the best means of liberating Palestine. The road to Palestine was to pass through the Arab capital cities. The Arab nationalists (Al-

Qaumiyun Al-Arab), founded and led by the Palestinian Dr George Habbash, also believed that Palestinian liberation could only be achieved after the unity of Arab states had been realized. The Arab nationalists, who can justly be described as pioneers of the Egyptian revolution, were based in Beirut, and had some influence at the American University there and at the University of Cairo.

At this time, the hopes of Palestinian refugees were pinned on the Arab states and, after the Egyptian revolution, on their undisputed leader Gamal Abdul Nasser.

The Ba'ath party and the Arab nationalists were the most influential political movements in the Arab world at that time. They were able to disseminate their political thoughts and ideas without hindrance and they both won over numerous sympathizers and recruited members in the Palestinian refugee camps.

After the Arab defeat in 1948, the only Palestinian organization tolerated in the Arab world was the Palestinian Students' Federation in Cairo. It was founded and led by Yasser Arafat, Abu Iyyad, Farouk Kaddoumi and also by members of the Ba'ath party and Al-Qaumiyun Al-Arab.

The Students' Federation was the first organization to provide the Palestinians with an opportunity to discuss the fate of their people with the various political movements and parties. Moreover, the federation's membership of the IUS (International Union of Students) enabled it to establish contacts with the 'outside world' and to make other students more aware of and sympathetic to the Palestinian cause. Yasser Arafat, president of the Students' Federation, travelled to the socialist countries, skilfully and persistently presenting the Palestinian case in Prague, Budapest, Warsaw, Bucharest and other European capitals. The most active members of the Students' Federation in those days now form most of the leadership of the PLO.

Parallel to this, Palestinians in the Gaza strip now began to form underground groups. The best-known of their leaders were perhaps Kahlil Wazir (Abu Jihad), commander of the al-Assifa forces, and Abu Youssef El-Najjar, who was killed in an Israeli commando operation in 1973.

In November 1956 Great Britain and France used the nationalization of the Suez Canal by Nasser as a pretext to attack Egypt. Israel joined in the attack and occupied the Gaza strip. Although the occupation lasted only six months, it was enough to sow the first seeds from which al-Fatah sprung.

The aim of these groups in the Gaza strip was to form a common front of all Palestinians, uniting all the resistance movements of the Palestinian people regardless of their political differences. The Palestinians were no longer content to pin their hopes on Arab armies and governments or on UN resolutions. These were the dominant motives which led to the foundation of the National Unity Front al-Fatah (Harakat al Tahrir al Watani al-Falestini Fatah) in 1955.

Al-Fatah had a very difficult time in the beginning. Gamal Abdul Nasser's success against the British and French and the prospects of a union between Egypt and Syria were virtually an affirmation of the policies of the Ba'ath party and the Arab nationalists. Hopes in Arab unity and the restoration of a powerful Arab empire had been sent soaring. The insistence on a separate Palestinian identity was regarded with suspicion, as a sign of a lack of Arab solidarity. But al-Fatah stuck to its conviction that the Palestinians would have no influence within a united Arab nation unless they could establish an identity and an organization of their own. Only when the entire Palestinian people were organized and the armed struggle against Zionist Israel began would the liberation of Palestine be possible. Al-Fatah regarded this as the only possible way of winning over the Arab masses to its struggle.

Al-Fatah's political convictions were well founded. Its leadership had studied the causes of the division of Palestine and analysed the reasons for their defeat. They had studied the history of Zionism, its organization and its connections with the imperialist powers. They had examined the role and the commitments of the Arab states and the consequences of the Second World War, such as the division of the world into spheres of influence at the Yalta conference. Neither then nor later did al-Fatah question the need for Arab unity; on the contrary, it was anxious to establish this unity. But it insisted that this unity should not only exist on paper. Lasting unity could only be achieved in the practice of a common struggle and in the confrontation with Israel. Al-Fatah regarded any further delay as time lost and wasted for the Palestinian cause. History has proved how correct its analysis was.

Al-Fatah's immediate aim was to win over more Palestinians to the cause of resistance and to widen its influence. Despite travel restrictions on Palestinians, there was no problem in maintaining contact between the Gaza strip and Cairo, the headquarters of the Students' Federation.

Abu Iyyad, for example, lived in Gaza, where he regularly met Abu Jihad; he also studied in Cairo. Yasser Arafat, who had already gained political experience abroad, was also a member of this group. Farouk Kaddoumi, a leading member of the Ba'ath party, was typical of many who joined al-Fatah from other parties and groups.

The movement now spread, making important recruits such as Abu Youssef El-Najjar and Kamal Adwan – both killed by the Israelis in Beirut in 1973.

But al-Fatah wished to go beyond the Gaza strip and Cairo and to bring Palestinians from other Arab states into the united front. A network of contacts was required if a broader-based organization of the Palestinian people was to be established. Palestinian students went to work as engineers, doctors and teachers in other Arab countries as soon as they had completed their studies. Once there, they set about recruiting new members and sympathizers. Cells were set up in Kuwait, where Yasser Arafat worked after his studies, in Saudi Arabia, where there were many Palestinian teachers, in the Gulf states, etc. The Palestinian Ba'athists and Arab nationalists pursued a similar policy. But whereas the latter organizations could work openly and present their viewpoint in Arab newspapers, al-Fatah's only method was to talk to and win over individual Palestinians. Its activities were to remain secret. However, it soon became clear that secret and selective contacts were not enough. Al-Fatah decided to take up the armed struggle against Israel. They sought inspiration in the recent examples of the Vietnamese, Yugoslav and Algerian revolutions.

The proclamation of this decision led to fierce controversy between al-Fatah on the one hand and the Ba'athists and Al-Qaumiyun Al-Arab on the other. The latter remained convinced that only a united Arab army could liberate Palestine.

Al-Fatah replied that armed operations would provoke Israeli reactions. This would force the Palestinians to defend and organize themselves. The Arab armies would also be forced to abandon their passive role and take up arms. Furthermore, Israeli settlers would be reminded that a people existed which had neither forgotten nor abandoned its rightful claim to its own land. And not least, these operations should be addressed to world public opinion, which had so long remained silent on the Palestinian tragedy.

A new problem now arose: the acquisition of arms. Following the 1956 war, al-Fatah had been able to stockpile and hide some weapons. More had to be bought – and these often proved to be antiquated or rusty. None the less, the first operations from 1 January 1965 had to be carried out with these weapons.

The process of organization gradually revealed shortcomings as well as indicating future tasks. Al-Fatah realized that an effective resistance movement would have to include engineers, doctors, students and, above all, workers. The Palestinian workers' clubs were consequently formed. Among the first of such groups supporting the aims of al-Fatah were those founded in the Federal Republic of Germany, in Frankfurt and Darmstadt, Stuttgart and Munich. Ironically, the Palestinians were now following in the footsteps of the first Zionists.

Ignored by the authorities, Palestinian workers met in the Federal Republic of Germany, Austria and Switzerland. Good access to information and intensive discussions soon provided the Palestinians in these countries with a comprehensive insight into the requirements of a resistance movement. They adopted and propagated the aims of al-Fatah. A struggle now broke out among the various Palestinian movements for the support of the student organization. The organization's leadership had been working closely with al-Fatah for some years. Its leaders, who were allowed to travel if they stated their reasons, had established important contacts. Apart from al-Fatah, Al-Qaumiyun Al-Arab in particular had a certain influence in the Palestinian students' organization. But as with the Palestinian workers, al-Fatah had substantial support among Palestinian students in the Federal Republic of Germany and in Austria. The third conference of the Palestinian students' organization in Gaza in 1963 would have to decide on the future political course.

Five months before this conference, a conference of Palestinian students in Europe took place in Mainz. This conference voted for armed struggle against Israel and the restoration of an independent Palestinian identity. With a mandate to this effect, the delegates Hayel Abdel-Hamid, Hani al-Hassan (both now members of the al-Fatah Central Committee) and Amin al-Hindi (a member of the al-Fatah Revolutionary Council) went to the Gaza conference. The heated discussions at this conference looked as if they might lead to a split in the students' federation. The Egyptian Secret Service intervened to prevent the Mainz resolutions from being passed, but the conference voted in favour of the al-Fatah proposals. The students' organization was the first mass organization to support al-Fatah.

Under Hayel Abdel-Hamid, who had been elected an executive member of the Palestinian Students' Federation and had moved to Cairo, al-Fatah began to gain increasing influence among students in Cairo. Hayel Abdel-Hamid, who combined considerable organizational talent with political acumen, now set up a number of new al-Fatah cells.

Al-Fatah also achieved its first 'foreign policy' success when, following the FLN victory against the French, it set up its first foreign branch in Algeria in 1963.

In September 1961, the United Arab Republic broke up; Egypt and Syria went their separate ways. The Palestinians now began to shed some of their illusions, as well as their hopes in Arab unity. Their uncommitted, partly sceptical, attitude to al-Fatah changed. The idea of independent Palestinian resistance began to gain ground. The cause was further helped by the scandal of the diversion of the Jordan waters into Israel. Apart from passing a few ineffective resolutions, the Arab states proved incapable of taking effective counter-measures against this latest act of Israeli aggression. Attempts by Syria and Jordan to divert the waters of the Jordan were frustrated by Israeli bombing.

The al-Fatah analyses of the fifties were now proved true. The division of the world into East and West and the influence of the Western super-powers did not permit Arab unity; the Arab states split up into pro-Western and pro-Eastern camps. The necessity for independent Palestinian resistance was clearer than ever. The movement began to win broader political support. But al-Fatah was still working underground with a tight-knit organization and in strict secrecy. Membership requirements were tough.

Those selected had to go through a one-year probationary period, during which they were set numerous, mainly political, tasks. Apart from fulfilling these tasks, members were required to have a thorough knowledge of Palestinian and Zionist history, to respect the feelings and traditions of the Palestinian people and to establish good contacts with the Palestinian masses.

Thanks to these methods, al-Fatah managed to escape the clutches of the Arab governments and establish an independent Palestinian organization. The national Palestinian identity had gained a new champion. This soon became abundantly clear.

The Founding of the PLO

On 1 June 1964 the 1st Palestinian National Council met. This assembly then founded the Palestine Liberation Organization (PLO).

The PLO's official aim was to liberate Palestine. A national fund consisting of donations and contributions was set up. The Palestine Liberation Army (PLA) was to be the military arm of the PLO.

The central feature of this first conference was the passing of the Palestinian National Charter and of the Basic Law, a kind of constitution. Both were drafted by Ahmad Shukairy.

Ahmad Shukairy, a diplomat and lawyer, became the first chairman of the 15-man PLO executive committee.

The members of the first Palestinian National Council had been nominated by Shukairy and invited to the inaugural congress as individuals. They were for the most part leading public figures, politicians, businessmen, industrialists, clerics, doctors, bankers and even some members of the Jordanian Parliament. Only a few representatives of farmers, trade unions, or students' and women's organizations were present. Guerrilla organizations were not admitted. The first Palestinian National Council had a total of 422 members.

The founding of the PLO was not unexpected. In September 1963 Shukairy had been accepted as the Palestinian representative by the Arab League.

On Nasser's initiative, the first conference of Arab heads of state, on 16 January 1964 in Cairo, had passed a resolution calling for the founding of an organization to 'embody Palestinian existence'. Nasser had entrusted Shukairy with the task of making the necessary preparations.

The PLO had been founded by the Arab states and in the first years of its existence it was also controlled by them. The move had been made for very specific reasons. The Palestinians in the refugee camps were growing more and more discontented and restless about the waiting tactics of the Arab states in the Palestinian conflict. They were tired of hearing nothing but speeches which did not change their situation in the least.

The break-up of the United Arab Republic, the inability of the Arab heads of state to prevent the diversion of the Jordan waters by Israel and petty internal political disputes in the Arab camp had all fanned the flames of discontent even higher. The idea of an independent, separate Palestinian resistance movement gained ground.

This idea now threatened to evade the control of the Arab states and to reveal the ineffectiveness of official Arab policy. Gamal Abdul Nasser tried to prevent this. He hoped that the founding of a Palestinian organization would not only provide an outlet and forum for Palestinian political ambitions but also be useful as an instrument for influencing pan-Arab policies. As long as Shukairy, a confidant of Nasser's, was head of the PLO, continued Arab influence was guaranteed. Shukairy made no important decisions in the PLO without first consulting Nasser.

Ahmad Shukairy was first the Syrian and later the Saudi Arabian representative at the United Nations. The Saudis dismissed him for refusing to bring a Saudi government complaint before the United Nations. But this won him the support of Nasser.

In the Western world, Shukairy was generally known as the man who 'wanted to drive Israel into the sea'. In fact, Shukairy was just a typical Arab politician of his time. He compensated for his inability to make any political impact on a superior enemy by a verbal strong-man act. His militant rhetoric must also be seen against the background of increasing military activity by the al-Fatah groups. Under Shukairy, the PLO had nothing comparable to offer.

None the less, Shukairy must be credited with drafting the Palestinian National Charter and thereby presenting a manifesto which for the first time formulated the ideas of a Palestinian identity. And in the so-called Basic Law he also created a provisional organizational framework for this identity.

However, the traditional Palestinian élite was unable to cope with the challenges and demands of a war of national liberation. On 24 December 1967 Shukairy had to resign.

As early as 1966, political and military developments emerged which prefigured the release of the PLO from the chains of Arab control two years later. Under the pressure of guerrilla activities, the third Palestinian National Council called for the unity of revolutionary organizations within the framework of the PLO. The credibility of this call can be judged by the fact that the PLA had not undertaken any military action against Israel. It was integrated into the Arab armies. And the Arab armies agreed with the traditional Palestinian élite in condemning fedayeen operations. The renaming of the PLO executive committee in December 1966 – it was now called the Revolutionary Council – was merely cosmetic.

The Arab defeat in the 1967 June war completely discredited the traditional leadership. Finally the Arab states were forced to withdraw their support for Shukairy. Yahya Hammouda, a lawyer, now succeeded Shukairy as PLO chairman. Under Hammouda's interim leadership – he had not been officially confirmed in office by the National Council – the PLO made cautious approaches to the guerrilla groups. A special committee was set up to make contact with these groups. But Hammouda, too, was a member of the traditional Palestinian élite whose policies had clearly failed by 1948. He was unable to develop new initiatives for the Palestinian liberation struggle. The age of the traditional élite was irrevocably finished, and it was soon overtaken by events.

The fourth congress of the Palestinian National Council, on 17 and 18 July 1968 in Cairo, again extended the existing executive committee's mandate. But now the resistance organizations claimed half the seats in the National Council. Al-Fatah and the Popular Front had 48 of the 100 seats. The Palestinian Workers', Students' and Women's Organizations had one seat each. This practically guaranteed a majority – a fact which was reflected in the resolutions. The National Council called for freedom of movement for the commandos in the states bordering Israel, an end to Arab control and support for military operations against Israel. It also rejected UN Security Council Resolution 242, in which the Palestinians and their rights were not mentioned. The Palestinians were referred to only indirectly as a 'refugee problem'. The word 'Palestinian' was not used, nor was 'self-determination'.

On the organizational level, the National Council was democratized – in particular the election of the executive committee and the powers of the PLO chairman.

The PLO now set out on a new path – the path of armed struggle and of a separate, independent Palestinian resistance movement.

Al-Fatah and the Founding of the PLO

The founding of the PLO by the Arab states in 1964 confronted al-Fatah with a new situation. It had every reason to believe that the PLO's primary aim was to keep the Palestinians under Arab control and to isolate the independent resistance groups from the Palestinian people – even to denounce them as 'adventurers' and 'enemies of Arab unity'.

Al-Fatah had to act or else lose the influence it had gained in the rising Palestinian national movement. The Political Office for the United Action of Palestinian Revolutionary Forces was founded, comprising a number of Palestinian resistance groups. In fact there were about 40 such groups in 1965 – which is not as surprising as it seems. Many Arab states were using 'their own' Palestinian resistance groups to gain influence on the movement as a whole. As soon as al-Fatah took up the armed struggle, many of these groups either joined al-Fatah or disappeared.

In May 1964, shortly before the PLO was founded, the Political Office issued a statement expressing doubts about the success of an organization which dissociated itself from the revolutionary organizations. The Office offered its help in transforming the Palestinian National Council into a revolutionary force.

Even before this, Arafat, Abu Jihad and others had been in contact with Shukairy, whom they knew from their student years in Cairo, to explain the al-Fatah position to him. They wanted the activities of the PLO and the work of al-Fatah to be coordinated and this coordination to be kept secret. Because of his commitments to the Arab states, Shukairy refused. In spite of this, al-Fatah sent a number of its leaders (Abu Jihad, Abu Youssef El-Najjar, Kamal Adwan, etc.) to the inaugural PLO conference to put the al-Fatah viewpoint. The main feature of the al-Fatah argument was the need for armed struggle.

The Beginning of the Armed Struggle

Al-Fatah carried out its first military operations on 31 December 1964. Three commando groups were to operate independently from Lebanon, Jordan and the Gaza strip. The first successful operations included the blowing-up of bridges, mine laying and attacks on kibbutzim.

On 1 January 1964 al-Assifa (the Storm), the military arm of al-Fatah, issued its first military communiqué. The name al-Assifa had been chosen to avoid compromising al-Fatah if the operation failed.

Initially, the commandos had to fight not only against Israel but against harassment from the Arab side. The group operating in the Gaza strip was discovered by the Egyptian secret service on 15 February. By 20 February, all its leaders had either been imprisoned or placed under house arrest.

The decision to take up the armed struggle had been preceded by fierce and controversial discussions within al-Fatah itself. There were two camps. One argued that it was too early to start guerrilla warfare and that they should wait until al-Fatah was a mass movement with substantial support and membership.

To this Arafat, Abu Jihad, Abu Youssef El-Najjar, Abu Lutf, Abu Iyyad and others replied that only through armed struggle could al-Fatah make itself a mass movement. The hopes that al-Fatah had aroused in the Palestinian people should not be disappointed. A decision was postponed. The adoption of military operations was not finally approved until another meeting of the entire al-Fatah leadership in Damascus in October 1964.

The spectacular operations of 31 December 1964 achieved the desired effect. After a few days of silent consternation, a storm of outrage and indignation broke out over al-Assifa. Almost all the Arab newspapers condemned the operations, describing them as the deeds of 'Muslim Brothers', 'CIA agents' or 'agents of international communism'. Press organs in various Arab countries were even forbidden to mention the name of al-Assifa. A resolution of Arab League defence ministers called on all Arab countries to prevent al-Assifa operations so as not to give Israel a pretext for an attack.

The first Palestinian revolutionary killed in action was shot by Jordanian army bullets. Ahmad Mussa was killed by King Hussein's troops when he returned to Jordan, where he thought he was safe.

Palestinians were now kept under surveillance, persecuted and imprisoned. In 1967, there were 250 Palestinians in Jordanian prisons on suspicion of membership of al-Assifa. Some al-Fatah leaders were also arrested.

In spring 1966, Yasser Arafat, Abu Jihad, Abu Ali Iyyad and others were arrested in Damascus. It was only after a one-month hunger strike and the intervention of other al-Fatah leaders such as Farouk Kaddoumi and Abu Iyyad that they were released.

Shortly afterwards Yasser Arafat was arrested by Lebanese security forces on suspicion of being an Israeli agent. Al-Fatah again managed to get him released. The Lebanese authorities had been unable to establish his identity.

Al-Fatah did not wish and could not afford to jeopardize the effective organization of the Palestinian people and the contination of the armed struggle. It had to normalize its relations with the other Arab countries.

The al-Fatah leadership visited Cairo to discuss political co-operation with Nasser. They hoped that Nasser would be able to use his influence in the Arab world to win support for Palestinian resistance. But in fact no meeting with Nasser took place. The Egyptian government was interested only in finding out as much as possible about the structure and leaders of al-Fatah.

Al-Fatah had to get by without such support until after the June war in 1967. But the military as well as the political struggle continued just the same. In the two years from 1965 to 1967 the fedayeen carried out more than 200 operations.

14. The Arab Defeat of 1967

The June War

On 5 June 1967, in a surprise attack, the Israeli army destroyed almost the entire Egyptian air force on the ground.

This coup dramatically highlighted the state of readiness of each side just before this new episode in the Arab-Israeli conflict. The Israeli army, government and secret service had been preparing for this war for years. Internal political wrangles had been settled in time for the war by the formation of a 'government of national unity'. The Israeli General Staff had been working out the details of this summer offensive for years and had begun the mobilization of reserves well in advance of the outbreak of hostilities.[1]

American newspapers reported that the Pentagon had gone over all the options in the June war as a map exercise in March 1967.[2]

Israel had without question the best-equipped troops in the Middle East. Their arms technique was vastly superior. By mobilizing its reserves, Israel could put 300,000 trained and experienced soldiers into the field.

In contrast, the Arab governments were as ill prepared for the war as the Arab armies. They did not want the war, knowing that they were inferior in every respect. The total troop strength of Egypt, Syria and Jordan together was no more than 180,000, although Egyptian radio claimed that 500,000 Arab troops had been mobilized. Western news agencies carried exaggeration to absurdity, claiming that three million Jews were faced by 60 and even 100 million Arabs.

Politically, the Arab states had been strengthened by their closer ties with the Soviet Union. They continued to insist that Israel should implement the numerous UN resolutions on the Palestine conflict; and in particular that it should return the territories conquered in 1948 and allow the refugees to return. However, the majority in the Israeli cabinet now favoured a policy of 'defeating the Arabs so comprehensively that they will be forced to accept the terms dictated to them at the conference table.'[3] In May 1967, Syrian as well as Soviet intelligence reports confirmed the probability of an imminent Israeli attack on Syria.

The Arab Defeat of 1967

Israeli Chief of Staff and later Prime Minister Rabin had said in April 1967 that Israel would not tolerate a socialist government in Syria. It backed up these militant threats with military attacks on Syria, which were even the subject of UN Security Council resolutions.[4]

Nasser now had to act or else lose his leading role in the Arab world, especially as he had signed a friendship and defence pact with Syria only a few months before.

By verbal threats, by reinforcing his army in Sinai (without the least attempt at secrecy), by calling for the withdrawal of UN troops along the ceasefire line – they withdrew on 24 May 1967 – and by blocking the straits of Tiran, Nasser hoped to intimidate Israel and prevent a war against Syria. Even Moshe Dayan had to admit in his memoirs that Egypt's military operations, including the troop reinforcements in Sinai, were purely defensive in nature.

However, the verbal escalation on the Arab side had now provided Israel with the arguments and pretexts it needed to justify its offensive blitzkreig in 1967.

The mass media in the West European capitals and in the United States gave the impression that the Arabs were preparing to wipe Israel off the face of the earth – with the result that West European and North American sympathies were almost entirely on Israel's side in its third expansionist war.

Israel's army and government ruthlessly exploited the military weakness and political errors of the Arabs. They struck so hard that they had attained all their tactical goals within a week.

International efforts to bring about a ceasefire succeeded only after this week had elapsed. Till then, Israel's Western allies had kept a conveniently low profile. Israel now occupied all Palestine, Sinai and the Golan Heights, and brought under its control an area several times larger than its original territory.

In Sinai, thousands of soldiers were buried in the sand, burnt to death by napalm or blown to pieces by bombs. Knocked-out tanks and guns remained in the desert as iron ruins. Israeli and foreign cameras – the contemptuous intention was clear – had previously taken shots of soldiers fleeing barefoot. The Arab disaster was complete. 700,000 Palestinians were again put to flight.

In 1956, Israel had fought together with France and Great Britain against Egypt. In the war of June 1967 it was alone. Israel thus proved that it was capable of playing the part of the former colonial powers single-handed. In the June war, Israel impressively demonstrated its worth as the bastion and ally of the United States to the entire world. From then on, Israel would not need to worry about military and financial aid.

The Second Expulsion

> One need not necessarily be the victim of propagandistic exaggeration to be reminded of the fate of Lidice.*5

If the Israeli triumph over the Egyptian air force had demonstrated the detailed preparation and precise planning behind the 1967 offensive, the Israeli army's operations in the newly-conquered areas showed an equally high degree of planning – not only in the military sense. The Israeli government was acting with definite political intentions and full awareness of the consequences.

Those Palestinians who had not been forced to flee by the threats and confusion of war were now deliberately and systematically driven out by the Israelis.

For many Palestinians, this was the second flight, following that of 1948; more misery, suffering, hardship and uncertainty. To take the example of Kalkiliya:

> A large proportion of the 16,000 inhabitants of Kalkiliya were refugees from 1948. With the aid of UNWRA they had built their own homes and started a new life. Having driven the inhabitants out of their town by 16.00 hours on 7 July 1967, the Israeli army used tanks and bulldozers to destroy two-thirds of the town. Foreign correspondents were not allowed to visit the town. After the destruction, an Israeli officer said: 'That was Kalkiliya; now it is Kfar Saba.'6

In the first days of the war, the Israeli army systematically blew up Arab houses and indeed entire villages. While the Israeli radio called on the refugees to return, the Israeli army hounded them from village to village and finally over the frontier.

A few names and facts will have to stand for many. Imwas, Yalu and Beit Nuba were blown up on 7 June. On 8 June, the villagers were driven out of Sufir near Hebron and 13 of the best houses were blown up. In Jerusalem, the inhabitants of the former Jewish quarter were ordered to leave their houses within 24 hours. This district, which is near to the Wailing Wall, was then flattened by bulldozers. 400 families, about 6,000 people, lost their homes and everything they possessed. On the Golan Heights, the villages of Kafr Elma and Al-Hurriah were destroyed. Eye-witnesses told of mass executions of Syrian resistance fighters. Summary shootings and executions were also carried out in other parts of the occupied territories. The population was seized by panic. The Ameri-

---

*Lidice, a village in what is now Czechoslovakia, was wiped out by the Nazis. All its inhabitants were murdered and the houses were razed to the ground.

can special correspondent of *Associated Press* wrote of the Israeli army: 'They behaved like cowboys driving a herd before them.'[7]

These operations by the Israeli army did not cease when the war ended. In the second week of November, the village of Jiftlik on the Jordan was destroyed. It, too, had housed 6,000 Palestinian refugees from 1948. The Israeli army took the Palestinians to Jordan in buses, lorries and even horse-drawn carts.

According to reports in the *New York Times* and *Le Monde*, columns of refugees were repeatedly bombarded and burnt by napalm fired from squadrons of Mirage jets. By another expulsion of hundreds of thousands of Palestinians, the Israeli military now created the conditions for the Zionist settlement of all Palestine. The Arab armies were defeated. Israeli expansion could continue unimpeded – with the entire world looking on.

Palestinian Resistance and the Arab Defeat of 1967

In the days immediately after the defeat, the mood throughout the Arab world was one of gloom and hopelessness. Nasser's resignation on 9 June was a symbolic acknowledgement of the failure of the strategy and tactics used hitherto and of conventional methods of war in the struggle for the liberation of Palestine. But Gamal Abdul Nasser, who embodied Arab unity, was to return to office, stung by the jubilation of his enemies and moved by the wild outbursts of grief among his supporters.

The defeat in the June war had confirmed the correctness of al-Fatah's analyses. The Arab armies were unprepared and far too weak to resist the Israeli army. Their interest in the liberation of Palestine was only indirect and their resistance was not sufficiently sustained. The Palestinian people needed a new organization under Palestinian leadership to set it on the path back to Jerusalem. By the defeat of 1967, the Arab governments had forfeited all claims to speak or negotiate on behalf of the Palestinian people.

On 12 June 1967, a few days after the end of the war, al-Fatah held a conference in Damascus. Delegates argued fiercely about whether to continue guerrilla warfare immediately. A group led by Abu Obeida regarded the continuation of the struggle against so superior an enemy as futile self-sacrifice. Arafat, Abu Jihad, Abu Lutf, Abu Iyyad and others completely disagreed with this view, arguing that the Palestinian people had gained new hope from the operations of the fedayeen. The defeat of the Arab armies underlined the need for Palestinian armed resistance. Resistance had to continue – and it did.

Al-Fatah's call to continue resistance met with a good response. Commando troops collected arms and ammunition from the battlefields and brought them to safe depots in Jordan. Leading al-Fatah representatives travelled to Arab states drumming up support for Palestinian resistance. Palestinians from all over the world responded to al-Fatah's call. Soon the military training camps in Damascus and Algiers were too small to cope with all the recruits. New recruits had to be taught in crash courses. The fedayeen conducted their operations in the occupied areas, underlining the Palestinians' determination to return to their country.

The al-Fatah resolution at the Damascus congress stipulated that everyone, including leading cadres, had to take part in military operations. No distinctions were to be made between leaders and ordinary members – there were to be no soft options behind the lines. It is no mere legend, for example, that Yasser Arafat lived in Jerusalem for a time after the Israeli occupation and carried out operations in occupied Palestine, as did Abu Jihad, Abu Sabri and many others. The mood of hopelessness was over and motivation for resistance renewed.

On 31 August 1967, the commandos carried out their first large-scale operation, soon to be followed by new operations and attacks. The Arab world was still paralysed by the 1967 defeat. The Israeli army was still enjoying the intoxication of victory, with all the arrogance of those who think they are invincible.

The political impact of the fedayeen operations was surprisingly great. The Arab armies were defeated but the Palestinians had not capitulated. The resistance organizations' prestige in the Arab world rose enormously and hundreds of young Palestinians swelled al-Fatah's ranks. The myth of the fedayeen now embodied the courage and the aspirations of the Arab nation.

The Arab defeat and the continuation of partisan warfare also had a unifying effect within the Palestinian ranks. The Arab nationalists (Al-Qaumiyun Al-Arab) – from which the Popular Front under George Habbash had been formed – now accepted the need for an independent armed struggle.

From today's perspective it might appear that many operations were only limited military successes. Betrayal sometimes led to operations being discovered in advance; claims were made of successful operations which were impossible to verify. None the less, the fedayeen won general sympathy and admiration. Israel itself ensured this, by frequently blowing up the homes of real or alleged guerrilla sympathizers, imposing curfews and deporting suspects.

In the first phase after the June war in 1967 the political, not the military, effect was the decisive factor. But military operations formed the basis for the widening of political resistance. Israel responded to fedayeen attacks with counter-attacks on alleged guerrilla bases. One of these bases was Karameh.

Notes

1. See: Fritz Schatten, *Entscheidung in Palästina* (Stuttgart), p. 34; also the memoirs of Moshe Dayan and Levi Eshkol.
2. Hans Henle, *Der neue Nahe Osten* (Frankfurt, 1972), p. 246.
3. Ibrahim Abu Lughod, 'La politique d'Israel à l'égard des Arabes', in Anis Sayegh (ed.), *La Confrontation israelo-arabe* (Paris, 1969), p. 133.
4. See UN Security Council Resolutions S/6248, S/6382, S/6392, S/6731.
5. Nathan Weinstock on the expulsion of the Palestinians in 1967.
6. Paul Gauthier, *Jérusalem et le Sang des Pauvres. 5−8 juin 1967*, pp. 13, 41ff.
7. Ibid., p. 50.

15. The Battle of Karameh: The Turning Point in Palestinian Resistance

In the early morning of 21 March 1968, 10,000 Israeli infantrymen, supported by tank units and helicopters, marched over the Allenby Bridge into Jordan. Their objective was Karameh.

Karameh is a small border town in the Jordan valley. Immediately behind the town, where the hilly countryside rises and the ground becomes stony and barren, lay Karameh refugee camp. After the June war, many Palestinians took refuge in emergency accommodation and tents here, only one hour's walk away from Palestine.

Karameh was no longer a sleepy border town. It was the political and military headquarters of al-Fatah and the base from which many commando operations in occupied Palestine were conducted.

The Israeli army had decided to 'take out' this base and eliminate the 'guerrillas' in a few hours. However, the fedayeen were not completely unprepared for this attack. The Jordanian General Khamanash had told al-Fatah leaders on 18 March that the Israelis were likely to attack in the next three days. He also advised them to avoid a confrontation with a superior enemy. From the military point of view, this well-meaning advice was certainly correct.

However, Arafat, Abu Jihad, Abu Iyyad and the fedayeen made a different and crucial decision: to stand their ground and fight.

The Israelis attacked on a broad front. In spite of a barrage from pro-Palestinian Jordanian army units, Israeli tanks broke through. The first houses in the town of Karameh were blown up. Infantry troops entered the refugee camp and tanks flattened huts and tents. The fedayeen fought with courage born of despair. Some even jumped with bomb belts around their bodies in front of Israeli tanks, blowing themselves and the tanks to pieces. Troops now fought from house to house, and often from man to man. By the afternoon the camp was destroyed and three-quarters of the town reduced to rubble. The Israelis withdrew in their remaining vehicles. They had not achieved their objectives. The battle had taken a heavy toll but the resistance had held its own – against a superior enemy with an aura of invincibility. This myth was now shattered, not by the Arab armies but by a small, determined group of revolutionary Palestinian guerrillas. The political motivation of ordinary Palestinian workers and students had proved stronger than the military drill, the training and the experience of the Israeli army. This battle was celebrated as a glorious victory throughout the Arab world.

The battle of Karameh was the political and military turning point in Palestinian resistance, especially for al-Fatah. Karameh restored the dignity and self-esteem of the Palestinians and of the entire Arab world. Karameh pointed the way ahead after the disaster of the June war.

Admiration of the fedayeen was now exuberant. In the refugee camps, people gathered and chanted 'Karameh, Karameh.' The UNWRA starvation rations, the cold tents and muddy roads – all this was forgotten. Pride, confidence and hope were written on every face. Even the older people in the camps held their heads up high and no longer walked around with shoulders bowed. The time of endless speeches and paper resolutions, of defeat and humiliations, of silent, helpless waiting – this time now seemed definitively over. Only a few hours after it ended, the battle of Karameh was a legend.

Thousands of volunteers now joined al-Fatah. Only about a fifth of them could be taken on in the training camps. Many Palestinians now joined other Palestinian organizations, such as George Habbash's Popular Front. This influx not only increased the military potential of the resistance movement, it also made possible greater political differentiation and the establishment of political and social institutions. Many Palestinians unable to take part in military operations became involved in these other areas and thereby strengthened the resistance movement.

Al-Fatah's first move was to set up a political department. Newspapers were started, books published and publishing companies founded. The people in the refugee camps were no longer an apathetic, longsuffering mass. They began to organize themselves. All kinds of committees were formed. Gradually, political and social structures began to take shape in the refugee camps. An independent medical care service was established, nurseries were founded, classes were started and all kinds of other activities were organized. A wave of enthusiasm and *élan* transformed the refugee camps into revolutionary centres. It was after the battle of Karameh that the political and organizational foundations were laid on which the PLO would build in the following years. The ripples from Karameh reached far beyond the Palestinian or the Arab nation. Karameh considerably boosted al-Fatah's international standing. Palestinians in West Europe and North America were given opportunities to argue their case and present their demands. In the universities of America and Europe, in Frankfurt, Paris, Rome and London, Palestinians found a hearing. Perhaps for the first time, they also found sympathy in those countries. They were greateful for these opportunities and used them to explain the programme and views of al-Fatah and the Popular Front. In the 1960s, Easter marches were very popular in West Germany. Palestinian students and workers took part in them and used them to win sympathy and understanding for their cause. The first Easter march in which

Palestinian students and workers were actively involved was in 1968.

These activities soon began to make an impact. Committees of solidarity with Palestine were formed throughout West Europe. Newspapers were started up: *Resistencia* appeared in Rome and Madrid; the magazine, *Free Palestine*, was published in London; a committee in Amsterdam produced its own bulletin, and the French *Comités de Solidarité* compared the Palestinian with the French resistance movement. In West Germany, a magazine, *Resistentia*, was published, later to be followed by others such as *Falestin al-Thaura* (Palestinian Revolution) in Bonn, and *Palästina-Nachrichten* and *Freies Palästina*.

Many students had pictures of Palestinian fedayeen hanging on their walls and the traditional *kouffiya* or Palestinian headcloth was worn throughout Europe.

16. Power Changes Hands in the PLO

At its fourth session on 17 and 18 July 1968 in Cairo, the Palestinian National Council had seen the military resistance groups take almost half the seats (see chapter 13, second section). The battle of Karameh was beginning to have its first institutional consequences. Admiration for fedayeen courage and determination and the creation of political and social structures in the refugee camps by al-Fatah had substantially increased their popularity and influence. Fatah representatives visiting other Arab countries after the June war found that doors were suddenly opening and that their arguments were no longer falling on deaf ears. Most Arab heads of state had cautiously indicated their recognition and promised support. The prestige of the resistance organizations had risen further.

This general change of mood and the vast improvement in morale in the camps deprived the traditional Palestinian élite of its power base. In the elections at the fifth congress of the Palestinian National Council, the resistance groups triumphed, notably al-Fatah which won about a third of all seats. In February 1969 Yasser Arafat was elected president of the PLO executive committee.

The Popular Front for the Liberation of Palestine (PFLP) and Saiqa (the Palestinian branch of the Syrian Ba'ath party) gained 12 seats each, while the Palestine Liberation Army (PLA) gained only five seats. Not yet represented in the National Council were the present-day Democratic Front (then the DPFLP) and the Popular Front/General Command, both breakaway groups from the Popular Front, and the pro-Iraqi Arab Liberation Front (ALF), which was only founded in 1969. The Independent Group with 28 seats was the second strongest in the National Council after al-Fatah.

At this fifth congress of the National Council, trade unions and federations such as the General Union of Palestinian Students (GUPS), the General Union of Palestinian Workers (GUPW) and the Palestinian Red Crescent together held ten seats. These seats reflected the groups' growing influence and the Palestinian people's increasingly active role in the struggle for Palestinian liberation.

The take-over of power by the resistance groups in the PLO marked the arrival of a new historical force on the world political scene. Through the Palestine Liberation Organization, the Palestinian people not only regained their courage and dignity but also their national identity in the struggle for the liberation of Palestine. They had created their own independent organization to lead the return to Palestine. After more than 20 years of defeat and humiliation, they had taken their fate into their own hands.

Al-Fatah now became the most powerful organization in the PLO. Its hopes and its analyses had been confirmed by concrete developments, so it is hardly surprising that in all essential respects the PLO's political programme was identical with al-Fatah's.

This programme, which al-Fatah first announced at a press conference in 1968, proposed that the Palestinian people should be organized in a single organization. All Palestinians were to be regarded automatically as members of the Palestine Liberation Organization. This organization of the Palestinian people regarded itself as separate and independent of other Arab states. The National Council was the supreme decision-making body and it was the responsibility of the executive committee to implement these resolutions.

Al-Fatah believed that the principle of non-intervention in the internal affairs of Arab states was an important guarantee of its own independence. The unity of the Arab nations was to be achieved in the struggle for the liberation of Palestine. Yet in precisely this area the PLO would have to face some very painful experiences in the years to come. The PLO had also drawn important conclusions from the experiences of the Zionist movement in the 1920s and 1930s, which underlined the importance of international connections and international recognition.

The success of these efforts is shown by the fact that more states now recognize the PLO than the State of Israel.

The declared aim of all Palestinians was to return to their country and to establish an independent, democratic Palestine in which Jews, Christians and Muslims could live together in peace and harmony. No one doubted, least of all the Palestinians themselves, that the path to this goal would be stony and difficult. The Palestinian people would have to face many bloody and bitter confrontations – the first of which took place in Jordan in the seventies.

17. The Civil War in Jordan

The Causes of the Conflict in Jordan

After the occupation of the whole of Palestine in the June war, Jordan became the base for the Palestinian resistance movement; its political and military leadership operated from Palestinian refugee camps. It was here that they trained most of their resistance fighters, organized their militias and built up their own social and political institutions. The resistance movement was responsible for administering and organizing life in the refugee camps. But the fedayeen dominated more than just the streets of the refugee camps. Heavily-armed Palestinian commando groups demonstratively patrolled the streets of the capital, Amman. Open conflicts and armed clashes between Jordanian state forces and these commando groups became increasingly frequent.

The Palestinian people, poorly administered by the Hashemite regime, had created their own structures in the camps and had thus taken the first steps towards their social and political emancipation. Their large degree of independence had made them a powerful factor in Jordan which the king could not control. The king's authority was now called into question. The Jordanian state apparatus could no longer impose the rule of the royal family as absolutely as before.

King Hussein realized that his throne was in danger – and not just because of the possible impact of social change on Jordanian society. A good half of his country's inhabitants were Palestinians. The Jordanian army and police had been virtually powerless for some months after the June 1967 war and during this time the standing, power and arms of the resistance groups had grown – in the king's eyes, to alarming proportions. King Hussein saw only one possible solution and from 1968 he began preparing for a confrontation. On 4 November 1968, élite Jordanian troops entered the large refugee camps of Djebel Ashrafiyeh and Djebel Hussein in Amman, where they killed 28 people. The massacre was prompted by an al-Fatah radio broadcast urging them to act on the king's words, 'we are all fedayeen now', and go over to the fedayeen side.

The Jordanian army now posed a serious threat to commando bases and attempted to prevent Palestinian resistance fighters infiltrating into the occupied areas. Al-Fatah at this time took advantage of the help of friendly Iraqi officers in Jordan to bypass Jordanian checkpoints and even to enter Israel via North Syria.

After this, the conflict escalated: verbal abuse, kidnappings and shoot-outs were the order of the day. Ceasefire agreements were reached only to be constantly broken. The Jordanian secret service operated very skilfully, smuggling *agents provocateurs* into the Palestinian ranks; and the Jordanian security services provoked incidents whenever this appeared to be to the king's tactical advantage. Certainly Hussein had good reason to be worried. The Popular Front led by George Habbash and the Democratic Front under Nayef Hawatmeh were openly calling for the 'overthrow of the oligarchy' in Jordan, wishing the king a 'well-earned' exile in the United States. In April 1970, when the Deputy American Secretary of State visited Amman, several Palestinian organizations led violent demonstrations in which the American cultural centre was burnt down and the US embassy attacked. These operations inevitably led to harsh reactions and the screw of violence was turned ever tighter. However, the majority of Palestinians under Yasser Arafat and al-Fatah were anxious to avoid open conflict with the militarily superior Jordanian forces. A Palestinian defeat in such a conflict might imply a pretext for Israel to expel Palestinians to Jordan. Jordan was not and would not be the home of the Palestinians. Their goal lay on the other side of the Jordan.

But all efforts to observe ceasefire agreements and achieve a political solution of the conflict were doomed to failure. By the early summer of 1970, civil war looked inevitable. King Hussein, certain of military support from the USA, was determined to settle the conflict by military force.

The Palestinian attitude was more complex. While al-Fatah was continually looking for a political means to a *modus vivendi*, others favoured the overthrow of the king. In August 1970, King Hussein announced on Jordanian television that he would give his backing to the 'peace plan' of American Secretary of State Rogers. This announcement was virtually a declaration of war on the Palestinians. That same night, Jordanian army units moved into new positions.

Events now came thick and fast. On 1 September, another attempt on King Hussein's life failed, the second in a few months. On 6 September, the Popular Front hijacked three aeroplanes; it later hijacked a fourth. One of the planes was blown up in Cairo in protest against Nasser's troop reduction agreements on the Suez Canal. The others landed at 'Dawson Fields', a former British military airfield 25 kms from Amman. The escalation of violence was now inevitable. On 16 September, Hussein dismissed the civilian government and appointed a military government in its place. On the morning of 17 September, the Jordanian army began its attack on Amman and the Palestinian refugee camps. Amman was reduced to rubble. The Jordanian army spared neither the civilian population nor the prisoners.

The fedayeen with their light weapons had no chance in street fighting against tank-backed Jordanian infantry. The guerrillas had been trained for quick commando attacks and rapid retreats, not for long positional and defensive warfare. Hussein emerged victorious from the one-week battle of Amman.

Despite assurances to the contrary from some Arab countries, the Palestinians had been abandoned when they needed help. Israel mobilized its troops and put them on the alert. Syria withdrew its tanks from North Jordan. The Iraqi forces stayed in their positions and waited for orders from Baghdad. Only the USA acted, conducting an airlift to Amman and supplying arms, ammunition, medicine and food – for King Hussein.

The Palestinian Resistance Movement Is Expelled from Jordan

On .27 September, at Nasser's insistence, a ceasefire agreement was reached between Arafat and Hussein. This was followed on 15 October by a formal agreement between the PLO and Jordan. This 14-point agreement gave the PLO complete freedom of movement in Jordan, although the fedayeen were barred from appearing openly in the towns. King Hussein officially committed himself to 'unreserved support for the Palestinian revolution'.

In reality, Hussein did everything he possibly could to restrict the Palestinians even further – and in Wasfi Tall, Prime Minister and Minister of Defence, he found a man admirably suited to help him achieve this aim. Wasfi Tall set up 'police posts' – in fact Jordanian army bases – near fedayeen bases. A new law – violating the agreement between Hussein and the PLO – stated that anyone found in possession of arms could be sentenced to death. Repression was intensified; the refugee camps were occupied and many people were imprisoned. Bulldozers of a Jordanian pioneer unit flattened the 'Tomb of the Unknown Fedayeen' – a monument to the 175 Palestinian victims of the bloody September fighting.

In accordance with the agreement, the fedayeen had withdrawn from Amman to Jerash and Ajlun, north of the capital. King Hussein was determined to destroy these bases too.

On 13 July, the Jordanian army began its final offensive against PLO units. Completely cut off, the fedayeen at Jerash and Ajlun fought a desperate rearguard action. The heroic stand of Commander Abu Ali Iyyad, a member of the al-Fatah Central Committee, at Tell Al-Akra, has become legendary. Guerrillas led by Abu Ali Iyyad defended their positions in the hills to the west of Jerash to the last bullet, till they were massacred by the Jordanian army. On 19 July, the Jordanian Prime Minister Wasfi Tall announced that there were no longer any guerrilla bases in Jordan. The PLO was defeated; its political and military presence in Jordan was destroyed. Thirty thousand Palestinians were killed in this bloody civil war. Reports of the fighting in September 1970 and in July 1971 are unanimous in their condemnation of the cruelty and brutality of the Jordanian army. Civilians in the refugee camps were cold-bloodedly murdered or crushed by Jordanian tanks. Thousands of wounded died on the streets because the Jordanian army would not allow any medical aid, stopping even the International Red Cross from giving help. Prisoners were appallingly mistreated, tortured and killed.

Many fedayeen obviously preferred to flee to Israel rather than fall into the hands of Hussein's troops. This was a truly tragic end to a sorrowful chapter in modern Arab history.

The Causes of Defeat

The defeat of July 1971 brought the PLO to the verge of collapse. Not only were its military units defeated and fragmented but the political and social work of the previous three years was practically destroyed. What were the causes of this defeat?

There is no doubt that one of the critical weaknesses of the PLO at that time was its lack of unity. There was no concerted and agreed position in the resistance movement on the conflict with the Jordanian regime. While al-Fatah was attempting to reach some kind of understanding and agreement with King Hussein and did not wish to intervene in Jordanian internal affairs, the Popular Front, the Democratic Front and other groups were trying to overthrow the king. King Hussein cleverly exploited these political divergences for his own ends.

A Palestinian Supreme Command did exist, but it lacked technical equipment and, more importantly, it had little authority. No concerted strategic decisions were taken, each group operating as it thought best. Palestinian operations were essentially a response to Jordanian army measures, and so the Jordanians were able to fix the time, the place and the circumstances of the decisive battles. They could achieve little military impact without a joint political position. The Palestinians fought without a united front and without a common strategy. King Hussein, on the other hand, could rely on a well-equipped, experienced and disciplined army. And he also managed to win the Jordanian people over to his side – or at least to keep them neutral.

The tactics of some Palestinian groups who hijacked aeroplanes to draw world attention to the Palestinian cause also contributed to the defeat. King Hussein took advantage of these actions to gain the support of world public opinion. The silence of world public opinion also suited his purposes admirably during the decisive battles against the fedayeen and the Palestinian people. Hussein also benefited from the fact that the PLO's relations with other states, parties and organizations in the international arena were still in the early stages. The support of the United

States, which provided Jordan with supplies of all kinds through its fleet, was a further advantage to the Jordanian army.

United States' intervention was not the only external factor in the Palestinians' defeat. The Israeli armed forces were on the alert at the Jordanian and Syrian borders. Israeli politicians several times threatened that their army would intervene if the Jordanian army looked like being defeated. This also intimidated Arab states which – despite previous verbal assurances – did not dare to intervene on the Palestinian side in this unequal struggle.

Finally, the death of Nasser on 28 September 1970 deprived the Palestinians of one of their most important friends in the Arab world. Nasser, while looking to Egypt's own interests, had always shown great sympathy for the Palestinian people's struggle for liberation.

Reflections on Terror and Resistance

The liquidation of the Palestinian resistance by the Jordanian regime was a bitter and bloody lesson. Thousands of Palestinians, men, women and children, had literally bled to death, with the fedayeen powerless to help. The survivors were deeply shocked by the silence of world opinion, especially of Arab governments, at the bloody massacre of fedayeen in Jerash and Ajlun.

The hopes of many Palestinians of returning to Palestine – hopes for which they had given up their jobs and studies, their security and in many cases their whole livelihood – were now dashed. Intense bitterness and resentment now became widespread. Faith in their own leadership was badly shaken and they had only contempt and mockery for their 'Arab brothers'. Many of these young men began to realize that the resistance had not been radical or hard enough – and in the leadership of al-Fatah and the PLO these feelings fell on fertile ground. Many Palestinians were reminded of the Israeli massacres at Kafr Kassem and Deir Yassin. They could note no difference between the actions of the Jordanian government and those of the Israelis.

If the world was not prepared to consider the fate of the Palestinians, then the world would not be spared the same fate which the Palestinians had suffered.

'In today's world, no one is innocent, no one is neutral. Either you are on the side of the oppressors or on the side of the oppressed.'[1]

These were the words with which the Popular Front justified its aeroplane hijacks in 1970. Of course it was clear that the situation of the Palestinians could not be permanently improved by hijacking aeroplanes. But the Palestinians saw that Europeans and Americans sat up and took notice when their interests were threatened so dramatically. The issue had been brought to public attention; the fact that a nation was living in misery and despair could not be concealed. But sensations are short-lived and less than a year later, in summer 1971, the world had forgotten the Palestinians again.

The names of Jerash and Ajlun were known only to the initiated. The Palestinians were again alone. Leila Khaled's words summed up the feelings of many Palestinians in those months following the defeat in Jordan: 'We are living in the age of violence. Justice cannot be enforced, it is powerless. Our strategy is to fight violence with violence.'[2]

Those responsible for the deaths of almost 30,000 Palestinians were to be called to account and the world was to be reminded that the injustice suffered by the Palestinians could not just be passed over in silence.

In autumn 1971 'Black September' was founded. The name commemorated the beginning of the civil war in Jordan in September 1970. Black September was not a closely-knit organization but a loose association of fedayeen from all Palestinian organizations. Its aim was to use violence to punish those responsible for the bloody massacre in Jordan.

At the end of November 1971, Wasfi Tall went to Cairo to take part in the meetings of the Joint Defence Council of the Arab League. Security measures were extremely strict. The Jordanian Prime Minister was a living symbol of the betrayal of the Palestinians and had to expect an assassination attempt at any time. Two days passed and nothing happened. On 28 November, the third day of the conference, just as relief at the lack of any incident was setting in and security was being relaxed, Wasfi Tall was shot down in the lobby of the Sheraton Hotel by four Palestinians, who were immediately arrested. When asked about their motives, they said they had killed an executioner of the Palestinian people. Their organization: Black September.

Another objective of Black September in those years was the liberation of Palestinian prisoners from the cells of the Jordanian secret service. A detailed plan to occupy the American embassy was worked out and the occupiers' demands were formulated. But on the day of the operation, all the commando members were arrested.

But there were also uncontrolled actions whose only motive was revenge born of blind despair. On 21 May 1972, three young Japanese shot passengers in the concourse of Lod airport, killing 25 and wounding 78. Most of the passengers were Christians from Puerto Rico visiting the Holy Places. The PLO condemned this operation in the strongest terms.

There were also actions for which Black September had no responsibility whatever. A motley group calling itself the 'Seventh Suicide Brigade' shot US citizens at Athens airport, allegedly to draw attention to the 'criminal methods of the Americans' in the war against the Palestinians.

Other groups such as the 'Phalanx of the People' and the 'Martyr Abu Mahmud' group claimed responsibility for aeroplane hijackings.

The al-Fatah leadership then decided to punish severely any future sky-jackings, in order to prevent the Palestinian resistance movement from being identified with such acts.

But before this, an event occurred which was to shock world opinion and cast a dark shadow over the Palestinian resistance movement for years to come: the attack on Israeli athletes at the Munich Olympics in September 1972.

It is common knowledge that this operation ended in a bloodbath at Fürstenfeldbrück airport. The German authorities lured the commando group and its hostages into a trap. There was no crew in the Lufthansa plane that was supposed to fly them all out. The commando group and its hostages returned to the helicopters 150 metres away. After more than one and a half hours' silence, the police opened fire on the helicopters. Hand grenades exploded, the helicopters burst into balls of flame. The hostages were all killed in the inferno. Three fedayeen survived.

The events leading up to the Munich operation are little known. Abu Iyyad describes them in his book *Home Country or Death*:

> At the beginning of 1972 the PLO in an official letter to the Olympic Committee asked for a Palestinian team to be allowed to compete in the Olympic Games. There was no reply, so a second letter was sent. This too was unanswered – the only response was contemptuous silence. This worthy organization, which claims to be non-political, obviously considered us to be non-existent. Perhaps they simply did not wish us to exist.
>
> This affront, coming about six months after the extermination of the last fedayeen at Jerash and Ajlun, angered and outraged our young supporters. The leaders of 'Black September' decided to take this matter into their own hands and devised a plan with three aims: first, to underline the existence of the Palestinian people; second, to use the many international press representatives in Munich to gain a hearing – positive or negative, it did not matter – for our cause throughout the world; third, to force Israel to release 200 resistance fighters.[3]

The Israeli government rejected the Palestinian demands out of hand, saying that it was at war with the Palestinians and that death was one of the risks of war. It categorically rejected negotiations.

After the operation, the Palestinian news agency Wafa published a 'Fedayeen Testament' which said:

> Our aim was to tell the athletes that there is a people whose land has been occupied for 24 years, whose honour has been trodden underfoot. It will do the world's youth no harm to reflect on the tragedy of this people for a few hours. So let the Olympic Games be interrupted for a few hours.

The Munich hostage taking triggered off an unparalleled wave of persecution of Palestinians living in West Germany. Students and workers were declared terrorists overnight and deported, without being given a chance to appeal and delay their deportation. The General Union of Palestinian Students (GUPS) and the General Union of Palestinian Workers (GUPW) in West Germany were banned. The Arabs were generally caricatured in the media as *'Untermenschen'*. It was to be some time before the name 'PLO' evoked any other association than 'terrorism' among West Germans.

The civil war in Jordan with its indescribable cruelties had opened up deep wounds. At this time of defeat, despair gave rise to violence by the weak and the humiliated. These operations were not under PLO control. And after the PLO had been reorganized in the mountains of Lebanon, the causes of this violence were removed. In 1973 the West was for the first time forced to sit up and take notice of the Palestinian problem and the Palestinian people. Since then, such operations have completely ceased.

Notes

1. *Black September* (Political Documents of the National Front) (Beirut, 1971), p. 113.
2. G. Konzelmann, *Arafat* (1981), p. 103.
3. Abu Iyyad, *Heimat oder Tod* (Düsseldorf, 1977), pp. 155–6.

18. Palestinian Resistance Reorganized in the Mountains of Lebanon

On 21 June 1972, Israeli army units landed by helicopter and attacked fedayeen bases in the Arkoub, the inaccessible mountains in the southeast of Lebanon. Israeli tank units entered southern Lebanon from North Palestine. Their aim: to smash Palestinian guerrilla forces in the Arkoub region.

The overwhelming defeat by the Jordanian army had occurred only a year before. The Israelis were not alone in expecting a rapid and easy victory. But, for the fedayeen, Lebanon was the last base from which they could carry the guerrilla struggle into Israel. Everyone realized that a second defeat like that in Jordan would mean the end of resistance and of all hopes of a return to Palestine in the foreseeable future. For decades to come, the Palestinian people would be banished to miserable refugee camps, condemned to an existence without hope and without a future.

For four days, the fedayeen in the Arkoub resisted the heavy assaults of the Israeli raiding party. Despite large-scale deployment of tanks and helicopters, the Israeli forces finally had to withdraw. The resistance fighters had held their ground, reviving memories of the battle of Karameh in March 1968.

Once again, the Palestinian fedayeen had surprised friend and foe alike. This victory gave the Palestinian people and the fedayeen themselves new faith and hope. The al-Fatah leadership and Yasser Arafat – who had even been the victim of an assassination attempt after the defeat in Jordan – now regained their standing and authority. The resistance movement, which was still going through a process of reorganization, had passed its first test.

The road to this achievement had not been an easy one. In summer 1971, the guerrillas had withdrawn from North Jordan to Deraa, a small border town in southern Syria. Their mood was one of disappointment and resignation. The structures they had carefully built up in the previous years had been destroyed. Fear and despondency had crept into the hearts of many Palestinians, who were now mistrustful not only of their Arab neighbours but of their own leadership. The question that weighed heavily on them all was: what to do next? The guerrilla war against Israel could not be conducted from Deraa. However, Arafat and the al-Fatah leadership had no intention of giving up. They reorganized their units, even forming a new brigade, the Yarmuk Brigade, from the large numbers of soldiers and officers who had deserted from the Jordanian army.

Clearly, Deraa could only be a temporary headquarters. The Palestinian guerrillas set up new bases in the Arkoub, the rough and inaccessible mountain area of Lebanon. There they were more or less safe from the attacks of the Israeli army, and, if necessary, they could use guerrilla warfare tactics to their advantage. The Arkoub was soon given a new name: Fatah land.

In Lebanon too, however, they faced tension and difficulties with the army and government. After 1967, commandos had gained influence, and could deny the Lebanese police and army access to the refugee camps in the south of Lebanon and on the outskirts of Beirut. For 20 years the Palestinian refugees in Lebanon had been in an extremely difficult political and economic situation.

The Cairo agreement gave the commandos in the south greater freedom of movement. The Palestinian camps were practically placed under the control of the PLO. The Cairo agreement between the Lebanese government and the PLO had been signed in November 1969, thanks largely to the efforts of President Nasser.

In the following years, the PLO, aware of the errors made in Jordan and determined to correct them, was anxious to avoid any confrontation with the Lebanese police or army. It also wanted to establish good relations with all the political parties in Lebanon.

Ever since the period of the French mandate, Lebanon had been split into two camps. This division had been institutionalized in a 'National Pact' between Maronite Christians and Sunnite Muslims in 1943, the year of independence. In drafting the agreement, they adopted the mandate practice of allocating political posts according to religion; this gave the Maronites a six to five advantage. The Maronites' political and economic interests were closely bound up with those of the former mandatory power, France, and later with the United States. Lebanese 'proportional representation' was based on a French census in 1932. The influential posts of president and supreme commander of the army were reserved for the Maronites. Lebanon was a Third World country and its development was not very different from that of any other such country. The Arab nationalist sections of the bourgeoisie and the oppressed and impoverished masses rebelled. In 1958, an armed uprising took place and the ensuing civil war was decided by a US army invasion on the side of the conservative forces. But the fires went on smouldering beneath the seemingly calm surface.

The progressive forces in Lebanon which were later to form the Lebanese National Movement had intensified their political activities since 1970. They demanded a revision of Lebanese 'proportional representation', which was based on religious affiliation. The conservative forces, worried by the presence of the Palestinian movement in the country, feared for their power and privileges. There had already been several armed confrontations. Nevertheless, the PLO's efforts to resolve conflicts and differences of opinion by peaceful means were remarkably successful – until 1973. The PLO had stuck to its resolution of non-intervention in the internal affairs of the Lebanese State. Lebanon was not, nor should it become, the home of the Palestinians – but it was a vitally important base for the PLO liberation struggle.

The democratic structures in Lebanon, unlike Jordan, gave the PLO opportunities for considerable political activity. Beirut was more cosmopolitan and enlightened than the Jordanian capital of Amman and here the PLO established many international connections and contacts.

From Beirut, PLO delegates travelled not only to other Arab countries but to Europe, Asia and America to present their case. Parties and delegations came to Beirut to talk to the PLO. A lively exchange of information and opinion had now become possible.

The PLO had rebuilt its political institutions near the Arab university of Beirut, not far from Shatila and Sabra refugee camps. It had created an information centre to inform world opinion about the Palestinian conflict; established its own news agency; founded SAMED, which originally concentrated on helping the relatives of fedayeen killed in action and today runs its own production centres providing training and work for Palestinians; here the Palestinian Red Crescent resumed its work, building hospitals and laboratories and providing medical care. The Palestinian Women's Union involved Palestinian women in the resistance movement and carried out social work such as looking after orphans. The General Unions of Palestinian Workers and Students included in their ranks a large proportion of all Palestinians throughout the world, wherever they had been forced to go and seek work. All these organizations took part in the reorganization of the Palestinian resistance movement, together with the military resistance organizations.

The PLO in Lebanon thus proved for the first time that it was capable of looking after the economic, social and cultural interests of the Palestinians. The resistance movement had not only reorganized itself – by the early seventies, it had grown and established itself on a much broader basis. The PLO now took on responsibility for all the needs of the Palestinian people. The reconstruction of the PLO in Lebanon was principally due to the determined initiative of al-Fatah, although this in no way detracts from the efforts of the other organizations within the PLO.

The resistance movement was now stronger – a fact which had not escaped the attention of Mossad (the Israeli secret service) and the Israeli government. They responded as the Zionist movement always had since the beginning of its struggle for Palestine: on 10 April 1973 – the 25th anniversary of the Israeli massacre in Deir Yassin – heavily armed Israeli special units landed on the Lebanese coast. In cars and trucks driven by drivers who knew Beirut well, Israeli troops reached the Rue

Verdun, home of a number of PLO leaders. Not far away is the headquarters of the Democratic Front.

On 9 and 10 April the PLO Central Council had met – this time, exceptionally, in Beirut. The meeting had ended late in the evening.

Shortly after midnight, Beirut was shaken by an explosion. The Democratic Front building was in flames. The guards had been killed but no one else was in the building. Eye-witnesses reported that the attackers wore fedayeen uniform but their orders were given in Hebrew.

Shots were also fired at the flat where Yasser Arafat was living, but the attacks were beaten off. But Arafat was not the attackers' main target. Three prominent PLO leaders lived in the Rue Verdun: Abu Youssef El-Najjar, a member of the al-Fatah Central Committee and leader of the PLO political department; Kamal Nasser, writer, member of the PLO executive committee, official PLO spokesman and editor-in-chief of *Falestin al-Thaura*; Kamal Adwan, engineer, member of al-Fatah Central Committee, responsible for the organization of the resistance struggle in the occupied areas.

The guards in front of the house were shot dead. The Israeli commandos took the lift to the sixth floor. The soldiers blew up the door and broke into the flat of Abu Youssef El-Najjar. His 16-year-old son escaped through a window into the flat below. Abu Youssef El-Najjar and his wife locked themselves in the living room. A hail of fire from automatic weapons blew out the door and the Israelis broke into the room. El-Najjar's wife threw herself in front of her husband. The Israeli troops cold-bloodedly shot them both. Kamal Adwan, his wife and child lived on the second floor. Warned by the noises on the stairs, he had his machine-gun in his hand. But before he could fire, he was killed by a grenade with his wife and child looking on. A group of Israeli commandos had entered the flat from the back. The poet Kamal Nasser lived on the third floor. He was still working on an elegy on his Palestinian colleague Issa Nakha, who had died a few days before. Kamal had only a revolver to defend himself and was mown down by Israeli machine-gunfire. The Israeli bullets tore into Kamal's books and collected poems, as if they hoped to silence his words too.

The murder of these three PLO leaders shocked the world. The Arab leaders expressed their outrage at the attack and many Lebanese were deeply shocked and angered.

They could not accept this flagrant violation of Lebanese sovereignty. Many people throughout the world were now for the first time confronted with the Israelis' real methods and began asking themselves questions.

The progressive Lebanese organizations backed the Palestinian and PLO demands for punishment of those who ordered and carried out the attack. Many suspected what was to be proven incontrovertibly two years later: that there were forces in the Lebanese army and in the *Deuxième Bureau* (the Lebanese secret service) who had collaborated in this terrible attack. Lebanese police headquarters were in the Rue Verdun – yet no Lebanese police or Lebanese soldiers were anywhere near that night to prevent the Israeli raiding party's atrocities.

Hundreds of thousands followed the funeral cortege of the three murdered PLO leaders, including tens of thousands of Lebanese. Church bells rang and the voices of the muezzin sounded from the minarets. The funeral procession became a demonstration for the Palestinian resistance movement. Under the pressure of public opinion, the Lebanese government was forced to resign and was succeeded by a military government.

On 3 May, after repeated skirmishes between Lebanese army units and the fedayeen, Lebanese tanks advanced on the PLO headquarters near the Arab university. Their objective: to occupy the PLO offices and disarm the resistance movement in a 'blitz' operation. But the Palestinians were no longer alone; they had political and military support from their Lebanese allies. Once the first Lebanese tanks had been knocked out by bazookas and access to the Arab university quarter had been blocked, the Lebanese operation came to a stop. The army could not conquer the district. Losses on both sides were high.

Lebanese aircraft even bombed the refugee camps. Yet the Palestinians were determined to defend their last 'base'.

Mediation by Arab states, especially Egypt and Syria, led to the opening of negotiations. On 17 May the 'Melkart protocols' were signed and hostilities ceased. These agreements – named after the hotel where negotiations were held – formulated the Cairo agreement more precisely. The conflict appeared to be over. But it had left deep scars on Lebanese and Palestinian society. The seeds of the next confrontation had been sown.

The Lebanese Civil War 1975–76

The Lebanese civil war was triggered off by a massacre. On 13 April 1975 a bus was stopped in the Christian quarter of Ain Rummaneh and its passengers – all Palestinians, among them women and children – were all killed.

This massacre was the beginning of a cruel war which was to last 18 months, during which 60,000 people were killed and the country was torn and divided.

Names such as Karantina, Maazra and Tel Al Zaatar exemplify the cruelty of this war. The first two were Lebanese slum areas attacked by Lebanese Front militias and razed to the ground. Hundreds of people were cold-bloodedly massacred in these attacks.

Tel Al Zaatar is the name of a Palestinian refugee camp in the east of the capital, Beirut. For 57 days, the people in this camp held out against a siege by right-wing militia. Many children died during the siege because of the scarcity of water. Mothers were shot dead trying to fetch water from the wells which were all in range of the besiegers' fire. In Tel Al

Zaatar a drop of water was as precious as a drop of blood.

Arab League mediation helped bring about an agreement to evacuate the camp. As they left, many of the refugees were killed in an appalling massacre.

That day, several hundred people were mown down by the militia of Gemayel and Chamoun. The Red Cross, which was responsible for organizing the evacuation, could only stand by helplessly as the militia caused a bloodbath. The survivors later took refuge in the town of Damour to the south of Beirut. They were to be driven out once again, in summer 1982, this time by the Israelis.

The Lebanese crisis was an internal Lebanese affair, centred on the revision of the 'National Pact', the system of proportional representation based on religion which guaranteed the Maronites domination and privilege. Yet in Lebanon, Arab and international interests played an at least equally important role.

Eric Rouleau wrote in *Le Monde* of 1 June 1976:

> *Moukhatat* – a key word which recurs in every political discussion in the Middle East. An observer who does not take this into account will probably be completely bewildered by the mentality and logic which to a large extent determine the responses of the protagonists and observers of the Lebanese tragedy. Ask a Syrian, a Jordanian, a Palestinian or a Lebanese what this war is about and they will always give the same resigned or outraged answer: 'Everything is determined by the rules of *Moukhatat* (Arabic for conspiracy). Do you think this war could have gone on for so long otherwise? Could the fighting have kept starting up again after every ceasefire?'
>
> . . . The unanimous view is that this conflict is being fanned by hidden, foreign powers. In most cases, one's interlocutors consider it superfluous to define the 'conspirators'. In this part of the world, even many right-wing circles openly admit that the Americans and their allies are directing the bloody Lebanese ballet. The plan that Washington has devised is said to be Machiavellian in its precision. The intrigue, it is argued, serves several purposes at once. In the short term, it will guarantee the 'Kissinger peace' until the presidential elections distract the Arab powers who question the Sinai agreement. Have not the Palestinian guerrillas, whose main aim is to survive the civil war, not interrupted their guerrilla operations against Israel? And has Syria not been forced to extend the 'Blue Helmets'' mandate on the Golan Heights without receiving any territorial or political concessions in return?
>
> The second phase of the American plan: the Palestinian resistance movement must be destroyed or, failing that, so weakened that it would be forced to recognize the State of Israel, and then take part in negotiations leading to a 'pax americana'.

At the beginning of the Lebanese civil war the main protagonists were the Lebanese Front on one side and the Lebanese National Movement on the other. The most important groups in the Lebanese Front were the Falangists under Pierre Gemayel, the National Liberal Party under Camille Chamoun, the militias of President Suleiman Franjieh and the National Block Party led by Raimond Edde.

The Lebanese Front's policy was to retain and defend the status quo. It attributed all Lebanon's internal problems to the presence of the PLO and demanded the expulsion of the Palestinian resistance movement from Lebanon. The PLO was even blamed for the many Israeli attacks on Lebanon. Rejecting close ties with the Arab world and inclining more towards Europe and the USA, it took an isolationist stance within the Arab world.

The Lebanese National Movement included socialist, Nasserist and communist parties and organizations led by Ibrahim Kuleilat, Mohsen Ibrahim and George Hawi; both wings of the Ba'ath Party and the Syrian Socialist-Nationalist party. This nationalist alliance was led by Kamal Jumblatt, Druse leader and chairman of the Progressive Socialist Party. Today the Shi'ite Amal movement led by Nabil Berri is also a member of the alliance.

The Lebanese National Movement called for political and economic reforms, the abolition of political feudalism and denominationalism, the introduction of a system of proportional representation and effective changes in the economic sphere. It also called for an Arab Lebanon and stronger support for the Palestinian Revolution.

After the massacre of Ain Rummaneh and the attacks which preceded it, the PLO could no longer remain neutral. The frontal attack by the Lebanese Front forced the PLO to intervene in the conflict.

The civil war split Lebanon into two camps. The state apparatus and the Lebanese army were also affected. Lieutenant Ahmed al-Khatib formed a Lebanese Arab army which joined the progressive forces.

After months of fighting, interrupted by ceasefire agreements which lasted for varying periods but never long, the Lebanese National Movement controlled almost three-quarters of the country. The conflict was as good as decided militarily when Syria decided to intervene on the side of the conservative forces.

The election of Elias Sarkis as the new Lebanese president on 8 May 1976 could not have occurred without Syrian protection. And US influence in Lebanon was plain for all to see.

The US administration's intentions had been highlighted by the appointment of Godey as US ambassador shortly before the beginning of the civil war. Godey was no unknown. He had already accomplished 'special missions' in Chile and Vietnam. As the conservative forces faced defeat, Dean Brown, the former US ambassador in Jordan, was appointed US mediator. His task, according to the US State Department, was to save the 'Lebanese system'.

But all attempts at negotiation broke down, and the intervals between the ceasefire agreements became shorter and shorter.

On 1 June 1976 the Syrian army intervened in the fighting and then began a painful and tragic confrontation which the Palestinians had never wished. The Syrian army advanced into Lebanon with tanks and heavy artillery. A first ceasefire agreement was reached on 8 June but it was not observed for long.

On 10 June the Arab League in Cairo decided to send an Arab peace force to Lebanon to restore security and political stability and to replace the Syrian forces. Eight Arab countries were to provide troops.

However, Syrian army support had given the Lebanese Front a new lease of life and they had regained lost ground. On 29 June they occupied Jisr El Bacha refugee camp in Beirut and on 6 August they occupied Nabaa, the Muslim quarter of Beirut. On 12 August the siege of Tel Al Zaatar ended with the massacre described above in which more than 3,000 people were killed.

The Syrian offensive continued and on 12 October one of the fiercest battles of the war was fought between the Palestinian and progressive forces and the Syrian army at Bhamdun.

On the initiative of Yasser Arafat, who persistently tried to mediate in the conflict, a 'small' Arab summit meeting was called for 16 October in Riyadh. The heads of state of Saudi Arabia, Kuwait, Syria, Egypt and Lebanon and PLO leader Yasser Arafat agreed on a definitive ceasefire in Lebanon. The conference upheld Lebanese integrity and sovereignty and agreed to the sending of an Arab peace-keeping force. The main contingent in this force would, however, be Syrian.

After the signing of the ceasefire agreement and intensive consultations, relations between Syria and the PLO were normalized. But the effects of the war could not be normalized.

The warring parties in this civil war were defined – especially in the foreign press – according to religion, Christian or Muslim. But the Lebanese civil war was certainly not a religious war. Its causes were purely political and social. It was complicated primarily by outside interference.

The division of Lebanon into sectors – their number increased after the Israeli invasion of 1978 when Major Sa'ad Haddad took control of southern Lebanon – meant the collapse of the Lebanese State. It could not survive in its previous form or under the system that had obtained till then.

A year after the civil war ended, Israeli support for the Lebanese Front became official. The Falangist leaders themselves admitted that they had co-operated with Israel. Israel had supplied the Falangists with arms and blocked PLO supply routes, in particular the ports of Tyre and Saida. For years to come, Israeli interference would prevent the country from achieving peace and a Lebanese solution for Lebanese problems.

The Israeli invasion of summer 1982 emphasized this fact.

19. The October War

'An Eye for an Eye, a Tooth for a Tooth'

From 1967 to 1973 a new form of confrontation emerged: between Israelis and Palestinians. Fedayeen guerrilla operations in the occupied areas hit Israel hard – and all too often its response was to bomb Palestinian refugee camps. But, particularly after Palestinian guerrilla operations abroad, Israel sought other methods. In 1972 a top-level decision was taken by the Israeli government and secret service to combat 'terrorism' (i.e. the PLO) by every means available. A fierce 'shadow war' now began.

One of the most prominent victims of Mossad was the Palestinian teacher, poet, writer and politician, Ghassan Kanafani, the official spokesman for the Popular Front for the Liberation of Palestine. His wife tells of his murder on the morning of 8 July 1972:

> Before he went off, he set up the model railway for Fayez and his two cousins. The three were playing that morning in the house. Lames, Ghassan's niece, wanted to go into town with her uncle for the first time since she had arrived from Kuwait with her mother and two brothers. She planned to visit her cousins in Beirut. But she never arrived. Two minutes after Ghassan and Lames had said goodbye, there was a terrible explosion.

A bomb had blown Kanafani's car to pieces.

Kanafani wrote many novellas and short stories as well as children's books, political analyses and literary essays. He is perhaps best known for his short stories 'The Boot Black', 'The Land of Sad Oranges', 'Men in the Sun', which was filmed as *The Dupes*, and 'Umm Saad' (The Mother of Saad). The day after the assassination the *Daily Star* wrote in an appreciation: 'Ghassan was the commando who never fired a gun. His weapon was a ballpoint pen, and his arena newspaper pages. And he hurt the enemy more than a column of commandos.'

By killing Kanafani, the enemy had struck at Palestinian culture and Palestinian identity. Yet the words Imad Shehadi wrote to his wife in 1972 have proved true: 'Ghassan Kanafani is dead. His people will make him immortal.'

The Israeli government's aim was to destroy the Palestinian identity and liquidate the PLO. Mossad now sent parcel bombs to PLO representatives throughout the world. In Algiers, the PLO representative was seriously wounded when a parcel bomb addressed to him exploded. In Tripoli a similar explosion blinded and paralysed Mustafa Awad. In Stockholm, Omar Sufan, director of the Palestinian Red Crescent, lost the fingers of both hands. Adnan Hamad, a student in Nuremberg, was seriously injured by a letter bomb. In Rome and Paris, PLO representatives Wahel Zuhaiter and Mahmud Hamchari were killed in Mossad attacks; and on 25 Janury 1973 Hussein Abu El-Kheir, PLO representative in Nicosia, was murdered.

The Palestinians now retaliated. On 27 January Israeli agent Baruk Cohen, suspected of involvement in the Nicosia murder, was killed. Unable to discover the 'leak', Mossad was forced to disband its entire spy network in Spain. On 12 March 1973 another Israeli secret service man was killed by Palestinian counter-espionage in Nicosia. In Brussels a Mossad officer was shot dead while making a contact in a café. The Palestinian secret service now started sending letter bombs to Israel, repaying the Israelis in their own coin.

However, generally speaking the 'shadow war' was a very unequal one. The Israelis had official embassies which they could use as bases – and they had support from Western secret services, including the CIA.

The Israeli government, undeterred by these setbacks, continued to pursue its goal: the liquidation of the Palestinian leadership. Their most spectacular success was the killing of three PLO leaders in Beirut in April 1973. Many other assassination attempts on PLO leaders failed. In later years, further attempts were to prove more successful.

For many years Mossad had been able to operate in Arab capitals almost unimpeded. The Palestinians, despite their extremely modest means, were the first to keep Mossad in check and to strike some dangerous and telling blows against it. In those years, Mossad had its hands full dealing with the Palestinians. This preoccupation was to have disturbing consequences for Israel.

In Syria and Egypt preparations had long been under way for a new war with Israel. Nasser had begun the reorganization of the Egyptian army, bringing in Soviet advisers, forming new, stronger units and modernizing and improving training. The Arab Frontline States, with the exception of Jordan, wanted to wipe out the memory of the humiliating defeat of 1967 and shake up entrenched positions to pave the way for a political solution. In Syria, too, the equipment and training of the army had been improved. Some of these new arms had been tested in the war of attrition on the Suez Canal in 1969–70. From 1971 onwards, Sadat declared that the next year would be the year of decision. Egyptians demonstrated frequently to demand the recovery of the occupied Arab areas and the fulfilment of Sadat's promises.

Foreign observers believed that this was simply impossible, especially

The October War

as Sadat had expelled Soviet advisers at the beginning of 1973. In May 1973 the Egyptian army held official manoeuvres to which all Western military observers were invited. The manoeuvres ended in fiasco, with all the Western observers looking on. Hardly a single missile hit its target. When the buttons of the electronic weapons systems were pressed, clouds of smoke billowed into the air. Tank units simply came to a halt somewhere or other or suddenly found themselves facing each other. The *Financial Times* and *Le Monde* wrote long reports on the incompetence of the Egyptian army. In June 1973 Sadat announced a general mobilization. By October, this was no longer taken seriously. But Western military observers and the Israeli secret service soon realized that they had fallen for a clever ploy.

The Fourth Middle East War

On the afternoon of 6 October 1973 the Egyptian and Syrian armies attacked. The Israelis were celebrating Yom Kippur. Contrary to all military rules, the afternoon had been chosen to increase the element of surprise – and there is no doubt that this gave the Arabs an advantage. Nothing highlights Mossad's failure more clearly than the fact that this attack took the Israelis by surprise. It also proves how preoccupied Mossad had been by its dealings with the Palestinians.

The Egyptian army faced two obstacles which were both considered insuperable: the Suez Canal and the Bar-Lev line. The Bar-Lev line, named after the Israeli Chief of Staff who had this defence line built at a cost of c.£60 million after the 1967 June war, consisted of 25 strongly fortified bunkers, surrounded by minefields. Along the banks of the Suez Canal. Against all expectations, losses were very low. Not even the with napalm. All the military theories and techniques of fortification had been taken into account in the building of this line.

In the first hours of the war, the Egyptian army achieved what military experts in both West and East considered impossible – it crossed the Suez Canal. Against all expectation, losses were very low. Not even the Egyptian officers believed it would be so easy to cross the canal. The Egyptian army had been restructured, with officers and soldiers fighting together and taking equal risks. It was now a modern, powerful force – as the Israelis were about to discover.

In the first days of the war, this army achieved another 'impossible' feat by taking all 25 bunkers of the Bar-Lev line. The first Israeli prisoners were taken. In the desert tank battle, the Egyptian army adopted the 'Chinese method'; instead of tank to tank fighting, they used bazookas against the Israeli tanks – a highly effective method. The elimination of the Israeli air force was a strategic masterpiece by the Syrian and Egyptian command. In the first three days of the war, the Israelis lost 85 of their most modern Phantom bombers. The Arab forces, instead of deploying

133

their technically inferior Mig 17s, 19s and 21s against Israel's American bombers, used Soviet Sam 6 and Sam 7 anti-aircraft missiles.

The Israeli Chiefs of Staff could no longer deploy their full air force strength to back up their infantry and tank units.

So they decided to strike at enemy morale by attacking its hinterland. The Israeli leadership now bombed the major Egyptian and Syrian cities: Damascus, Latakia, Tartus, Homs, Cairo, Port Said, etc. Fragmentation bombs and napalm were dropped on residential areas, killing civilians.[1]

The Syrian army also had considerable success in the early stages, penetrating up to 35 kms into enemy territory in places – as far as the slopes of the Golan. The Israeli counter-attack three days later pushed the Syrians back a few kilometres but failed to make a decisive breakthrough. The Syrian soldiers remained in their positions, supported by Iraqi tank units who held the crucial Mount Hermon front. And on the Golan Heights near Kuneitra stood the PLA units, who were to play a key part in various places along the front.

After seven days of war, the Israeli state coffers were empty. Not even the huge donations by Jews in Europe and the United States – over $2,000 million – could cover the cost of continuing the war. However, the United States government did not present the bill but instead went on sending replacements for knocked-out tanks and aeroplanes. From their European bridgeheads in Frankfurt (West Germany), Portugal, Italy and other countries, the USA flew arms and ammunition into Israel daily. US Hercules carriers no longer landed in Tel Aviv but flew straight on to the desert airport of El Arish. The USA risked its entire military strength to establish a balance between the warring parties. Henry Kissinger confirms this in his memoirs: 'I was playing for time. For two weeks we had stood by Israel, filled its arsenal and risked and finally suffered an oil embargo . . .'

Thanks to this massive support, the Israeli counter-attack in Sinai succeeded. By the eleventh day of the war, the Israelis had occupied a 25-km stretch of the bank between Ismailia and Suez. But elsewhere the Israeli counter-attack was brought to a halt.

The impact of this war in Israel was staggering. It caused a psychological earthquake. The Israelis had not expected such a disciplined and successful Arab attack. This was a severe blow to their arrogance and sense of superiority. The myth of the Israeli army's invincibility was shattered. The pictures of hundreds of Israeli prisoners shown on Arab television proved this point. The surprise element, the panic and confusion in the first days of the war, the high losses and the prospect of defeat shook Israel deeply.

On 22 October the United Nations Security Council called on the belligerent parties to: 1) cease fire and refrain from any further act of war; 2) immediately after a ceasefire was agreed to comply with Security Council Resolution 242; 3) to take up negotiations immediately with a view to finding a lasting and just solution to the Middle East problem.

Israel and Egypt formally complied with the call immediately and Syria followed suit on 24 October.

Despite the ceasefire, the Israeli army under Ariel Sharon continued the war on the west bank of the Suez Canal. The Egyptian Third Army was surrounded near Ismailia and on the following day the Israelis made a 40-km breakthrough towards Cairo.

A second mediation attempt did not succeed until 26 October, when the fighting finally ceased.

The PLO in the Fourth Middle East War

The PLO leadership was first informed of preparations for another Middle East war in May 1973. On 12 September, after a meeting of the Non-Aligned States in Cairo, Sadat assured Arafat that he would inform him of the precise date of the Arab attack. On 30 September a message asking the PLO leadership to come to Cairo was transmitted via the Egyptian embassy in Beirut. However, Abu Lutf and Abu Iyyad did not arrive in Cairo until 4 October. They were received by Sadat and told about the imminent attack. Instead of a code, a messenger was sent to Yasser Arafat, who received the news shortly before the outbreak of war. All PLO units were immediately put on the alert. These units consisted of guerrillas, with no training for conventional warfare. Their task was to open up a new front in the occupied areas.

As soon as war broke out, tens of thousands of Palestinians went on strike in the occupied areas, despite harsh Israeli repression. The Israelis did not want to lose the services of these rare Arab workers. But the Palestinians were determined to back the Arab struggle by every means available.

The fedayeen's military task was to attack Israeli supply bases and prevent transports from reaching the front. This was an extremely difficult mission, yet the Israelis counted more than 200 PLO operations during the war. The Israeli ambassador to the United Nations publicly stated that the Palestinians attacked 43 kibbutzim. Fedayeen operations were by no means confined to the occupied areas. On Mount Hermon, the Golan Heights and along the Suez Canal fedayeen units fought side by side with Iraqi, Syrian and Egyptian troops.

PLO operations in the occupied areas were a kind of pinprick tactic which sometimes posed the Israelis serious problems. PLO leader Yasser Arafat has described the Palestinian role in the fourth Middle East war as follows:

> Of course fedayeen operations are less spectacular when compared with high-calibre grenades exploding on the battlefields. But the Israelis had to admit that it was the PLO who opened up a third front after the Egyptian and Syrian fronts.[2]

King Hussein of Jordan refused to take part in this fourth Israeli-Arab war and the Palestinians took his place on the Arab side. This increased the political standing of the PLO in the Arab world. Sooner or later, this was bound to have consequences.

A New Weapon: Oil

The ceasefire between Israel and the Arab states was extremely fragile on all fronts. The Egyptian army was still encircled at the end of November. The Israeli troops under Ariel Sharon on the west bank of the Suez Canal threatened to strike back at any moment.

On 3 to 4 November 1973, the Organization of Arab Petroleum Exporting Countries decided to reduce crude oil production by 25%.

Oil now became a weapon. The Arab countries imposed a total oil boycott on the USA, the Netherlands and South Africa because of their strong pro-Israeli sympathies. Friendly states – including France and Great Britain – continued to receive normal supplies, with the rest of the oil being shared out among the so-called neutral countries.

Arab states had not formerly had the power to enforce such a decision. It was not until 1972 and 1973 that the power of the major oil companies in the oil-producing countries was systematically reduced. It is now the Arab countries themselves, and no longer the bosses of the oil corporations, who fix the prices and production levels of their 'liquid gold'.

The formation of OPEC (Organization of Petroleum Exporting Countries) meant that no oil country, however small, was alone in its negotiations on prices and drilling rights with the powerful corporations of the industrial nations. For all these countries, OPEC meant protection and strength.

The Arab states were now for the first time able to use their natural resources to lend force to political demands – internationally recognized demands backed by United Nations resolutions. From now on, the Sword of Damocles hung over the heads of the world's industrial nations.

These industrial nations were dependent on Arab oil. European, American and Japanese industry had only just switched their industrial production to oil, which had become a crucially important raw material.

In 1973, West Germany imported 60% of its oil from Arab countries. A quota was now imposed on exports to West Germany as well – and it was only political consideration for West Germany, which was well respected in the Arab world, which prevented a total boycott. It was no secret that American tanks had been loaded on to Israeli ships at Bremerhaven – though the Bonn government did at least protest about this to the American authorities.

As oil quotas were cut, the Bonn government took measures to reduce oil consumption, the most spectacular being the ban on Sunday driving for four weeks from 25 November to 16 December 1973. Driving was prohibited from 3 o'clock on Sunday morning till 3 o'clock on Monday morning.

From now on, war and peace in the Middle East directly affected Europe. The interests of the major European industrial powers were at stake.

By using the oil weapon, the Arab governments forced the powerful industrial nations to think. A change in these states' attitudes towards the Middle East now began to emerge.

The first major success for the Arab states and the PLO after the October war was the EEC's 'Joint Declaration' of 6 November 1973 which called for a peace settlement on the basis of United Nations Security Council Resolution 242. It stressed that the acquisition of territory by violence was inadmissible, called for the return of the Arab territories occupied in 1967 and for a lasting peace in which the legitimate rights of the Palestinian people were taken into account.

The European Economic Community had now for the first time officially recognized the Palestinian problem in its essence and acknowledged the rights for which the Palestinian people had been fighting for more than 50 years.

Relations between Europe and the Arab world were now transformed. The Arabs were able to claim a second major success when, on 4 March 1974, the Conference of EEC Foreign Ministers passed a resolution calling for a 'European-Arab dialogue'. The aim of this dialogue was long-term European-Arab co-operation in the economic, technological and cultural spheres.

The deployment of the oil weapon had led to political, diplomatic and economic successes. Europe was forced to admit that it could not get by without the Arab world. The Arabs and the Palestinians now expected Europe to come up with an independent initiative for lasting peace in the Middle East and a just solution to the Palestinian problem.

Political Effects of the October War

The 1973 October war had not been fought to liberate Palestine from Israeli occupation. President Sadat of Egypt, the driving force behind this war, was pursuing goals in home policy as well as attempting to create a better starting point for the expected American 'peace solution' in the Middle East. This meant that Egypt's war aims were limited, the main objectives being to shake up rigid fronts and to force the USA to make an approach to the Arabs.

None the less the October war had its effects – in many respects.

The oil boycott put the United States under pressure, even though they finally benefited from the rise in oil prices. The concerted action of the Arab states and above all the initial Arab successes in the war had shown the United States that Israel was not, in the long term, able to guarantee US interests in the region. The USA now began to look for Arab support.

Kissinger's notorious shuttle diplomacy now began – and produced results. On 18 January 1974 the troop withdrawal agreement between Egypt and Israel was signed. Israeli troops withdrew from the west bank of the Suez Canal by 21 February. After long and difficult discussions Syria and Israel signed a troop withdrawal agreement on 31 May 1974. From now on, American interests were to be concentrated on Egypt.

The Arab states had gained ground with the October war and the use of the oil weapon. Their main interest now was to bring about a peaceful settlement of the Middle East problem. They expected Europe to make a substantial contribution, especially as the European attitude in the October war had been more nuanced and a dialogue on equal terms had been initiated.

At their fifth summit conference in Algiers in November 1973, the Arab states agreed on a joint strategy. They demanded Israeli withdrawal from all occupied Arab territories and recognition of the Palestinian right of self-determination.

The most sensational result of this summit conference as reported in the world press was its recognition of the Palestine Liberation Organization (PLO) as the sole legitimate representative of the Palestinian people. Yasser Arafat was received as a head of state at this conference and his status was equal to that of all the other Arab heads of state.

The breakthrough for the PLO had now been achieved. The PLO's claim to be the sole representative of the Palestinian people was firmly backed, with the Algerian President Boumedienne giving particularly strong support. The only dissenting voice was that of the Jordanian Prime Minister – King Hussein was not present. He explained Jordan's reservations but was completely overruled.

The PLO had gained strength as a political factor in the October war. It was now an equal partner with the other Arab states. And the strikes and demonstrations by Palestinians in the occupied areas had been a vote for the PLO. The PLO was the undisputed representative of the Palestinian people. The political-diplomatic offensive could now begin.

Notes

1. G. Konzelmann, *Die Schlacht in Israel* (Munich, 1974), p. 66ff.
2. G. Konzelmann, *Arafat*, p. 165.

20. International Recognition of the PLO

Recognition by the Non-Aligned Countries

The PLO had no illusions about its recognition at the Arab summit in Algiers. Although the PLO had fought underground for ten years and for an almost equal period had been carrying on open political and military confrontation, yet the Arab states' recognition of the Palestinians and the PLO as an independent political force was still only half-hearted. The PLO leaders knew only too well that the intensive efforts of Algerian President Boumedienne had played a key role. Boumedienne had given the Arab states generous support during the October war and his proposal to recognize the PLO carried considerable weight.

The PLO had now been recognized and was determined to seek further international recognition for its claim to be the sole representative of the Palestinians.

The meeting of the Co-ordination Bureau of the Non-Aligned Movement in Algiers from 19 to 21 March 1974 provided an excellent opportunity. The PLO systematically prepared for this meeting. Palestinian representatives accompanied every delegation and were able to talk to them effortlessly in their mother tongues – one positive result of the world-wide Palestinian diaspora. It is hardly surprising, therefore, that the delegations were thoroughly immersed in the Palestinian problem. And journalists from all over the world who attended the conference had an opportunity to hear – in many cases for the first time – the Palestinian view of the Middle East conflict. The PLO and the Palestine problem became the major topic at this conference.

PLO influence within the Non-Aligned Movement was further increased by Yasser Arafat's successful mediation in a dispute between Muammar Gaddafy and Fidel Castro. It was definitely in the PLO's interest to help the Non-Aligned Movement out of the stagnation it had fallen into since the deaths of Nehru and Nasser.

The conference ended in complete success for the PLO. In the 'Statement on the Middle East and the Palestine Problem' – part of the Co-ordination Bureau's final resolution – the Non-Aligned States expressed their 'full recognition of the Palestine Liberation Organization as the sole legitimate representative of the Palestinian people and its struggle . . .'

All member states in the Non-Aligned Movement were called on to break off diplomatic relations with Israel if they had not already done so.

This resolution effectively blocked any attempts by the Arab heads of state – and such attempts were quite likely – to go back on the Algiers resolutions.

The Ten-Point Programme

The PLO now faced new challenges. The issue of PLO participation in the Geneva Peace Conference had led to controversial debates within the PLO. At the Non-Aligned Conference, the PLO delegation had frequently been asked its plans for peace in the Middle East, and its specific claims and demands. If the PLO was to avoid international isolation and new military confrontations in which the civilian population would be exposed to more massacres, it would have to reconsider its 'all or nothing' policy. An adjustment to the political requirements of the international situation was absolutely essential.

Intensive discussion on the best policy to pursue now began among the Palestinian leadership – and these discussions were soon heatedly and passionately taken up in the refugee camps, the fedayeen organizations and the press.

Al-Fatah and the Democratic Front – the latter even more resolutely – declared their determination to establish a Palestinian State on any territory evacuated by or liberated from the Israelis.

A political process was now triggered off among the Palestinians, many of whom argued that the PLO's policy should now be to achieve their objectives step by step instead of trying to force through all their demands at once. Others were less convinced of the wisdom of the gradualist approach. Would the million refugees of 1948 now have to give up their rights to their country, to their homes in Jaffa, Haifa and Akko, to their land? Did this proposed new strategy not mean a renunciation of these rights?

The Popular Front and other Palestinian organizations firmly rejected any strategy involving the possible foundation of a 'mini-state'. Their slogans were: 'No negotiations', 'No surrender', and 'No Palestinian mini-state'. In summer 1974, these organizations formed the so-called Rejection Front. The questions were discussed at all levels and in all institutions. The PLO's democratic structure not only allowed such discussions – it insisted on them. The Palestinian National Council would have to decide. And the members of the Palestinian National Council were chosen by the Palestinian people.

The twelfth Palestinian National Council met on 1 June 1974 in Cairo. This session, which lasted until 8 June, was attended by many experts and scholars who presented papers to help the delegates reach a decision. The National Council's decision would be of historic importance. Discussions went on every day from 10 in the morning till late into the night, with heated arguments about every word of the political statement which was later to become the ten-point programme.

The final vote on the programme showed a clear majority for the new strategy. Only 14 members of the National Council voted against it – two al-Fatah members and 12 delegates of the Popular Front for the Liberation of Palestine.

Five years later the controversy had died down completely. In 1979 and 1981, the National Council's resolutions on this question were passed unanimously.

The controversial and decisive changes in the 1974 Political Programme were:

> 2. The PLO fights with all means, the first of which is armed struggle, for the liberation of Palestinian territories and the establishment of a militant, independent popular administration in every part of Palestine which is liberated. We wish to stress that this can only be achieved by a change of the balance of power in favour of our people and its struggle.

And:

> 4. The PLO regards every act of liberation of Palestinian territory as a step on the path to the realization of its strategy, the establishment of a democratic Palestinian State as laid down in previous congress resolutions of the Palestinian National Congress.

Admittedly the PLO, in point 2 of the programme, did reject 'any partial state solution . . . the price of which would be renunciation of a historical right and the revocation of our people's right to a return to, and self-determination in, our country.' None the less, in this programme the PLO for the first time made it clear that it regarded the creation of a democratic Palestine as a lengthy process – and the first step in this process would have to be the establishment of a Palestinian State in any part of Palestine which was liberated. Here, for the first time, methods other than armed struggle are expressly mentioned. However, in real terms, a change in the balance of power in favour of the Palestinian people remained the pre-condition for a political solution.

With this programme, the PLO revised its 'all or nothing' attitude. It had shown the world its willingness for peace and a political solution of the conflict. And it had expressly allowed its leadership the scope to work out and determine 'on the basis of this programme . . . the tactics best suited to the realization of these objectives.'

Discussions among Palestinians did not of course end when the National Council session closed on 8 June 1974. There were further developments and discussions continued throughout the world, wherever Palestinians lived. Palestinian workers and students, and engineers', lawyers', doctors' and women's organizations discussed the new resolutions with their friends and with the parties. National Council delegates also travelled to various capitals to explain the resolutions.

The Cairo ten-point programme formed the corner-stone of the PLO's continuing diplomatic offensive; many new contacts in the international political arena were now made. The Arab states, too, were relieved at the results of the Cairo congress, which took the wind out of the sails of the opponents of the Arab nation and of the PLO. The oft-repeated claim that the PLO wished to destroy the Jews, was an enemy of peace and an obstacle to any political solution was now effectively belied. The coming years would prove again and again, often dramatically, that the main obstacle to a comprehensive and just peace was not the PLO.

The Arab Summit Conference in Rabat

The Arab states could not ignore the new situation and the substantial improvement in the PLO's international standing and recognition. On 28 October 1974 the Arab heads of state unanimously passed a resolution recognizing the PLO as the sole legitimate representative of the Palestinian people. The conference also confirmed the Palestinian people's right to return to their country, to self-determination and the establishment of an independent national authority over all the liberated areas under the leadership of the PLO. Jordan, Syria and Egypt were expressly called on to reorientate their relations with the PLO in accordance with these resolutions. The Arab heads of state committed themselves not to interfere in the Palestinians' internal affairs, to preserve the unity of the Palestinian people and to support the PLO in its national and international responsibilities.

Palestinian identity had again taken real shape. The word 'Palestine', which the Israelis wanted to wipe off the map, was now fully accepted in political discussion. At last, the Palestinians were equal with other states and the Palestinian leadership had to be accepted as equal to others. Even King Hussein of Jordan was forced to recognize this.

The Rabat resolution radically changed the structure of the Arab world. The PLO was now, for all practical purposes, a 'Rejection Front' state, which is why the US Secretary of State warned before the summit conference that recognition of the PLO would make any solution of the Middle East problem impossible. This may have been true of any 'American solution'. It would objectively have been more correct to say: there could be no political solution which did not include the Palestinians.

The Palestinian people was no longer, as UN Security Council Resolution 242 put it, a mere 'refugee problem'. National self-determination and the establishment of a separate and independent

Palestinian State – these were the new Arab demands. A nation's identity had been restored.

The defeat of 1948 had destroyed the structure and unity of Palestinian society. For decades, the Palestinians had had no recognized leadership. Recognition by the Arab states marked the end of the period in which the Palestinian people had been ignored, without rights. The Palestinians were now recognized as a people and they had created a new political and social structure with a new leadership. This the Arab states now recognized.

Yasser Arafat at the United Nations

On 16 October 1974 the United Nations General Assembly invited the PLO, as the representative of the Palestinian people, to take part in discussions on the Palestinian question. 105 states voted in favour of this proposal, with only four – Israel, the USA, the Dominican Republic and Bolivia – voting against.

On 13 November 1974 Yasser Arafat addressed the United Nations General Assembly, where delegates from 140 nations gave him, the PLO and the Palestinian people a standing ovation.

Arafat's speech was an impressive plea for the Palestinian people's national rights, their right to self-determination, to return to their country and to establish an independent Palestinian State in which Jews, Christians and Muslims could live together in peace and harmony. Yasser Arafat founded this dream and this hope on the history of Palestine and the history of the Palestinian-Zionist conflict.

Arafat's speech was constantly interrupted by applause – applause, too, for the PLO's willingness to find a political solution to the conflict. The PLO's ten-point programme had produced results. Arafat's assurance 'that when we are talking of our common hopes for the Palestine of tomorrow, we also include all the Jews living in Palestine today who wish to live together with us without discrimination on Palestinian ground' was also greeted with applause and approval.

Arafat stressed that if a just peace were attained, he did not wish to see a single drop of Jewish or Arab blood shed.

World opinion was sympathetic to the PLO dream of a secular, democratic State of Palestine. It seemed a more human alternative to the 'purely Jewish' State of Israel. Arafat's concluding words, which were interrupted by thunderous applause lasting for minutes, have often been quoted:

> I came to you today with the olive branch in one hand and the rifle of revolution in the other. Do not make me drop the olive branch, do not make me drop the olive branch . . . Mr President, war flames up in Palestine and yet it is Palestine where peace will be born.

After a two-week debate the United Nations General Assembly passed Resolution 3236, in which it affirmed the 'inalienable rights of the Palestinian people', including 'the right to self-determination', 'the right to return to its country' and the 'right to national independence and sovereignty'. It further acknowledged the Palestinian people's right to fight 'with every means' for the realization of its rights – a phrase which clearly meant that the United Nations sanctioned armed struggle as a legitimate means.

The very fact of its invitation to the Palestine debate implied the PLO's recognition by the United Nations as the representative and spokesman of the Palestinian people. It confirmed this in Resolution 3237 in which the PLO was granted observer status at the United Nations – the first liberation organization ever to receive this status. The PLO later became a full member of all United Nations sub-organizations. This meant that the PLO now enjoyed world-wide recognition.

The United Nations' attitude to the Palestinian conflict had now changed fundamentally. It had been faced with this seemingly insoluble problem ever since the British relinquished the Palestine mandate in 1948. Since then, the Palestinian problem had always been on the agenda at every session of the United Nations General Assembly. In 1948 the United Nations decided to divide Palestine without even consulting the Palestinian people, and for many years the UN had either ignored or misjudged the crucial factor in the conflict: the Palestinians. For almost 30 years, the United Nations treated the Palestinian problem as a refugee problem, the most prominent examples of this attitude being Security Council Resolutions 242 and 338 in 1967. From March 1950 to November 1966 the UN Armistice Committee condemned more than 60 serious cases of Israeli attacks and raids on neighbouring Arab states. But no effective measures were taken to prevent them, mainly on account of the veto in the Security Council of the USA and its Western allies.

By 1974 the Palestinian people's struggle under the leadership of the PLO had forced the United Nations to do a 180-degree turn in its judgement of the Palestinian question. The former colonies of Africa and Asia, in particular, and, more gradually, the socialist countries now recognized the PLO and most of these countries have given the PLO full diplomatic status ever since. The PLO became a full member of the Non-Aligned Movement, and representatives of the Palestinian National Council were invited to conferences of the Inter-Parliamentary Union, an organization in which parliamentarians from all over the world are represented. More than 110 states have now recognized the PLO as the sole legitimate representative of the Palestinian people. Only 70 countries still maintain diplomatic relations with Israel. Since 1974, the United Nations has regularly passed resolutions expressing broad support for Palestinian demands. On 2 November 1979 the United Nations proclaimed 29 November – the anniversary of the UN partition of Palestine – a day of international solidarity with the Palestinian people.

The UN therefore recognized in international law the Palestinian people's demand for its national rights. In doing so, it created an important precedent for the recognition of the PLO by other states; many followed shortly afterwards.

Palestinians in occupied Palestine, in the Arab countries and throughout the world celebrated Yasser Arafat's address to the United Nations as a great victory for their cause. In the occupied areas, huge demonstrations were held in support of the PLO. The confidence and self-esteem of Palestinians in their occupied home country, in the refugee camps, in the other states where they were exiled and even in areas annexed by Israel in 1948 increased, and so did their loyalty to the Palestinian people. They said they were Palestinians despite the identity papers imposed on them by the Israelis. Many now began to hope that the end of Israeli occupation was approaching – and the hope of some day returning to Palestine seemed more than just a distant dream.

The PLO was the first liberation movement to be officially invited to a United Nations debate and to be granted observer status at all UN institutions. It was now treated as equal to all the other states in the world. The PLO was no longer just a regional military force that could be dismissed as a 'disruptive factor'; it was now a recognized political factor in the international arena. The world had done more than accept that the Palestinian problem lay at the core of the Middle East conflict; it had confirmed the legitimacy of the Palestinian people's national rights.

The Palestine Liberation Organization (PLO)

The vast majority of world states today support the Palestinian struggle for their legitimate national rights, and recognize the PLO as the sole legitimate representative of the Palestinian people. It is no accident that the PLO has achieved this status. Yet in the West the PLO is frequently regarded merely as a resistance organization, its political and military aspects being stressed to the exclusion of all others.

It is generally unknown, or at least unnoticed, that it was only the PLO's democratic legitimation – its work for the Palestinian people in the fields of social welfare, medical care, cultural and trade union activities, its representation of the political and economic aspirations of Palestinian society – which enabled the PLO to gain this world-wide recognition. The PLO is not an organization in the strict sense. It represents the structure of the Palestinian State. Before this Palestinian State can be proclaimed, Israeli occupation must end.

The supreme constitutional body of the PLO is the Palestinian National Council, which has 301 members, representing the Palestinian people on a broad basis.

The PLO and Palestine

1. STRUCTURE OF THE PLO

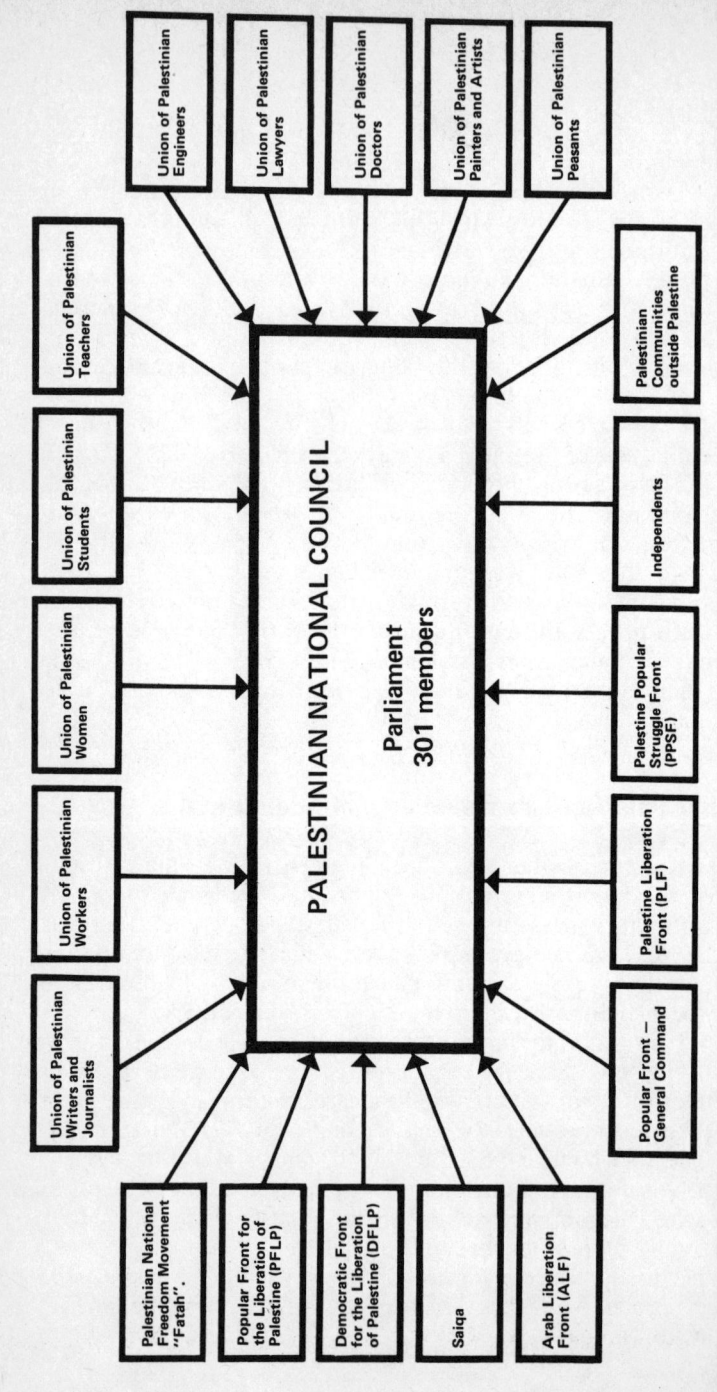

2. STRUCTURE OF THE PLO

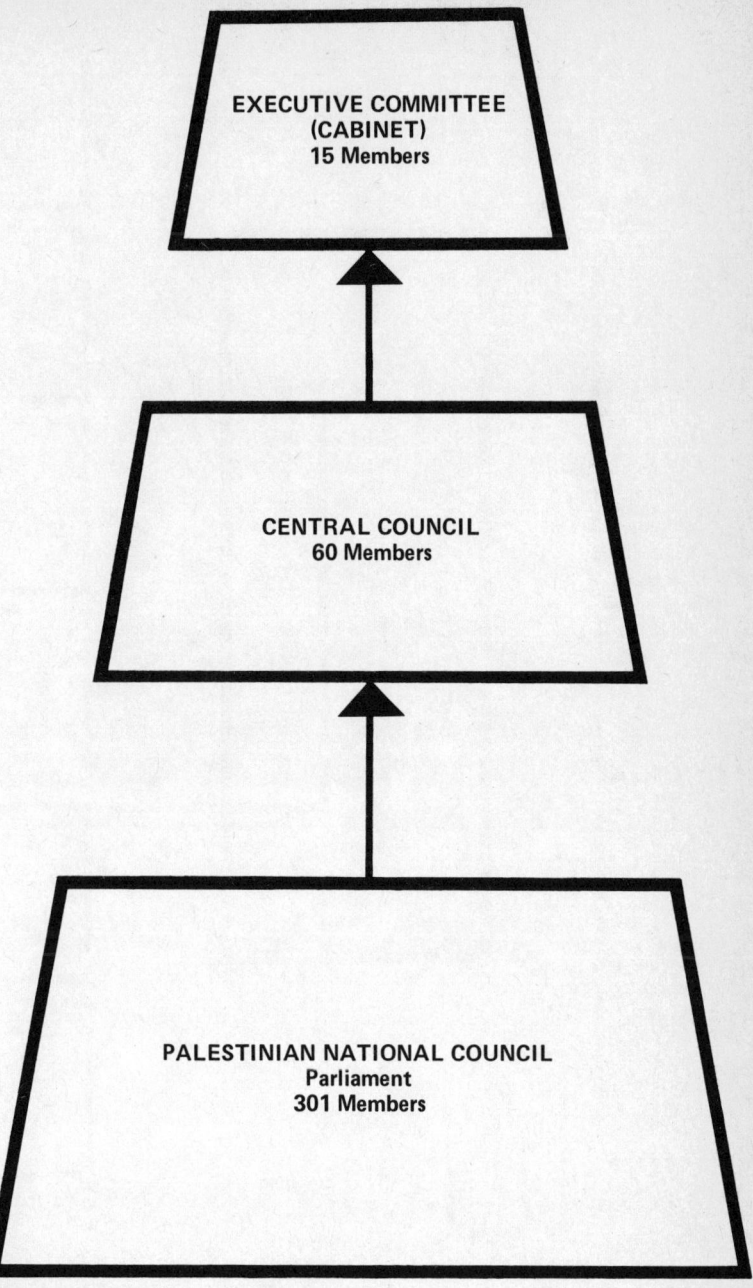

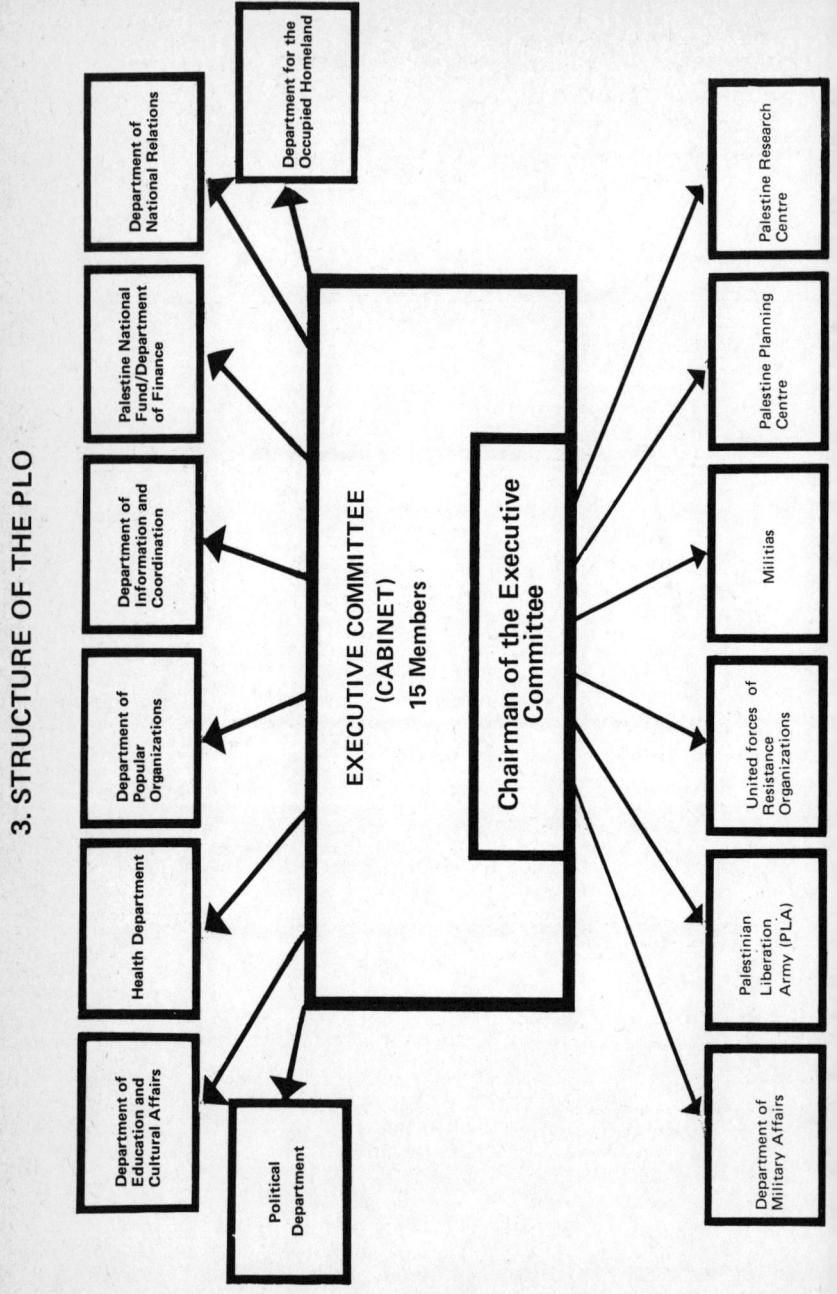

International Recognition of the PLO

4. STRUCTURE OF THE PLO

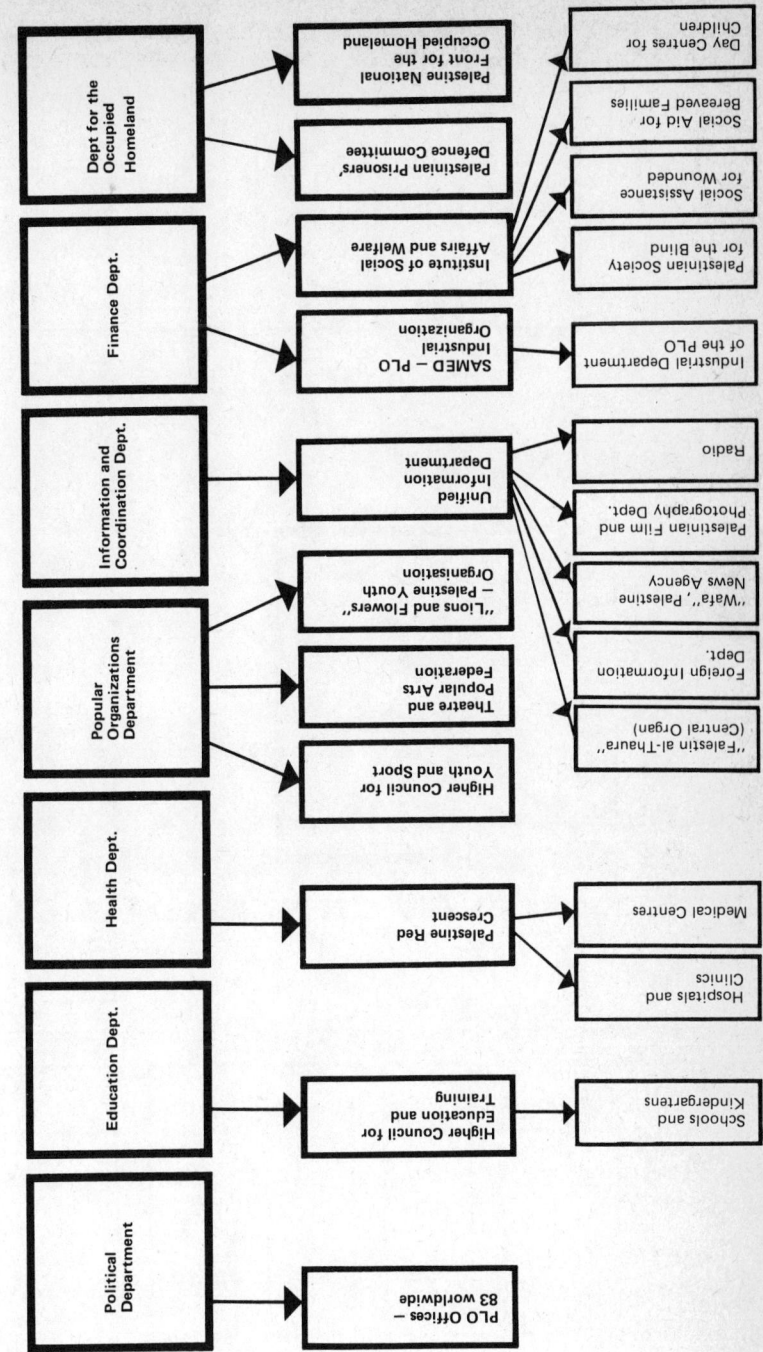

The PLO and Palestine

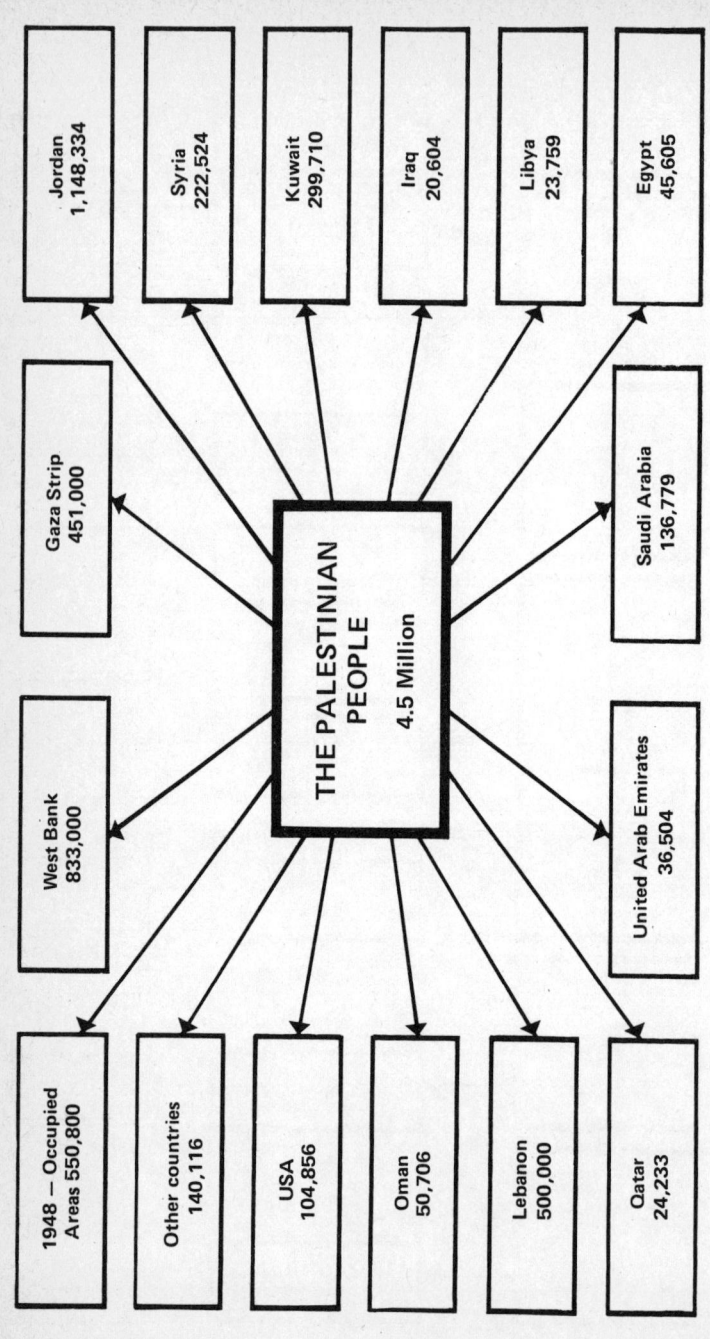

There are eight Palestinian resistance organizations, which in fact means eight political parties. The political parties are all based on democratic principles. They each hold general assemblies to which the various constituent associations send delegates. These general assemblies then elect the central council or central committee of the organization, which in turn elects a political bureau or executive committee. This means that all the representatives of these organizations on the National Council have a democratic mandate. Al-Fatah is by far the largest of these parties. The Popular Front (PFLP) and the Democratic Front (DFLP) also have considerable influence. The other five parties are: Saiqa, the Arab Liberation Front (ALF), the Popular Front/General Command (PFLP/GC), the Palestinian Liberation Front (PLF) and the Palestinian Popular Struggle Front (PPSF).

Despite all the bloody confrontations in its history, despite exile and political disagreements among the organizations, the PLO has managed to establish a structure which is stronger and more united than that of many a state with land and a flag of its own. And Palestinians throughout the world, in the United States, in West Germany and in other countries, are loyal to the PLO. The Palestinian people's ties with the areas of Palestine occupied by Israel in 1948 and in 1967 are today stronger than ever – as the huge demonstrations on 'Land Day' prove. The Palestinians in Israel have celebrated 'Land Day' on 30 March of every year since 1976. On this day, Palestinians protest against Israeli appropriation of Arab land, a process which is still continuing. The Israelis even dispossess Palestinians who officially hold Israeli citizenship.

The Palestinian people's broad identification with the PLO has enabled it to create an important second pillar of support in the trade unions and professional associations. The oldest of these organizations are the General Union of Palestinian Students and the General Union of Palestinian Workers, both of which were founded – under different names – in the 1950s. They both played crucial parts in the formation of the Palestinian resistance movement, and many of the leading figures in the PLO today were once members of these organizations. On the initiative of al-Fatah in particular, other organizations were founded in the sixties and seventies. There are now ten in all. The General Union of Palestinian Women, whose history, though under a different name, goes back to the British mandate period, has an extremely important role to play – particularly in an Arab society. Palestinian artists, writers and journalists, teachers, lawyers, peasants and engineers all have their own organizations which in turn are part of corresponding Arab and international institutions. Marwan Abdel Hamid, president of the Palestinian Engineers' Union, has been elected to the executive committee of the World Federation of Engineers for the period 1981–85. The social and political importance of these associations is enormous. The Association of Palestinian Doctors, for example, is the second largest in the Arab world – after the Egyptian. A remarkable achievement when we consider that Egypt's population is ten times greater.

Palestinian engineers have made indispensable contributions to the development of Arab industry and economies and today occupy leading positions throughout the Arab world. Many of the leading figures of the Palestinian revolution today were teachers in their younger years. The Palestinian Teachers' Association now has 80,000 members and is one of the largest organizations in the PLO.

All these organizations have formed national associations wherever Palestinians live in large numbers. The national associations elect their leaders according to their statutes, and these leaders form the association's central conference. This conference elects the central council or leadership of the union, which then represents the organization on the Palestinian National Council, according to the strength of its membership. Here again we see these ten organizations all democratically electing their representatives on the National Council.

At preparatory meetings of the National Council a committee is chosen which then visits all countries where substantial numbers of Palestinians live. In each country, they nominate Palestinians who enjoy high standing in their community. A vote on these nominees is then taken in the Palestinian National Council. Palestinians abroad are thus also represented on the National Council.

The problem of representation for those Palestinians forced to live under Israeli occupation also has to be solved. The Israeli occupying forces ban anyone who has taken part in National Council meetings from returning to Palestine. The National Council has therefore reserved 50 empty seats for the population of the occupied areas. The last time the population of the occupied areas was allowed to elect its own mayors and town councillors was in 1976, when PLO candidates won overwhelming victories. The executive committee has set up a special department for maintaining relations with the population of the occupied areas.

To sum up, the Palestinian National Council is rightly regarded as the representative parliament of the Palestinian people. This was confirmed in 1974 when the Palestinian National Council became a member of the Inter-Parliamentary Union. The PLO owed this significant political recognition largely to the efforts of Khaled al Hassan, one of its most brilliant and internationally reputed politicians and diplomats.

The Palestinian National Council elects its 'government', the executive committee, which comprises 15 members. At the last National Council meeting (April 1981), it was decided that the chairman of the PLO should also be elected by the National Council. It voted unanimously for Yasser Arafat.

The executive committee takes on all the responsibilities of the PLO in accordance with the directives and resolutions passed and laid down by the National Council. It is bound to implement these resolutions.

Members of the executive committee are each responsible for a department (or ministry) and they are individually and collectively responsible to the National Council. The dispersal of the Palestinians and the difficult, protracted electoral procedures for the National Council mean that it cannot be in permanent session and so a committee – the PLO Central Council – has been formed to conduct business between National Council sessions, which are held every two to three years. It comprises 60 members chosen by the National Council, including the PLO executive committee. However, this Central Council has only advisory functions.

The chairman of the PLO executive committee is also supreme commander of the Palestinian forces and head of the Military Department. The forces of the Palestinian revolution consist of guerrilla units, militias and the Palestine Liberation Army (PLA). The Planning and the Research Centres are also under the direct control of the executive committee chairman. Their function is to work out recommendations and provide advice to help the executive committee in its decision making.

The executive committee departments are in effect ministries – as their names imply: the Political Department, responsible for foreign affairs and the PLO's foreign relations; the Education Department; the Health Department; the Palestinian National Fund, i.e. Finance Department; the Military Department; the Information and National Guidance Department, responsible for newspapers, news agencies, radio stations and other media; the Department of National Relations – equivalent to a ministry of home affairs; the Occupied Areas Department, which includes for example the Political Prisoners' Defence Committee and maintains contact and relations with the National Front in the occupied areas; finally, the Department of Youth and Culture, responsible for youth organizations, sport, theatre and popular arts.

All these departments are, of course, subdivided further. The heads or directors of departments are representatives of the executive. They may be voted out of office or dismissed at any time.

The Palestinian revolution has concentrated particular attention on developing social and health care and education. Three institutions in these areas will serve as examples of the PLO's achievements: the Palestinian Red Crescent (PRCS), SAMED (Workshops of the Children of the Martyrs of the Palestinian Revolution) – now the PLO's economic institution – and Beit as-Soummud and Souq al-Gharb, PLO orphanages.

The Palestinian Red Crescent was founded in Jordan in 1969. Its aim was, from the beginning, to provide medical care for the Palestinian people and for the fedayeen. The PRCS has established fully-equipped clinics and hospitals (c.130 in all) in many Arab countries but especially in Beirut and the refugee camps. About 3,000 patients on average are cared for daily. Apart from hospitals and out-patients' departments, the PRCS runs a school of nursing, a training centre for medical and technical assistants, a central laboratory and a central blood bank in Beirut. It established a centre for the production of artificial limbs and physiotherapeutic treatment of the handicapped and war victims in Ramleh hospital. The staff are in many cases former patients passing on their experience.

The PRCS also has centres in which it runs courses in secretarial work and dressmaking. PRCS 'social workers' practise preventive medicine in the refugee camps, teaching and informing the people there about hygiene and first aid. As most of these social workers also live in the camps, their work is highly effective.

Treatment in clinics and hospitals, named after Palestinian towns (Haifa, Jaffa, Nazareth, Ramleh, etc.), is free for all fedayeen, for the families of those killed in action, and for victims of Israeli bombing and other military operations. Anyone requesting treatment is admitted, regardless of religion or nationality.

The Palestinian Red Crescent has observer status within the International Red Cross and is a full member of the Arab Health Organization.

The House of the Children of Steadfastness (Beit as-Soummud) was founded by the General Union of Palestinian Women (GUPW) during the Lebanese civil war. During this war, Tel Al Zaatar (Thyme Hill) refugee camp withstood siege by Falangist militias for 53 days. Thousands of civilians were killed during the siege or brutally murdered when it ended. Hundreds of children were left without parents – and it was for them that the House of Steadfastness was founded.

A remarkable childcare system was developed in the house – that of the 'alternative mother' and the 'alternative family'. It meant that groups of eight children, usually brothers and sisters, were cared for and looked after by a 'mother' in family units. These mothers, specially trained for the purpose, are for the most part themselves survivors of Tel Al Zaatar and therefore familiar from their own experience with the traumatic experiences and shocks to which these children have been subjected. The house runs nursery schools; school-age children attend UNWRA schools, to prevent them from becoming isolated from other Palestinian children.

The House of Steadfastness provides a wide range of activities for its children. Volunteer teachers give sports, painting and embroidery instruction, teach music and folk dancing and many other courses. Experienced psychologists, doctors and sociologists are part of the house staff. The work of this institution is exemplary by any standard.

The PLO runs another orphanage, Souq al-Gharb, in the mountains near Beirut. Souq al-Gharb is a modern, well-equipped boarding school preparing more than 500 children for a new future in Palestine.

The Society of Sons of the Palestinian Martyrs (SAMED) was founded in 1969, mainly to provide work and financial aid for the families of those killed in action. Today, SAMED is the main economic arm of the PLO – the embryonic force of the future Palestinian economy. SAMED comes under the jurisdiction of the Palestinian National Fund (Finance Ministry).

After first concentrating on embroidery and dressmaking, SAMED has now developed into a broad-based production co-operative in which woodwork and metalwork are coming to play an increasingly important part alongside the traditional textile sector. SAMED also runs a film department and SAMED films have won prizes at several international festivals.

Apart from consumer goods such as clothes, blankets, leather goods, furniture, toys, etc., SAMED produces capital goods and machines. It has signed co-operation agreements with the socialist countries and with various member states of the European Economic Community.

SAMED products, which in recent years have improved greatly in quality, are exported to all Arab countries, the socialist countries and the entire Third World. It also has contacts with France, Italy, the Federal Republic of Germany and Norway. SAMED is a full member of the International Workers' Conference and the Food and Agriculture Organization.

In the agrarian sector, SAMED has established close ties between the African countries and the PLO. Palestinian experts are involved in agricultural projects in many African countries, as well as helping to train African specialists and develop agricultural technologies. This close cooperation underlines SAMED's political character – SAMED is developing and practising new forms of mutual development aid in the Third World.

SAMED's organization also underlines its political character. Its workers are not only workers but Palestinian revolutionaries, and they decide on all important issues of management and production. Its workers are represented by elected revolutionary committees which are accountable to their fellow-workers and can be voted out of office at any time. The revolutionary committees function as mediators between directors and workers. Directors have, at various times, been dismissed at the request of workers. Revolutionary committees also run political courses, improving workers' qualifications and at the same time politicizing them.

But a people's identity is more than the sum of its political and social institutions. Culture and tradition are also crucially important. Palestinian artists and writers have achieved international repute and won international awards in the fields of painting, the plastic arts and literature in recent years. The paintings of Ismail Shammout – especially his Tel Al Zaatar sequence – and the designs of Burhan Karkutli are particularly well known in West Germany. The work of writers such as Ghassan Kanafani and Mahmud Darwish are also familiar. Studies and analyses by historians and writers such as Saddam Hadawi, Walid Khalidi and Faris Sayegh have made considerable impact throughout Europe. Indeed for many people these works were the first authentic information describing the Palestinian conflict from a Palestinian perspective which they had read. All these artists and writers are members of the General Union of Palestinian Writers and Journalists or of the General Union of Palestinian

Painters and Artists and are therefore part of the Palestinian revolution and the PLO.

Palestinian culture and tradition is very ancient – but it is above all original and independent. In recent years, the PLO has brought it to a new flowering after the years of dispersal and exile.

In SAMED workshops, Palestinian women are again embroidering clothes and dresses with traditional designs and motifs which vary in Palestine from town to town and from one area to the next. This style of embroidery was also widespread in the Balkans. Palestine is also famous for its silver jewellery and for glassmaking, an art invented in Hebron around 4000 BC. Ceramics, pottery, olive-wood carving and mother-of-pearl work – all these traditional handicrafts can today be admired in SAMED exhibition rooms. These works have been displayed at major exhibitions of Arab work in Spain, West Germany and other countries.

Dancing and singing are also an integral part of Palestinian culture and today Palestinians still sing and dance on festive occasions, at marriages and official and religious feasts. The best-known Palestinian dance is the *dabka*, of which there are several variations.

The main popular musical intruments are string instruments, flutes and rhythm instruments.

There has always – long before the Palestinian problem arose – been a close connection in Palestine between music, dancing and singing and political and social subjects.

The PLO has revived this traditional connection in its dance and folklore group, which has performed in many countries, including two tours of West Germany, and won many prizes and cultural awards.

The above-mentioned medical, social and educational achievements and the revival of an independent Palestinian tradition and culture, only briefly outlined here, demonstrate that the PLO has, with great success, become involved in all the concerns of the Palestinian people. These aspects of the PLO's work are scarcely known in the West, yet they have contributed decisively to its recognition and international legitimation.

Many people are puzzled about where the PLO gets its money from. Many millions of dollars are needed to finance all its organizations and institutions. To raise these sums, the PLO has created a complicated system whereby Palestinians throughout the Arab world pay a 5% income tax to the PLO. Palestinians in other countries make voluntary contributions. The Arab League also has a PLO support fund into which Arab states make payments, and various Arab states give the PLO financial backing over and above this. But it is the Palestinians themselves who provide most of the finance.

All incoming funds are administered by the National Fund (Finance Ministry) and distributed according to the political resolutions of PLO committees.

Though in exile, the PLO has already established the embryonic structures of the future Palestinian State. And these political institutions and organs of the PLO prove categorically that this future State will be democratic. The PLO is the first liberation organization which – thanks largely to its origin and history – has created democratic structures in its own ranks. And it has held true to these structures, even though internal discussions and disagreements have all too often been interpreted as lack of unity or a sign of weakness. The PLO is the first quasi-state institution in the history of Palestine which genuinely practises democracy – and this is a major reason why the Palestinian people regard the PLO as their sole legitimate representative.

Self-determination for the Palestinian people is, politically, culturally and economically, no longer a seemingly impossible goal. This is the historic achievement of the PLO.

21. Europe and the Arab World

Relations between Europe and the Orient have existed for thousands of years. The history of these relations is one of a constant interchange of products and goods, ideas and inventions. But it is also a history of wars and conquests.

Alexander the Great conquered large parts of what is now the Arab world; the Arabs reversed the process some thousand years later, when they penetrated as far north as Poitiers and established a flourishing culture and economy in southern Spain. Later, the crusaders occupied Jerusalem and from the mid-19th Century European colonialists penetrated into the remotest corners of the Arabian peninsula.

It is generally acknowledged that developments in Europe could not have taken place as early as they did without the achievements of Arab scholars, their scientific experiments, their writings and their philosophy.

Medicine, science and education: the great cultural achievements which Europe regards as its own were in fact taken over from the Arab world in the Middle Ages. Baghdad, Fez and Cairo boasted institutes of learning which were the forerunners of modern universities. Even today, Al Azhar in Cairo is one of the finest universities in the entire Arab world.

Nor is it coincidental that the three great monotheistic religions all had their origins in the east Mediterranean region.

This region was characterized by a common image of mankind, a shared conception of civilization. A great deal of cultural cross-fertilization and interchange of ideas took place. But this did not continue. The Arab world played no part in the great changes of the 19th Century. Political oppression, economic lethargy, poor administration, institutional weaknesses and unfavourable economic conditions combined to cause stagnation in the Arab world.

The European advance was inexorable, and the Arab continent sank in the darkness of colonial rule.

In the 20th Century, the Arab struggle for independence began, and the Arab states all won national sovereignty – with the exception of Palestine; a fact for which the European states, England and France in particular, must bear historical responsibility.

After the Second World War, England and France, abetted by the United States, brought about the division of Palestine and the establishment of a Jewish State on Palestinian territory. The European powers, now including the Federal Republic of Germany, supported the State of Israel with financial aid or compensation payments. And they supplied Israel with arms in the June 1967 war.

It was not until the October war in 1973 that the first signs of a change in relations between Europe and the Arab world began to emerge.

Since November 1970, the European Economic Community had been considering a declaration on the Middle East. The October war and the impending Arab oil boycott undoubtedly speeded up the publication of this declaration. In summer 1974 the Arab League and the European Economic Community agreed to start a dialogue. But the European position on the Palestinian problem was ambivalent and so it was two years before the European-Arab dialogue really got under way. Finally, the two sides reached agreement on the composition of each delegation. This agreement, the so-called 'Dublin formula', said that the dialogue would be conducted between a joint European delegation on the one hand and an Arab delegation, including the PLO, on the other. There would be no direct talks between representatives of single member countries or organizations. This formula enabled the Europeans to take part in talks without officially recognizing the PLO. The existence of the European Economic Community and the Arab League meant that discussions could be held between two parties and not 30.

Common historical experience, close cultural ties and current political and economic interests guaranteed that this dialogue would benefit both sides. Europe's interest was and still is to ensure its traditional political sphere of interest and advantageous economic relations – in particular to guarantee European energy supplies and create a thriving Arab market for European products.

Oil is crucially important for the Arab states, too. It is the indispensable motor of their economic development. The Arab states finance most of their home investments with the proceeds from oil sales. Europe and the Arab world are therefore both to a large extent dependent on oil.

The Arab states looked to Europe for an independent policy of unreserved co-operation, which would make possible rapid and balanced industrial development in the Arab world. They also expected the European Economic Community to develop an independent Middle East policy which would help to bring about a just and lasting peace.

These goals were laid down in a joint memorandum drafted by high-ranking political officials in Cairo in June 1975. It says:

> The political dimension of this dialogue consists mainly of the attempt to re-discover, renew and develop relations between the two regions . . . and in the determination to provide a basis for mutually advantageous political co-operation in a wide range of areas. This agreement must form the basis of

economic co-operation between the European and the Arab countries and thereby contribute to greater stability, security and a just peace in the Arab world and to peace and security in the world.

On economic co-operation the memorandum says:

> In the economic sphere the primary aim of the dialogue is to make co-operation possible and thus to create the conditions for the development of the Arab world as a whole and for bridging the gap which at present exists between the Arab and the European countries. For this purpose we must endeavour to achieve specific measures and decisions in all areas on the basis of a fair division of labour.

The possibilities for co-operation between two regions separated only by the Mediterranean, whose interests are otherwise complementary and convergent, are considerable and could certainly prove mutually beneficial, politically and economically.

The European Economic Community and the Arab states have signed a number of economic co-operation agreements. The Arab world is today the major importer of the European Economic Community's products. The economic results of the European-Arab dialogue have undoubtedly been highly satisfactory for the Europeans. The pattern of trade relations has been maintained, and continues to favour West European countries. Import restrictions on Arab textiles still apply, and Arab exports remain heavily dominated by oil. On the other hand, Europe need no longer fear energy supply problems.

Despite these reservations, it must be acknowledged that the European-Arab dialogue has provided important impulses for friendly co-operation – and in the economic sphere this has benefited both sides.

The political side of the dialogue is far more complicated. From the beginning, some Europeans wished to exclude the Palestinian problem from the discussions. In 1978, Claude Cheysson, then European Commissioner for Co-operation and Development and later French Foreign Minister, said: 'We started the European-Arab dialogue for political reasons. It is a kind of political exercise.' The main feature of this dialogue has been a slow and cautious recognition by the Europeans of the political realities of the Middle East.

At the end of June 1977 the EEC made a second declaration on the Middle East conflict. It went further than the first declaration of 6 November 1973 in that it spoke of the 'national identity of the Palestinian people' and the 'necessity of a homeland for the Palestinian people'. Since 1975, the member states of the EEC had accepted Palestinian representatives in their countries as part of Arab League delegations. In this period, the PLO set up information offices in practically all West European countries. And in most such countries these offices are recognized *de facto* as PLO representations. Senior staff in these bureaux have conducted talks with West European political parties and governments. The PLO made a further European breakthrough at the 'Vienna Meeting' in July 1979. The Socialist International in 1980, led by Willy Brandt and Austrian Chancellor Bruno Kreisky, received Yasser Arafat as head of the PLO and held discussions with him lasting several days. The response to this meeting exceeded all expectations, with most West European media regarding this as at least *de facto* recognition of the PLO. Many leading journalists, including some in West Germany, now openly criticized Israeli expansionism. In *Die Zeit*, Theo Sommer even spoke of 'the Germans' moral commitment . . . to the Palestinians who if it had not been for Hitler would now be living in their ancestral home country.' Sommer went on to criticize those 'who act as if we can only fulfil our much-invoked historical responsibility by signing the Gush Emunim programme.'

After the meeting between Brandt, Kreisky and Arafat, contacts between European politicians and PLO representatives intensified. Portugal and Spain had already recognized the PLO and in 1980 Austria followed suit, officially recognizing the PLO and giving it diplomatic status.

In 1981 the Greek socialist government officially recognized the PLO – the first EEC member state to do so.

In spring 1981 other European countries began to support the official inclusion of the PLO in all Middle East negotiations. Giscard d'Estaing called for 'joint European approaches to the PLO'. And Lord Carrington, then British Foreign Secretary, described the PLO as 'an important factor in the Middle East' in a speech in the House of Commons. In September 1979, the Irish Foreign Minister, speaking on behalf of the EEC, had described the PLO as a 'party in the Middle East conflict' in a speech to the United Nations.

The last EEC declaration to date on the Middle East came in Venice on 13 June 1980. It called for 'the participation of the Palestine Liberation Organization (PLO) in Middle East peace negotiations.' And it 'acknowledged the Palestinian right to self-determination.' This is the nearest the Europeans have come so far to recognizing the Palestinians' national rights – but it does not mention the right to establish a Palestinian State, nor does it recognize the PLO as the representative of the Palestinian people.

The Camp David negotiations were still going on at this time and the Europeans, though sceptical about the separate peace agreement between Egypt and Israel, were still not independent enough to develop an initiative of their own. Statements on the Palestinian right to self-determination, such as those made by Giscard d'Estaing and Helmut Schmidt, served mainly to provoke violent reactions from the Israelis, who promptly came up with their standard accusation of anti-Semitism. Begin's tirades against Helmut Schmidt violated all the rules of civilized political behaviour, but none the less they had their effect. When Reagan was elected president of the USA, the European scope for an independent Middle East policy was further restricted. The EEC again subordinated itself to the interests of the USA – as the sending of European troops to Sinai to uphold the Camp David agreements illustrated.

The Americans are exerting massive economic, political and military pressure on Europe. American high-interest policies, the attempts to scotch the German-Soviet gas pipeline deal, the installation of new American atomic missiles on European soil – these examples all show how narrow are the limits of European action, even when it is trying to pursue its own interests in Europe itself. However, Europe cannot, in the long term, secure its interests in the Middle East through the military power and confrontation policies of the United States. Europe and the Arab world – the EEC's major trading partner, before the USA – are condemned to co-operation. They cannot, in the long run, ignore each other – nor their political problems.

This is why the Palestinian problem cannot and must not be excluded from the European-Arab dialogue. Communiqués are no substitute for policies. A lasting and just peace in the Middle East can only be achieved if talks, contacts and agreements benefit both sides. A reversion to the system of separate talks between individual European and Arab states would merely be a waste of time, money and energy. The internal problems in both communities must be overcome; both the European and the Arab communities must be strengthened. Not until this happens will the two sides be able to take on political responsibility with a real prospect for a just and lasting peace.

The PLO and the European-Arab Dialogue

The European-Arab dialogue is unthinkable without PLO participation. The PLO has been involved in this dialogue since the beginning, i.e. since the Arab summit conference in Algiers in 1973. PLO experts played a leading part in working out the texts outlining the basis of the European-Arab dialogue.

The importance the PLO attached to this dialogue determined its positive attitude and explains the important role it wished to play and did play in it – especially in the preparatory and initial discussions on the Arab side.

The PLO nominated a high-powered commission for these discussions. Commission members included Dr Dajani, a member of the PLO Central Committee, Mohammed Rabiya, a member of the PLO Central Council, and Naim Khader, PLO representative in Brussels.

Whenever necessary, these delegates were joined by the PLO representatives in Paris, Rome, Bonn and London, whose advice was indispensable in areas such as economics and information.

The PLO's main interest was to stress the political nature of the dialogue and to ensure that the Palestine problem was on the agenda. The Arab states were unanimous in their support for the PLO's demands.

As various European representatives insisted that the Palestine problem should be excluded from the dialogue, the discussions frequently had to be adjourned or interrupted.

These blocking tactics failed – thanks to the patience and consideration the PLO showed towards the European states. Access to Europe remained open for the PLO. Dr Dajani, the head of the Palestinian delegation, was received by high-ranking politicians and officials in Rome, Brussels, Bonn, Paris and other European capitals. Yet the European attitude to the Palestinian problem – in particular their voting tactics at the UN – constantly led to stagnation and interruptions in the dialogue.

Distrust and criticism of the Europeans now became rife within the Arab delegation and the PLO. Even Arab delegates began to urge an adjournment or termination of the dialogue.

The Palestinian leadership, and Yasser Arafat in particular, managed to keep the dialogue going, in spite of meagre results, especially on the Palestinian question. The Abu Dhabi conference in 1975 underlined the importance of the PLO in the dialogue. Here, the PLO drafted the conference text, which was adopted by the Arab states.

The Europeans took little or no note of the increasing international importance of the PLO, its success and widespread recognition. Europe was under American pressure, with Kissinger demanding that the dialogue should be confined to economic and cultural subjects. The USA allowed Europe no scope for political participation in finding a solution. This led to disagreements within the EEC. Relations between the USA and France cooled perceptibly.

The US Administration clearly stated its displeasure at the Venice Declaration, warning the Paris-Bonn axis against taking any independent initiative.

This American attitude has remained the same until the present day. New Israeli aggression and the change of government in France have made the EEC's weakness on the Middle East question even more evident. Here, too, Camp David was a touchstone. Though the Europeans realized, and publicly stated that the Camp David agreement would not lead to lasting peace, they ceded to American pressure and sent troops to Sinai to enforce the agreement.

Europe no longer speaks with one voice on the Middle East. When he came to office, President Mitterrand of France promised a change in the French attitude to Israel. Admittedly, he did visit Saudi Arabia. But otherwise the 'balance' of French policy has tilted towards Israel. Mitterrand underlined the change in French policy by his state visit to Israel, which is largely isolated internationally. The EEC initiative on the Middle East has rapidly lost ground.

The Arab world viewed these developments critically. Klibi, the president of the Arab League, has repeatedly expressed these Arab criticisms on his visits to European capitals. The PLO, too, has responded to this change in the European attitude. Yasser Arafat and Farouk Kaddoumi invited all PLO representatives in West Europe to conferences in Tunis and Beirut. The conclusions of these discussions were clear: the European Community is not in a position to develop its own initiative on the Middle East independently of the United States; this does not, however, mean that the PLO denies or underestimates the importance of a continuing dialogue; but the realities make it necessary to seek new ways and methods in this dialogue.

This was not an easy decision for the PLO, which had made a major contribution to the European-Arab dialogue and paved the way for a deeper understanding between Europe and the Arab world. Some of the PLO's most outstanding and respected representatives were killed in the process. Ezzedine Kalak, PLO representative in Paris, was murdered in August 1978. Said Hammami, PLO representative in London, was killed in January 1978 and Naim Khader, the Brussels representative, in June 1981.

Yet even today the European states refuse to face facts, using diplomatic skill and verbal subterfuge to avoid recognizing the PLO.

All PLO representatives are members of the Arab League; their position in European capitals is no different from that of any other Arab ambassador, whether on the political, economic or cultural level. The Arab side insists that the PLO (Palestine) should be regarded as a full member and that the Europeans should accept this fact.

The PLO will continue its efforts to gain full diplomatic recognition throughout Europe. This should be much easier now that the PLO is fully recognized in the socialist countries, in the non-aligned states and, not least, by Spain, Portugal, Austria and EEC-member Greece, a fact which has had its impact in other West European capitals. In the long run, West Europe cannot ignore the facts.

Since the Israelis withdrew from Sinai, it has become clearer than ever that the critical problem between Israel and the Arab states is Palestine.

In spring 1982, the Belgian Foreign Minister Tindemans made a statement on the Israeli withdrawal from Sinai and called for a European initiative. Now that the Sinai problem had been solved, he said, the way was open for new moves. Tindemans did not mention the inescapable fact that the real confrontation in the Middle East is now between the Israelis and the Palestinians – thanks mainly to the continuing resistance of the Palestinian people in the occupied areas.

If Europe wants to take a meaningful initiative, it will have to establish more open relations with the PLO – on the diplomatic level. It is simply illusory to attempt to promote a peace settlement without speaking to those directly involved. Relations between Europe and the PLO cannot continue on present terms. The EEC must establish direct contacts with the PLO leadership, at governmental level, if it is to help achieve a peace settlement for the Middle East.

22. Camp David: A Blind Alley

In November 1977 Yasser Arafat, a guest of President Sadat, was listening to his host speaking to the Egyptian Parliament. In the course of this speech, Sadat said that he was prepared to speak with the devil himself and to travel to Jerusalem for the sake of peace. This assertion appeared to be improvised – a spontaneous overflow of words.

Yet Şadat did what he promised. Until the Egyptian president's aeroplane landed at Lod airport on the evening of 19 November 1977, no one took his words very seriously. The world was taken aback.

On 20 November, Sadat addressed the Knesset, the Israeli Parliament. He said it was understood that Israel would have to withdraw completely from the territories occupied since 1967, that the Palestinian problem was at the heart of the Middle East conflict and that peace could not be achieved without the Palestinians. A separate agreement, he said, was out of the question. He accepted Israeli demands for peace and security; he wished to end the state of war and never to wage war again.

Menachem Begin's reply was tactical and guarded. He spoke of peace negotiations with all Arab states, of the Jews' return to their homeland and of Israel's right to 'Eretz Israel'. Begin said that the only point at issue was the definition of frontiers and that these frontiers should be discussed in their negotiations. Begin referred to the Palestinians as 'Arabs in Eretz Israel'.

Begin paid a return visit to Ismailia. Finally, about a year later, Sadat, Begin and President Carter met at Camp David near Washington. After exhaustive preliminary talks, the official peace negotiations began on 5 September 1978 under the auspices of the United States. After days of negotiation in which the discussion partners were hermetically sealed from the outside world, the conference ended with the signing of two documents, on 17 September 1978. These documents were: 1) A Framework for Peace in the Middle East; 2) A Framework for the Conclusion of a Peace Treaty Between Egypt and Israel.

The first of these documents contains the Egyptian-Israeli declaration of their intent to reach an agreement covering all aspects of the Middle East problem on the basis of United Nations resolutions 242 and 338.

Regarding the West Bank and Gaza strip, it is agreed upon:

> Egypt, Israel and Jordan will agree on the modalities for establishing the elected self-governing authority in the West Bank and Gaza. The delegations of Egypt and Jordan may include Palestinians from the West Bank and Gaza or other Palestinians as mutually agreed. The parties will negotiate an Agreement which will define the powers and responsibilities of the self-governing authority to be exercised in the West Bank and Gaza.

Israel was to withdraw its troops to security positions. After an administrative council had been elected by the people of the occupied territories, a five-year period would begin at the end of which the definitive status of the West Bank and Gaza would be decided.

In the second document, Israel and Egypt undertook to sign a peace treaty after a three-month period. In this treaty the states would recognize each other and promise to observe all the regulations of the United Nations Charter. They further agreed to a withdrawal of Israeli troops from Sinai within three years and restrictions on the stationing of troops along the border.

The peace treaty between Israel and Egypt was formally signed in Washington on 26 March 1979 under the auspices of the United States. The treaty guaranteed normal relations with full diplomatic recognition, economic and cultural relations, an end to the state of war between the two countries and the definition of the borders between the two countries.

As for the West Bank and Gaza, the treaty merely refers to the Camp David agreements.

The costs of 'peace' were borne by the United States, which paid Israel $3,000 million for withdrawal from Sinai and the transfer of Israeli air bases to the Negev desert. Furthermore, Israel was to receive $1,800 million annually in financial aid and 75 F-16 fighter jets. Egypt would receive $2,000 million per year from the World Bank, towards which the United States would contribute $1,100 million. The *New York Times* estimated the value of US arms deliveries to Egypt at $2,000 million. There were good reasons why the United States was prepared to pay so high a price for its 'pax americana'. Camp David considerably increased American influence in the region. The USA saw Egypt as the new bastion of American influence there after the fall of the Shah. Moreover the USA now has several military bases in the Middle East. On 25 February 1979 the US Defence Secretary publicly stated: 'Protection of our oil supplies from the Middle East is clearly one of our vital interests. We will take any appropriate measure, including the use of military force, to guarantee these vital interests.' American and Egyptian forces have already held joint military manoeuvres in Sinai in preparation for a possible occupation of oil-fields. Egypt also opened its ports to the American navy. The USA emphasized its military importance and presence in the Middle East with the establishment of its 100,000-man rapid intervention force. The importance of the military aspect of the Camp David agreements was underlined by the military and strategic agreement which the USA and

Israel signed in 1981.

Ever since Sadat's journey to Jerusalem, the Arab world had become extremely distrustful and hostile towards his solo effort. The Arabs argued that the visit could only serve to strengthen the right-wing Likud government. They said it would end in the signing of a separate agreement which would split the Arab ranks and mean an Egyptian capitulation to an Israeli diktat.

Sadat's initiative did not meet with universal approval in Egypt either. The Egyptian Foreign Minister Fahmi resigned on 17 November, the day on which Sadat's journey was officially announced. And his successor Khamel resigned before the Camp David agreements were signed.

In the occupied areas, Sadat's visit to Jerusalem triggered off huge protest demonstrations. The Palestinians were afraid that they would be abandoned by Egypt, the most important Arab State, and that decisions about their fate would again be made above their heads.

Three days after the signing of the Camp David agreements, the Steadfastness Front (sometimes referred to as the Rejection Front) was formed in Damascus. Its members were Algeria, Libya, the People's Democratic Republic of Yemen, Syria and the PLO. The conference rejected the Camp David agreements because they renounced the principle of a just peace in the Middle East; this could only be achieved by complete Israeli withdrawal from all occupied Arab areas and the recognition and realization of the inalienable national rights of the Palestinian people. But the Steadfastness Front members were not the only Arab states to reject the Camp David agreements. Other Arab states generally referred to in the West as moderate also rejected the Camp David agreements and the signing of the Egyptian-Israeli peace treaty.

The Arab summit conference met in Baghdad from 27 to 31 March 1979. The Arab foreign ministers decided on the immediate recall of all Arab ambassadors from Cairo, suspension of Egyptian membership of the Arab League and the transfer of the Arab League General Secretariat from Cairo to Tunis. An economic boycott was imposed on all Egyptian firms, institutions and organizations collaborating with Israel.

The PLO, too, firmly rejected the Camp David agreements, which it regarded as a victory for Israeli interests and a negation of its legitimate national rights. The formal signing of the agreements in Washington was marked by huge protest demonstrations throughout the Arab world. Indeed, the agreements were also greeted with scepticism and rejection throughout the non-Arab world. Even the EEC was cautious, calling for the participation of all the parties involved 'including the representatives of the Palestinian people'.

It further declared that Israeli settlement policies hampered efforts to achieve peace. The UN also indirectly rejected the Camp David agreement, passing a resolution which called instead for a peace treaty in which the major powers and all parties involved – including the PLO – would take part. The Islamic and Non-Aligned States rejected the Camp David agreements and issued public statements stressing their support for and solidarity with the Palestinians. The Islamic Conference followed the example of the Arab League by suspending Egypt's membership.

Events since 25 April 1982 have proved that these reactions were by no means exaggerated. What the PLO and the Arab states have repeatedly warned against since 1978 is now a reality. The treaty between Egypt and Israel has remained a separate treaty. It has remained a separate treaty because Sadat achieved nothing for the Palestinians. Israel and the USA dictated the course of the talks in accordance with their own wishes. The Camp David autonomy plan is extremely vague and susceptible to wide interpretation. It is precise only in what it excludes. The plan quite clearly does not implement Security Council resolutions 242 and 338, which demand complete Israeli withdrawal from all occupied areas. It quite clearly conflicts with all UN resolutions to date on the Palestinian problem. It simply denies the existence of the Palestinian people, its right to self-determination in accordance with the United Nations Charter and its right to return to its home country. It rejects the PLO as the sole legitimate representative of the Palestinian people and expressly excludes it from negotiations. And it denies the rights of more than two milion Palestinians forced to live in exile in refugee camps.

Israel and Egypt have been negotiating on this autonomy plan since 1978 – and after all these years there is still not the faintest glimmer of an agreement in sight. There have been more than enough negotiations in this period, and time and again the Palestinians have been discussed. But these were negotiations *about* the Palestinians. The Palestinians themselves – as so often in the history of this conflict – were excluded from negotiations. Palestinians in the occupied areas have stressed again and again that only the PLO is entitled to negotiate in their name on the future of Palestine. As the American special envoy in the Middle East complained in October 1980: 'We simply could not find any moderate Palestinians who weren't in the PLO.'

The Israeli 'self-government plan' – officially approved by the Israeli cabinet – confirmed Palestinian fears that self-government would be no more than a legalized form of Israeli occupation.

Israel's major and publicly stated goal is to use this autonomy plan as a means of preventing the establishment of a Palestinian State and extending its domination and control of the occupied territories. On 27 December 1979 Begin told Israeli soldiers in Jerusalem: 'Everyone makes statements, but we are here! And if we say there won't be a Palestinian State, that is what counts.' And he added: 'No part of the country will be excluded from Jewish settlement.'

Therefore – according to the Israeli government plan – 'self-government' could only apply to the inhabitants, not to the land itself and not to Jewish settlers. The Israeli army would maintain control of the 'self-governed areas' and Jewish settlement would continue. An Israeli body would be responsible for the question of access to and use of water –

a critical factor in the agricultural development of the occupied areas.

Arab candidates for the 'Administrative Council', the executive organ of 'self-government', are vetted by Israeli security to ensure that there are no pro-PLO candidates among them. The administrative council is responsible for social and religious affairs, education and health and supervision of 'local police bodies'. It may not issue passports, issue its own currency or grant export and import licences. It is also forbidden to run radio or television stations. Registration and approval of land possession remains in the hands of the Israeli authorities.

The list of prohibitions and restrictions is in fact much longer. One Palestinian mayor in the occupied areas summed up the self-government plan by saying that it permitted at best 'a self-governed Palestinian refuse disposal department'.

The plan scarcely conforms to the United Nations Charter which affirms every people's rights to self-determination. It does not represent even a first step towards the granting of the right to self-determination – as the Israelis ruthlessly demonstrated by dismissing the democratically elected mayors of Al-Bireh, Nablus, Ramallah and Anabta in spring 1982.

International law has no provisions for self-government in cases where a country is under foreign occupation. Self-government implies the recognition of a central government – and recognition of such a government would be tantamount to approval of foreign occupation. 'Self-government' is therefore nothing but a first step towards annexation of the occupied territories. This would get round the problem of the Palestinian people's right to self-determination.

Sadat and Begin were awarded the Nobel Prize for this 'peace' in 1980. It is surely one of the ironies of history that Menachem Begin, once on the British wanted list as a terrorist, should receive such a prize for a peace which is no peace at all.

Less than four months after Sadat's visit to Jerusalem, 30,000 Israeli troops, supported by tanks and aeroplanes, attacked the PLO in Lebanon. South Lebanon was occupied and only evacuated after United Nations' intervention. However, Sa'ad Haddad's enclave in southern Lebanon provided the Israelis with yet another base from which to launch military operations in that country. Even after the official signing of the 'peace treaty', Israeli bombings of Palestinian refugee camps continued unabated. Time bombs disguised as toys were dropped on the refugee camps and children who picked up these 'presents' from the sky had their arms and legs blown off. Fragmentation bombs rained down from the sky, hitting first and foremost the civilian population. Hospitals and schools collapsed like packs of cards beneath Israeli bombs. The Camp David 'peace' had a truly terrifying face for the Palestinians.

But this was not all. The Israeli cabinet had officially approved the murder of PLO leaders as a 'protective measure against terrorism'. In January 1979, Abu Hassan Salameh, one of Yasser Arafat's closest advisers, was blown up and killed by a car bomb in the Rue Verdun in Beirut. Three people with him and four pedestrians were also killed and 18 people were injured. The bomb was detonated by remote control. Investigations centred on a British passport-holder, Erika Mary Chambers, who had rented a flat in the Rue Verdun and disappeared after the assassination. The Volkswagen car in which the bomb was hidden had been hired by an Englishman, Peter Scrivers. Further investigations showed that the assassination had been prepared and planned in the Federal Republic of Germany.

Abu Hassan Salameh came from a Palestinian family with a tradition of struggle for the Palestinian cause. His father had been a Palestinian resistance leader in the 1930s and was killed in action by the Haganah.

At the funeral, Abu Hassan's son stood beside Yasser Arafat at the graveside. Though he was still only a child, his face showed his determination to continue in the tradition of his father and grandfather.

The Israeli secret service used Golda Meir's vow to avenge Munich as their pretext for this murder. Abu Salameh was, it is true, concerned with security questions, but everyone knew that he had nothing whatever to do with the Munich attack. Abu Hassan Salameh was a Palestinian politician with good connections in the US State Department and with many other important international political contacts. The purpose of the attack was to reduce the PLO's political influence.

While the autonomy negotiations dragged on and the word 'peace' was mouthed and devalued in the press, Israeli bombers attacked Lebanon, Israeli gunboats shelled Palestinian refugee camps and Lebanese towns from the sea and Menachem Begin's henchman Sa'ad Haddad used Israeli artillery to reduce towns and villages in southern Lebanon to rubble.

Under the Camp David 'peace umbrella', Begin annexed Jerusalem in July 1980, ordered the bombing of a nuclear reactor in Baghdad and, in July 1981, ordered the bombing of the Fakhani district of Beirut. More than 300 people were killed in this attack alone. The 14-day war in July 1981 resulted in 2,000 deaths among the Palestinian and Lebanese civilian population. In 1981 the Knesset annexed the Golan Heights. Today, it is even threatening to annex the West Bank and the Gaza strip.

Even the most prejudiced observers must find it difficult to see this as a policy of peace or even as a single step towards peace. The Camp David agreement has simply provided Israel with convenient cover to continue its intransigent policy, launch new military operations in Lebanon, consolidate its annexations and continue its expansionism.

Israel blatantly violated the armistice agreement reached with the PLO in November 1981 after United Nations' mediation. Two days before the final evacuation of Sinai, the Israeli air force again bombed targets in Lebanon. This was a thinly disguised attempt to provoke the PLO into further military confrontation and thus gain a pretext for postponing withdrawal from Sinai.

Camp David: A Blind Alley

The Israelis have applied their savagely repressive policies not only against the PLO in Lebanon but also against Palestinians in occupied Palestine. Children have been shot dead in demonstrations, youths have been abducted by settlers and their mutilated bodies have been found later, democratically elected mayors have been dismissed from office, assassinated or simply deported.

In recent years the Begin government has given the go-ahead for 85 new Israeli settlements. Up to 1980 Israel had appropriated and brought under its control 40% of the occupied West Bank and of the Gaza strip.

Only two days after the evacuation of Sinai, Menachem Begin again stressed that Israel would never abandon its claims to sovereignty over the occupied areas and that Israel's right and claim to 'Eretz Israel' was valid in perpetuity.

Today, all responsible politicians know – whatever statements they may make for reasons of political opportunism – that Camp David has not brought peace. The Palestinian problem remains unsolved. The uprisings and protests of the Palestinian people in the occupied areas, which date from the introduction of 'Civilian Administration' on 1 November 1981, have directed world attention to the critical issue in the Middle East.

Today, Israel has one front less to defend. There is no longer any talk of 'border disputes' and negotiations. Right to the end, the Israeli government connived with supporters of the extremist settlement movement Gush Emunim and the fanatic Meir Kahane who were attempting to stop the withdrawal from Sinai.

On 25 April 1982, the anniversary of Israeli withdrawal from Sinai, Israeli Defence Minister Ariel Sharon issued an order of the day to the army revealing the reason for the spectacular manoeuvre to evacuate the Yamit settlement. He said that Israel had reached the 'red limit of concessions'. From then on, there would be no more withdrawals from Israeli settlements.

Peace has got lost up a blind alley. And the burden of occupation has again fallen on the Palestinian people alone.

The verdict of Shimon Peres, leader of the Israeli Labour party, on Camp David: 'It was like a Hollywood film the wrong way round – the happy ending came at the beginning.'

23. Occupation or Liberation? Israel in the West Bank and Gaza

'If one wishes to colonize a country in which people are already living, one has to establish a garrison in this country or else find a benefactor to establish this garrison for you. Zionism is a pioneer adventure and it therefore stands or falls with the question of armed force.'[1]

Zeev Jabotinsky, the great teacher of Israeli Prime Minister Menachem Begin, wrote these words in 1925. He was to be proved right. Great Britain provided the garrison until the founding of the Jewish State in 1948; and thereafter Israel ran its own garrison with support from the United States.

The State of Israel was created by force of arms in 1948. And in the war of June 1967, the West Bank, Gaza, the Golan Heights and Sinai were conquered and occupied by force of arms.

The Israeli occupying forces have ruled the West Bank and Gaza for 16 years. In the first years after 1967, Israel regarded itself as an occupying force, dubbing itself 'the most liberal occupying force in the world'. This view has now changed. Today the official Israeli terms for the West Bank are the biblical names of 'Judaea and Samaria'. The occupying force has now declared itself the 'liberator' of these areas.

The consequence of this liberation is that Israel has declared its intention never to leave the West Bank and Gaza.

This is today the official strategy of the Israeli government and the settlement department of the World Zionist Organization. For the past 16 years, Israel has massively increased its presence in the occupied areas, taking control of every sector. Politically, the areas are under military rule, and the Israelis have brought the industrial, cultural and educational systems completely into line with the requirements of the Israeli market, and of Israeli settlement and land acquisition policies.

The key feature of Israeli strategy has remained unchanged since the beginning of Zionist immigration to Palestine: land acquisition. Official propaganda cites military and strategic reasons for the Israeli occupation or else invokes, as it did before 1948, the familiar magic word 'security'. In reality, the Israeli goal is the gradual expulsion of the inhabitants and appropriation of the conquered lands. The trusted methods of the past are once again proving their worth.

On 12 June 1967, two days before the armistice, the Israeli army destroyed the villages of Yalu, Beit Nuba and Imwas. The villagers, now refugees, were left to wander for days without food or drink before they were sent to Beit Sira. There, too, Israeli bulldozers had already started their work of destruction. Israeli journalist Amos Kennan wrote: 'The children dragging along the road crying will be fedayeen in 19 years. On that day we lost our victory.'[2]

Today, the land on which these three villages once stood has been turned into the Canada Memorial Park and Israeli fields.

As General Dayan said at the time: 'We must bring about accomplished facts in these liberated areas without formally proclaiming annexation.'[3] This is precisely what has happened.

However, Israel faced a considerable problem. When the State of Israel was founded in 1948, the vast majority of Palestinian inhabitants either fled or were expelled. But in 1967, about 750,000 Palestinians remained in the occupied territories. Direct annexation would have created serious demographic problems for a 'purely Jewish State'. Annexation would have to be a carefully planned, long-term process.

Security Council Resolution 242 calling for Israeli withdrawal from the areas conquered in 1967, comparatively speaking, was the least of Israel's problems. The West never put the Israeli government under any serious pressure to implement the resolution and so Israel has to this day avoided complying with it.

Even before the end of 1967, the Labour government started building new Israeli settlements in the occupied territories – mainly in strategically important areas. Their main purpose was to ensure a military and physical Israeli presence in those areas, which in the long run were to become part of 'Eretz Israel'. Social Democratic Foreign Minister Yigal Allon said in 1976:

> Settlements will be established in strategically important areas, along existing borders or near areas which will probably be border areas in the future . . . I regard these settlements as a major contribution to the security of our State.[4]

And in fact the first settlements were concentrated in the very fertile Jordan valley, on the Golan Heights, in northern Sinai and in certain strategic points on the West Bank. This settlement policy in the early years of occupation constituted a victory for the 'populationists' as opposed to the 'territorialists'. Populationists regarded maintaining the Jewish majority as the prime goal, whereas territorialists argued for the acquisition of as much territory as possible. The main concern of the 'populationists' was the higher Arab birth rate. Golda Meir, the former Israeli Prime Minister, expressed this concern with remarkable honesty when she said how sad she was to wake up every morning and think how many Arab children had been born in the West Bank during the night.[5]

Menachem Begin's coming to power in 1977 represented a victory for the territorialists, who were not prepared to make territorial concessions in the West Bank and Gaza as part of a peace treaty. He said:

'We will establish new settlements in Judaea, Samaria, the Gaza strip and the Golan Heights.'[6]

'Settlement is a right and a duty. We must and we will continue to exercise this right and carry out this duty.'[7]

Settlement and judaization of the West Bank and the Gaza strip were and still continue to be central features of the Likud government's programme. In six years of office, Menachem Begin has allowed about 80 new settlements to be built. The 15,000 to 20,000 settlers now living in the West Bank and the Gaza strip will be joined in the next five years by another 80,000. Eleven new Nahal settlements, paramilitary strategic villages, were established in Israel and the occupied territories in 1982 to mark the 35th anniversary of the founding of the State of Israel.

The settlement policy was masterminded by the Israeli General and Minister of Defence, Ariel Sharon, who also controlled all the major departments concerned with settlement policies. The 'Sharon Plan' is the Israeli government's official settlement policy. It envisages several north-south settlement strips, reinforced by several settlement belts running from west to east. The plan has two main objectives: to encircle the heavily populated Arab areas and to break up or fragment the West Bank. One of the consequences of the Israeli plan to build a canal from the Mediterranean to the Dead Sea would be further fragmentation of the country. The purpose of the plan is to exclude any possibility of territorial compromise on the West Bank and Gaza and to prevent the establishment of a whole and undivided Palestinian State. The Palestinians would be forced into enclaves where, like the Palestinians in Israel, they would be a minority whose rights were not worth the paper they were written on.

Jerusalem, according to this plan – already largely realized – was to be surrounded by satellite towns, thus establishing a 'Greater Jerusalem' and altering the demographic structure to Israel's advantage. Further settlements are also planned for the already over-populated Gaza strip, to compensate for the settlements lost in the evacuation of Sinai. In a World Zionist Organization report on 'Settlement in Judaea and Samaria: Strategy, Policy and Plans' (1978), Matityahu Drobless, head of the Settlement Department, confirmed Israeli policies:

> There can be no doubt whatever of our intention to keep the areas of Judaea and Samaria for ever. Otherwise the minority could become discontented, with the result that repeated efforts would be made to establish an Arab State in these areas. The best and most effective method of crushing all doubt about our intention to keep Judaea and Samaria for ever is to strengthen the settlement movement.[8]

When the five-year transition period of the Camp David agreement has expired, the Israeli government will press its 'claims to sovereignty' over the occupied territories. The annexation of Jerusalem and the Golan Heights has already demonstrated what this will mean.

Two further conclusions may reasonably be drawn from settlement activity and settlement plans: 1) the settlement policy in the occupied territory is based not on 'security requirements' but on the declared intention to make the occupied territories into 'liberated' areas; 2) the purpose of the Camp David agreements was not to introduce Palestinian 'self-government' but to legalize occupation, i.e. to incorporate the West Bank and the Gaza strip into Israeli territory.

And the only Western democracy in this region has also introduced a law, to make matters absolutely watertight and 'constitutional'. This law states that in future no Israeli settlements may be demolished or disbanded, not even within the framework of a peace treaty! The Israeli government's actual settlement policies go even further than this. Settlers are to be encouraged not only to settle around Arab centres of population but actually *in* these centres. Kiryat Arba, for example, is a 4,000-man settlement near Hebron. In Hebron town centre, several buildings have been occupied by Gush Emunim fanatics who drove out the original Palestinian inhabitants. This illegal occupation was later given the blessing and financial backing of the Begin government. Israeli settlement projects cost thousands of millions of dollars – yet despite Israel's precarious economic situation and high inflation rate of 130% per year, funds always seem to be available for settlements. The Sharon settlement plan envisages the building of 10,000 to 15,000 dwelling units each year for the next five years – and this will cost £(Israeli)150,000 million. These policies could hardly be financed without donations from Jews throughout the world and preferential treatment for Israel from the Western powers (capital loans, favoured nation status, etc.). The problem of 'judaization' and settlement is not confined to the areas occupied in 1967. In Galilee, Arabs constitute almost 50% of the population – and the increase in the Palestinian population there is regarded as a 'demographic time bomb', which has to be defused. In 1977 Sharon said that he had 'begun to take drastic measures to prevent foreigners taking over national territory.'[9]

These drastic measures conform to a secret memorandum on the 'judaization of Galilee' written by Israel König, Commissioner for North Galilee. This so-called König Plan, which opens with a grotesquely racist description of the 'Arab mind', contained recommendations which have since become Israeli government policy. They include increasing appropriation of Arab land, control of education and other Palestinian institutions, a discriminatory tax on large Palestinian families, a break in all connections between Galilee and the West Bank, refusal of permission to build houses, etc.

The conquest of Palestine by no means ended with the foundation of the State of Israel. The 'vision' of a 'purely Jewish State' and the legitimation of the Zionist claim to Palestine will tolerate no 'foreigners'. Palestinians are either expelled or forced to leave.

Israeli settlement policy is both means and end in this process of displacement. The building of new settlements robs the Palestinians of their land and brings Israel nearer to its goal of gradually replacing the native population with its own settlers. The method of land acquisition in the areas conquered in 1967 differed little from that of 1948: the use of armed force.

Today, 40% of the West Bank and Gaza has been appropriated and colonized by Israeli settlers or brought under Israeli army control. 85% of the land appropriated or confiscated in the occupied areas belongs to Palestinian farmers, for whom the loss of land means the loss of their livelihood.

The most common method of appropriating Palestinian land is that of 'legal' dispossession, which operates as follows: the military commander of the area in question declares it a 'prohibited zone', for 'security reasons'. This procedure accords with Article 125 of the British mandatory government's emergency decrees of 1945. In issuing these decrees, the British aimed to limit freedom of movement in order to prevent conflicts and confrontations in 'restive areas'. Israel has been applying this decree since 1967 to prevent Palestinian farmers from having access to their land. After three years, the military administration found it convenient to apply a Jordanian law under which land left uncultivated for three years running had to be registered as state land. This enables the Israeli government to claim that it is merely using state land for the establishment of settlements. However, according to the Hague War Convention on Land, state land cannot become the property of an occupying power, whether the appearance of legality is kept up or not.

Another frequent pretext is that land has to be confiscated for military purposes (bases, barracks, etc.). The army then builds houses and barracks in the area; and after two or three years it leaves to make way for settlers.

Another method of land acquisition that seems tailor-made for Israeli requirements is that laid down in the law on 'absentees'. According to this law, all land and buildings whose owners left before, during or after the June war are regarded as 'abandoned property', even if the owner was only away on a business trip. This law has been extended since 1978 to apply to Palestinians living abroad. As Israel refuses to allow Palestinians abroad or Palestinian refugees to return, Israel has been able to take a further 500,000 *dunam* of land under its 'trusteeship', and this is also used for Jewish settlements. A Jewish settler gives the following account:

> Here in the Jordan valley we are cultivating a thousand *dunam* of rich, fertile farmland. This is – let's be honest about it – Arab land . . . , the land of 'absentees', people from Nablus and Tubas who fled to Jordan during the six-day war. These people cannot come back to Judaea and Samaria be-

cause the troops at the bridges have lists of names. The people in charge at the bridges are strict, and if you are an absentee landowner they just won't let you in . . . Some of the absentees' land wasn't suitable for settlement, either it was too stony or too remote . . . so we exchanged it for the land of Arabs still living here. Do you think they wanted to move out? We put, as you might say, pressure on them – we, the government, the military administration, the army.[10]

Another not infrequent method of Israeli settlement and occupation is the blowing up of Palestinian houses and villages. Since the foundation of the Israeli State on Palestinian territory, 478 villages have been completely destroyed. In the 16 years of Israeli occupation of the West Bank, more than 20,000 houses have been blown up – some as a collective punishment of Palestinian families.

Another common tactic is to demolish houses because of extensions for which no planning permission was granted. Thus the Palestinians lose not only their land, but the roof over their heads.

It must be stressed that these are not 'regrettable incidents' or isolated acts of violence by the occupying forces. In *Mahanaim*, the official publication of the rabbinate to the Israeli armed forces, the strategy of expulsion is described as follows:

> We therefore have to carry out an orderly and humane policy of resettlement over a relatively long period – not abruptly. This should be done in accordance with the fertility of the Israeli population and its capacity to replace evacuees and thus ensure that the land is not left uninhabited . . . The Arabs who live in this country represent an essentially alien element in it and in its destiny and should be treated according to the rules by which foreigners were treated in ancient times; our wars with them were therefore inevitable.[11]

This may have been largely theoretical in 1969. Today it is everyday practice in the occupied areas.

One of the direct methods of 'resettlement' is deportation. Since 1967, more than 2,000 people – mainly lawyers, teachers, doctors, town councillors and mayors – have been deported. One of the most effective methods of displacing Palestinians and depopulating the land is economic control over the occupied areas and political repression of Palestinians.

Israeli land acquisition deprives Palestinian farmers of their work and their livelihood, forcing them to emigrate or seek poorly-paid unskilled work in Israeli industry.

Israeli control of the economy of the occupied areas has led to serious structural changes. One is that the West Bank – which has virtually no industry – has become the most important export market for Israel's industrial products. On the other hand, agricultural products from the West Bank are subject to strict controls such as import restrictions, high customs duty etc.

Agricultural production in the occupied areas has not yet returned to pre-1967 levels. The number of agricultural workers dropped by a third between 1969 and 1977 and emigration rose.

Water is a decisive factor in the development of agriculture in the occupied territories, in the settlements and in Israel itself. The Israeli water authorities pump most of the water from the West Bank to Israel itself. The Israeli water authority or Mekorot has been responsible for the public water supply in the West Bank since 1967. This gives it a key position of economic and political power in a predominantly agricultural area.

The new wells which Mekorot has drilled are often right next to the old Arab wells. And as the Israeli wells are deeper, the Palestinian farmers literally have the water taken away from their mouths. There has not been a single case to date of a Palestinian being allowed to sink a new well for agricultural purposes – only seven wells for drinking water have been permitted.

The water supply in Palestinian villages has severely deteriorated in recent years. Many wells have dried out. Whereas many of the Israeli settlements have swimming pools and extensive irrigation plants, Palestinian villages and towns often have to rely on water-tankers for their meagre water supply. Seventeen wells sunk in the Jordan valley for exclusive Israeli use provide half as much water as the Palestinians throughout the entire West Bank are permitted to use.

This situation will continue according to the Israeli autonomy plan. Indeed it may get worse: with the number of Israeli settlements increasing, water will become an ever rarer and ever more expensive luxury.

Israel has boasted for years that Palestinians under Israeli rule are far better off economically than they ever were before. And it is correct that the wage level of Palestinian 'commuters' has risen under occupation in a relatively short time, so that they can now afford refrigerators and televisions – imported from Israel of course. However, wage and price differences between Israel and the occupied territories have now practically disappeared – and with it the short-term material advantage.

Palestinians today have no prospect of any improvement in their material situation, which is still worse than that of the poorest sections of Israeli society.

There can no longer be any doubt that the Palestinian economy under Israeli occupation has been completely geared to Israeli requirements. The vast majority of goods are imported from Israel. The West Bank exports labour and produces only a limited range of agricultural goods, which are promptly bought up and exported by Israeli companies. The deformation and dependence of the West Bank and Gaza strip economies are the result of Israeli occupation. In the political context, the Israeli 'integration' of the Palestinian economy is an important step towards final annexation of the occupied territories.

Israeli cultural and educational policies are such that they can, without exaggeration, be interpreted as a form of annexation.

The Israeli military government has here pursued, or rather combined, two courses of action: open repression and the creeping takeover and control of all decisions in the educational sector.

It is open repression when Israeli soldiers break into schools and universities, forcibly close them and arrest students and pupils. In the six months from 1 November 1981 to 1 May 1982, Bir Zeit, the best-known Palestinian university, was twice closed for two months. The closure of the university meant not only loss of time and money, delays in the period of study and postponement of examinations but also a stifling of political protests and demonstrations.

As Palestinian students and pupils are the most active protestors for the national cause, they are especially liable to persecution and imprisonment. A Committee for the Defence of Palestinian Rights report says:

> It often happens that soldiers or border police, who are notorious for their brutality, enter the campus and arrest students. They then take them outside the town and mistreat them so badly that they never recover from their injuries. (Mohammed Samhad, a 15-year-old from Nablus, lost the use of his right hand in such an incident in November 1976.) It also happens that students returning from abroad are arrested at the bridges and imprisoned, without explanation and without their parents being informed; the purpose of this exercise is to make them recruitment agents or Israeli police spies. A frequent method is to impose heavy money fines as a means of punishing their families. During the wave of demonstrations, hundreds of students and senior pupils were fined between £(Israeli)600 and 1,000, and now fines of £(Israeli)4,000 to 10,000 are being imposed. The purpose of this is to plunge people into poverty, forcing them to leave the country, and to break the resistance of the young people.

The military government controls the appointment and dismissal of teachers, admission of students and the curricula of schools. Many books which are freely available in Israel are banned from use in Palestinian libraries, even if they are scientific works or works of scholarship. Officially there are 3,000 books on the Israeli index for the occupied areas. Curricula and school textbooks are censored. The word 'Palestine' does not appear in them, nor do the Arab names of Palestinian villages and towns. Palestinian history has been abolished – to be replaced by the word 'Israel'. All school textbooks are riddled with the ideology of Jewish racial, religious and cultural domination and stress the political, economic and technical superiority of the Israelis.

The differences between Palestinians and Israelis – which are here presented as natural and God given – are in fact simply the result of Israeli control of education and training.

Palestinian universities are not allowed to establish technology faculties. Qualified Palestinian teachers are dismissed and replaced by less qualified Israelis. Of the 12,000 pupils who leave secondary school each year, at best only a quarter can go on to study at the universities.

Many of the textbooks are out of date, but the authorities refuse permission for new ones to be bought. The building of new schools or the extension of universities is also prohibited. A request for permission to build a new Palestinian university has been gathering dust in the military authorities' offices for years.

Israeli occupation has made the Palestinians what Zionist ideology claims they always were: inferiors and underdogs.

The tactics used in the educational sector are also used to crush Palestinian efforts to preserve their identity and culture. Exhibitions of Palestinian culture have been closed because of their 'inflammatory propaganda', or else stormed and smashed by Israeli troops. A picture painted in the colours of the Palestinian flag is regarded as sufficient justification for such action.

Many occupying forces adopt the culture of the land they have conquered, and Israel is no exception. The hostesses and stewardesses of the Israeli airline El Al, for example, wear uniforms similar to the traditional embroidered clothes of Palestinian peasant women.

Israeli archaeologists – including Generals Dayan and Yadin – have a remarkable reputation. In their quest for traces of the past in Palestine, they declare every shard or fragment they find to be evidence of their cultural heritage. The occupying forces even appropriate the cultures of the past and declare them their own.

Journalists, writers and artists are all subjected to strict Israeli military censorship in the occupied territories.

Israeli occupation implies the negation of Palestinian national rights – indeed the denial of the Palestinian people's existence. There is no place in the system for political opposition which questions the presence of the Israeli military or of settlers.

The Palestinians were and still are excluded from all decisions on their future and the future of their land, including discussions and plans at an international level. Violence is no longer the final resort – it is the constant, everyday means of enforcing Israeli intentions. In the occupied areas, this violence is embodied in military government and in the presence of the Israeli army. Israel rules with an iron hand.

It resurrected the British Emergency Defence Regulations of 1945 and has made them even more stringent. Former Israeli Minister of Justice Ya'acov Shapiro said of these laws in 1945 that they 'destroyed the principles of justice in this country'. He added that 'No government has the right to pass such laws.'[12] The climate in the occupied areas is one of constant repression. Palestinians live in daily fear of arbitrary arrest and humiliating controls by the army or by armed settlers. Political demonstrations are brutally repressed. In the demonstrations in spring 1982, 25 people, mainly pupils and students, were shot by Israeli settlers or by the army. One of the victims was a seven-year-old child. Cases of young people being abducted by settlers and their mutilated bodies being found later are becoming increasingly frequent in the West Bank.

Democratically elected mayors (the elections were organized by the Israelis) such as Fahd Kawasameh and Mohammed Melhem from Hebron and Halhoul have been deported. Four United Nations resolutions have called for their return and reinstatement, but so far they have still not been allowed back.

Bassam Shaka'a and Karim Khalaf – the mayors of Nablus and Ramallah – were injured in assassination attempts. No efforts were made to bring their assassins to justice – and there are strong suspicions that the planning and execution of these attacks was the joint work of the Israeli army, Kach and Gush Emunim (terrorist settlers' movements). The settlers need not worry: they know that the army and the government will not bother them.

Consequently they destroy Palestinian farmers' harvests, smash the windscreens and slit the tyres of their cars, break into their houses and beat up the inhabitants. The settlers of Kiryat Arba demonstrate their strength by marching up and down the streets of Hebron armed with batons and rifles and with Alsatian dogs at their side.

Israeli tactics in the occupied areas are remarkably similar to the Zionist *modus operandi* between 1945 and 1948; this includes co-operation between the government and the terrorist movements.

Israeli General Yariv revealed at a symposium at the Hebrew University that these similarities are not accidental but part of a definite plan:

> There are some who think that a war situation could be exploited to drive out 700,000 or 800,000 Arabs. Such views are widespread. They are discussed and the corresponding measures have been prepared.[13]

All these examples – from settlement policy to school teaching, from imprisonment to the smashing of cultural exhibitions – underline clearly that the Israeli government is doing everything in its power to prevent peaceful co-existence between Palestinians and Israelis. And one is forced to admit that they have been remarkably successful.

Notes

1. Zeev Jabotinsky, 'The Iron Law', in *Shahak Papers No. 31: Collection of Jabotinsky: His Life and Excerpts from his Writings* (1925), p. 16.
2. From *Israel and Palestine*, No. 43, October 1975.
3. Eric Rouleau, Hawks and Doves in Israel's Foreign Policy, in *The World Today*, 1968, p. 497.
4. *Yediot Aharonot*, 14 May 1976.
5. *Ha'aretz*, 25 October 1977.
6. Menachem Begin, in *Jerusalem Post* and *Ha'aretz*, 20 May 1977.

7. Menachem Begin, in *Jerusalem Post International Edition*, 3–9 June 1979.
8. *Vorwärts*, 6 May 1982.
9. *Ma'ariv*, 9 September 1977.
10. *Ha'aretz Supplement*, 20 October 1978.
11. 4/1969.
12. Quoted in: Sabri Geries, *The Arabs in Israel* (Beirut, 1968), p. 6.
13. *Ha'aretz*, 23 May 1980.

24. Palestinian Resistance in the Occupied Territories

Until 1967 the West Bank was under Jordanian control and the Gaza strip was administered by Egypt. During this period, political developments in each area differed markedly, but they had one thing in common: the traditional Palestinian élite were the leading personalities and held the key posts in local administration. However, whereas the Gaza strip in the late fifties and the early sixties developed into a centre of Palestinian resistance, all opposition in the West Bank was systematically muzzled. As late as 1966, the entire Palestinian opposition leadership was arrested and imprisoned.

In the first phase of Israeli occupation after 1967, the Palestinian population of the West Bank hoped that the Israeli army would soon withdraw. Resistance took the form mainly of memoranda, petitions and protests against specific actions such as the blowing up of houses, arrests, etc. Israel responded with harsher repression. A small number of leading Palestinians then decided to conform and accept the seemingly inevitable fact of Israeli occupation.

As the PLO gained strength, political resistance in the West Bank grew, especially after the battle of Karameh. Its inhabitants had begun to realize that the Israelis were entrenching themselves, preparing for a long stay.

The first protests came in 1968–69. Boy and girl pupils in many schools went on strike. Palestinian women demonstrated in Nablus and Jerusalem and committees to campaign against arbitrary arrests were formed. The first strikes by shops and businesses took place. The northern West Bank – especially the towns of Nablus, Tulkarem, Jenin and Ramallah – was the main centre of resistance, but there was also strong resistance in Bethlehem and Hebron in the south.

Black September in Jordan weakened the position of the pro-Jordanian notables in the West Bank, and gradually a new, more radical political leadership emerged. Its main demands were: an end to occupation, the right to self-determination and the establishment of a democratic government.

The first local elections under Israeli occupation were held in 1972. Only males aged over 21 who owned property or paid wealth tax were allowed to vote. Although there was resistance to elections under Israeli control even from traditional leaders, the Israelis used political and economic pressure to force them through.

Jordan greeted the election results as proof of the close ties between the West Bank and Jordan. Israel regarded the results as a step forward in the process of normalization. But nothing had changed.

The first years of occupation in the Gaza strip were quite different. In the June war, Egyptian and Palestinian units had offered fierce resistance to the Israeli army, and even after the armistice, several Palestinian guerrilla groups remained, with plentiful supplies of arms and ammunition.

Israel made its intentions of annexing the Gaza strip quite clear from the start. Thousands of Palestinian refugees were forcibly resettled, the majority in Jordan, the rest in Sinai. In 1976, Israel was condemned in the UN General Assembly (even by the United States) for this forcible resettlement, in flagrant violation of international law. The resolution called on Israel – in vain of course – to allow the refugees to return to their camps. The resettlement policy also had a military purpose. The huge refugee camps in the Gaza strip were a safe hide-out for Palestinian guerrilla units, and the Israeli army did not often dare to enter the camps.

The military government now used every possible means to break guerrilla resistance. Curfews were imposed for days and even weeks on top of the general ban on leaving the camp at night which was already in force. Collective punishments were frequent. The houses of relatives of fedayeen were blown up or their families were taken off to Sinai. The army had official permission to shoot on crowds if it suspected that there was a terrorist among them. The number of killed and wounded was especially high in 1969, when the occupying government allowed troops to fire at demonstrators, most of them women and youths.

When even these policies failed to break resistance, the army started to 'thin out' the refugee camps in 1971. Bulldozers flattened the corrugated iron and clay houses, tearing wide tracks through the camps and often not even giving the inhabitants time to collect their few miserable possessions.

The Israeli army, in tanks and armoured vehicles, could now move along these tracks combing the refugee camps for fedayeen. Military resistance was broken. Political resistance was only just beginning.

In 1972, at the tenth meeting of the National Council in Cairo, the PLO decided to intensify its political work in the occupied territories. For the first time, 100 leading personalities from the West Bank and the Gaza strip were invited to meetings of the National Council. The Israeli government responded by threatening to prevent anyone who attended the meetings from returning.

None the less, the gesture helped to unify Palestinians in the occupied areas.

In August 1973, the Palestinian National Front (PNF) was founded, comprising all Palestinian groupings and political tendencies. The National Front regarded itself as the political leadership in the West Bank and the Gaza strip. Its aims were to resist the Zionist occupying forces, to defend Arab land and to uphold Arab culture and history. It called for the 'restoration of the legitimate rights of the Palestinian people, especially of the rights to self-determination and return.'

From the beginning, the PNF regarded itself as part of the PLO. Though working underground, it succeeded in building up an organized resistance movement in the occupied areas.

During the October war, it organized the passive resistance of the Palestinian people. Tens of thousands of workers stayed away from their jobs in Israeli factories, thus paralysing many Israeli companies.

The Israeli government realized that the PNF was becoming increasingly influential and took steps to reduce its influence. In the first half of 1974, several PNF leaders were arrested and deported.

The PNF had extended and consolidated its influence by founding trade unions, professional associations and social institutions.

The PNF's position was also strengthened from outside. The recognition of the PLO in Rabat and Algiers, Yasser Arafat's speech to the United Nations and the passing of the ten-point programme in 1974 led to a series of sympathy demonstrations for the PLO and protests against Israeli occupation. The attitude of the PNF also influenced discussions and decisions within the PLO's committees; the passing of the ten-point programme is an obvious example of this.

The real test of the PNF's influence was to come in the 1976 local elections. That these elections were held at all can only be attributed to a would-be cunning manoeuvre by the Israeli government – a manoeuvre which backfired.

After the international recognition of the PLO and its political and diplomatic successes on the international scene, the Rabin government hoped that the elections would bring victory for the traditional Palestinian élite, whose attitudes to the PLO ranged from open resentment to total rejection. The Israelis reckoned with a PLO boycott of the elections. The PLO decided to leave the decision to the PNF. Only the 'Rejection Front' of the time called for a boycott of the elections.

The PNF, after heated discussions, finally decided to take part in the elections. Despite much Israeli harassment, culminating in the deportation of two popular PNF candidates, and despite the extension of the deadline for nominations (a concession to the very reserved traditional leadership), the election results were an overwhelming triumph for the PNF and the PLO, which won 148 of the 191 mayoralties and town councillorships. Karim Khalaf, mayor of Ramallah, explained the election victory thus:

> We are for the PLO, and we say this in our electoral speeches. This is our main electoral issue. The people who come along to our meetings do not ask about road improvements and new factories; we want an end to occupation.[1]

In the 1976 elections, everyone who paid communal taxes (rates) could vote. So, too, could women. This led to an extremely high turnout.

The Israeli newspaper *Ha'aretz* commented: 'The elections have become a national demonstration – and that means an anti-Israeli one.'[2]

The elections had wide-ranging consequences, especially for Israeli policies in the occupied territories. Nine years after the beginning of Israeli occupation, Palestinian identity was even stronger than before and the population openly acknowledged the PLO as its sole legitimate representative. The mayors of the West Bank maintained that negotiations on the future of the occupied territories could only be conducted with the PLO.

From then on, the mayors co-ordinated their declarations and activities in all Palestinian-Israeli confrontations. This concerted, consistent leadership strengthened the people's determination to resist; this manifested itself in increasingly open demonstrations against the occupying forces. The mothers of Palestinian prisoners held sit-ins at the Red Cross to protest against torture and inhuman conditions in Israeli prisons. Pupils protested against Israeli troops entering their schools. Shopkeepers went on strike in protest against the introduction of value-added tax or closed their shops to protest against atrocities by Israeli soldiers.

The most active street fighters against the Israeli occupation were and still are Palestinian pupils and students, as the events of spring 1982 confirmed. They are acutely conscious of political repression; and their individual and material prospects under occupation are bleak.

In the first weeks after the 1976 elections, six people were killed in the West Bank, two of them children. Some had been protesting at the provocative 'Eretz Israel' march by Gush Emunim. The resistance of these young people, many of whom were born and have grown up under occupation, remains unbroken, despite the high death toll.

The increasing protests and the co-ordinated resistance of the mayors soon prompted an Israeli response. Gradually the mayors were deprived of important rights such as the right to represent the town in relations with the military government, the right to grant building permission, control over municipal utilities, etc.

The purpose of these measures was to discredit the mayors in the eyes of the population and to reduce them to mere administrative functions. The Israeli authorities refused to give mayors any information on the whereabouts of arrested or imprisoned citizens of their towns – yet they readily gave this information to local notables who were less hostile to the occupying forces. This was meant to give the impression that mayors and town councillors were powerless to do anything for the local population. None the less, Israel still refuses to hold the local elections which have been due since 1980.

Even mayors who were not in the PNF or are considered 'moderates', such as Elias Freidsch of Bethlehem and Rashid Al-Shauwa of Gaza, have been forced to admit that the Israelis are doing everything in their power to prevent peaceful co-existence with the Palestinians.

The military authorities deported Fahd Kawasameh and Mohammed Melhem, the popular and established mayors of Hebron and Halhoul, as well as Sheikh Tamimi, the religious judge of Hebron. These three were spirited away at dead of night in Israeli helicopters, taken across the Lebanese border and left there.

The Israelis have had no hesitation in trying to physically eliminate mayors. The attempted murders of Bassam Shaka'a of Nablus and Karim Khalaf of Ramallah shocked and horrified world opinion. Bassam Shaka'a, who lost both legs in the assassination attempt, said: 'They may take my legs, but they cannot pull up my roots.'

The decisive reason for the Israeli military authorities' unscrupulous treatment of Palestinian West Bank leaders was the leading part they played in the rejection of the Camp David agreements.

On 1 October 1978, the mayors, town councillors, the various national institutions, the professional associations and the trade unions in the occupied areas signed a declaration condemning the Camp David agreements as 'the legalization of occupation, the incorporation of the occupied territories and intensification of Israeli control over the Palestinian people.'

The mayors formed a special committee, the National Leadership Committee, to organize broad and effective opposition to the Camp David agreements. The Israelis immediately stepped up repression, making the mayors personally responsible for civil disobedience. They severely restricted their freedom to meet and freedom of movement. The military government stopped payment of remittances from abroad in an effort to 'dry out' the towns and communes. And they refused to give permission for communal projects, such as road and school building.

The mayors, in speeches, appeals and manifestos to Palestinian citizens, international organizations and world public opinion, had pointed out the drastic effects that the Israeli autonomy plan would have on the Palestinian right of self-determination. This meant that these mayors posed a 'security threat' to Israel.

But resistance could no longer be repressed. In spring 1979, after the signing of the Egyptian-Israeli separate treaty in Washington and in spring and summer 1980, after the assassination attempts on the mayors and the Kiryat Arba settlers' attack on the Ibrahim mosque, a wave of demonstrations, strikes and violent confrontations with the occupying forces took place.

After the introduction of so-called 'civilian administration' on 1 November 1981 and the dismissal of the mayors of al-Bireh, Nablus, Ramallah and Anabta in spring 1982, all-out strikes paralysed the West Bank for weeks. In these demonstrations which spread to almost all the towns of the West Bank and Gaza, Palestinian youths with stones and sticks faced heavily armed Israeli troops. Yet the youths feared the Israeli bullets less than the Israelis feared their stones. These confrontations were filmed and shown on television throughout the world.

The united resistance of the Palestinian people in the occupied territories proved that the Palestinian problem cannot be solved by Israeli methods.

The growth of Palestinian resistance in the territories occupied in 1967 and the whole-hearted support for the PLO as the sole legitimate representative of the Palestinian people had even further consequences. The Palestinians in the areas conquered in 1948 – now third-class citizens in Israel – also became active. One of their best-known representatives is Tawfiq Zayyad, writer and mayor of Nazareth.

Palestinians in Israel fiercely resisted the König Plan attempts to expropriate Arab land and judaize Galilee. They founded the Arab Land Defence Committee and declared 30 March 1976 'Land Day'. Israeli police and military dispersed the demonstrations held on that day. In Sakhnin they killed six people.

Since 1976, the 'Land Day' has been celebrated on 30 March every year by huge demonstrations. A Jewish sculptor produced a statue to commemorate the Palestinians killed on 30 March 1976. This statue was set up in Sakhnin; Israeli settlers have since destroyed it.

However, criticisms of occupation policy and the harsh treatment of Palestinians were growing even in Israel itself. Israeli reservists wrote to the prime minister in 1980 that their officers ordered them, as a matter of policy, to humiliate and beat Arabs. Some refused to serve in the occupied areas. They were condemned to prison sentences.

Two Israeli lawyers, Felicia Langer and Lea Tsemel, have performed inestimable services on behalf of political prisoners. Their brave and committed defence of these prisoners has gained them world-wide respect.

One of the best-known and fiercest Israeli critics of the Begin regime and of Zionism is Dr Israel Shahak, a professor of chemistry and former president of the Israeli Human Rights League. Professor Shahak has written extensively on Zionism, discrimination against Palestinians, Israeli arms sales to the world's most notorious dictatorships, and the Zionist State's close co-operation with the apartheid regime in South Africa.

In his book *Non-Jews in the Jewish State*, Dr Shahak makes use of Israeli newspaper articles to reveal everyday discrimination against Palestinians and the latent racism of Israeli society.

Movements such as the Black Panthers and Peace Now also call for an end to occupation and for peaceful co-existence. The Front for Peace and Democracy, which has four deputies in the Knesset, is also an important political force.

This is not the place to mention all the Jews and Israelis who are resisting the policy of expansion and conquest, occupation and expulsion. Yet it would be invidious not to mention the two most prominent critics of Israeli policy in West Germany: politics professor Dan Diner, whose best-known books are *Israel in Palestine* and *On Barter and Violence in the*

Near East, and, above all, the Jewish poet Erich Fried. His poems contain insights and exhortation – not only for Jews.

These names and examples give cause for hope – hope in the possibility of equal co-existence between Jews and Palestinians.

The 'purely Jewish State' and the exclusiveness of Zionism negate the Palestinians, deny their rights and their existence. Palestinian resistance in the occupied areas has confronted Israeli usurpation for the past 16 years. In these 16 years, the movement has been tried and tested – and has emerged all the stronger. It is now a broad popular movement. The Palestinians in the occupied areas are a political force which, despite repression, has successfully resisted collaboration and capitulation.

Notes

1. *Financial Times*, 20 May 1976.
2. *Ha'aretz*, 14 April 1976.

25. Israel's Ideas on Peace

Attempts to find a political – or a military – solution to the Palestine problem are as old as the problem itself. There has certainly been no shortage of proposals, especially from the Israeli side. Ben-Gurion, Dayan, Allon and Begin – to mention just a few well-known names – have all put forward plans to bring peace to this region which have been much discussed in the West.

The problem is that all these proposals, regardless of their content, suffered from one serious flaw. This is undeniable when we look at them in retrospect. This flaw was their timing. The initiatives were always put forward when Israel was practising large-scale land expropriation, conquering new areas, extending its borders – or just before a war. In short, these proposals were always made when Israel had brought about *faits accomplis*.

This meant that the Palestinians and the Arab states always had new discussions, new positions and new conflicts imposed upon them. And of course Israel always had the best cards in its hands.

'Israeli peace' always involved new demands: from a 'national homeland' to an independent State, from the 1948 partition plan to the lines of the 1949 armistice; from there to the borders of 1967; today even Jerusalem and the Golan Heights have been annexed and Israel regards the border with Lebanon as 'open'.

This tactic of step-by-step conquest has meant that the word 'peace' has been flogged to death. Proposals which could have formed the basis for negotiation and compromise were rapidly overtaken by events. However, the vast majority of states today believe that if the Palestinian right of self-determination is to be realized, then an independent Palestinian State must be established in the borders of 1967, i.e. in the West Bank and the Gaza strip.

The most recent Israeli peace proposals have also concentrated on the future of the occupied areas. Though these proposals differ in form, they all have one objective in common: to prevent the establishment of a Palestinian State next to Israel.

The late General Moshe Dayan is often regarded in the West as a man of compromise, occasionally even as a generous friend of the Arabs.

Dayan, a hero of the 1967 war, was a minister in several Israeli cabinets. In 1980, he resigned from the Begin cabinet over disagreements on the Camp David negotiations. This seemed to confirm his reputation as a politician who sought compromise and reconciliation.

But Dayan was not really a moderate at all. In 1955 he said to Moshe Sharett: 'Let us hope for a new war with the Arab countries, so that we can get our land at last.'[1]

Shortly after the end of the June war, Dayan stressed the need for Israel's physical and military presence in the occupied areas.

His aim was to judaize and finally to annex the West Bank. He was one of the advocates of settlement policy in the Labour government: massive projects such as the settlements at Yamit in Sinai and Kiryat Arba in Hebron were started largely on his initiative. One of his most ambitious schemes was a plan to make the Gaza strip Israel's 'granary'. Dayan explained the fundamentals of his political ideas and his plans for peace in an interview with the Israeli daily *Ma'ariv*.[2]

His central premise was remarkably simple: Israeli military strength should always be great enough for the State to be able to rely on it for support for its policies.

Dayan demanded international security guarantees for Israel. But he added that these guarantees would only be acceptable if Israeli troops were allowed to stay on the Golan Heights. Dayan rejected demilitarized areas on military grounds. He also rejected any solution brought about by the UN or the major powers; he considered that Israeli policy should aim to prevent a situation in which a choice could be made between Israeli wishes and Arab wishes on the future of the occupied areas.

Dayan rejected out of hand any partition of Jerusalem, which he had played a leading part in conquering in 1967. For Dayan, the purpose of the settlement policy was to prepare the annexation of the occupied territories. This long-term strategic objective has become increasingly evident in the policies of Israeli governments since 1967. The intention is to bring about an almost total 'exchange of population' in the occupied territories. This argument, frequently presented by Dayan, is based on the thesis that the Palestinians were not driven out but that an 'exchange of population' occurred. According to this thesis, Jews from Arab countries immigrated to Israel and Palestinians from Israel emigrated to Arab countries. (This argument is quite clearly a retrospective rationalization, as there was no connection whatever between the expulsion of the Palestinians and the immigration of Jews from Morocco or Yemen.)

According to Dayan's ideas of peace, Palestinians who had not taken part in the 'exchange of population' would only be an unwelcome minority in the military fortress of 'Eretz Israel'.

Moshe Dayan, once a member of the Labour party and later a minister in the Likud government, did not seriously disagree with Menachem Begin's policies. Many observers interpreted his resignation in 1980 as an electoral manoeuvre rather than a protest against Begin's policies.

Dayan's response effectively prevented a territorial compromise, and Begin went on to make this official policy. According to Begin, the Camp David agreements will enable Israel to establish complete sovereignty over the liberated areas of Judaea, Samaria and the 'Gaza district', once the five-year transition period is over. This would mean the annexation of these areas.

The autonomy plan, on the other hand, looks like an attempt to appease over-zealous Western politicians and critics. The Israelis certainly never intended to allow the Palestinians any real indendence. Menachem Begin stamped on anything that suggested even a spark of independence, whether it affected the army, land, water, control of the education system, currency or the press.

Israel will not lay down the sword of occupation and annexation. Palestinians are regarded merely as undesirable 'Arabs in Eretz Israel'. The Likud party proposals backed by the United States owe much to the 'Eretz Israel' plans of Jabotinsky's Herut party and of the World Zionist Organization, plans which included parts of Jordan and Lebanon in 'Eretz Israel'. Menachem Begin and Ariel Sharon have not yet fixed Israel's borders. They have merely declared that they will never surrender what they have gained.

The Likud government has parliamentary and extra-parliamentary supporters for this kind of 'solution' of the Palestinian problem. The right-wing Hatchiyah (Rebirth) party even resisted the evacuation of Sinai and the Camp David autonomy plan. The fanatical Gush Emunim and Kach settlers' movements with their extremist demands give the Begin government further room for political manoeuvre in the international arena. Ariel Sharon and Chief of Staff Eytan are the unofficial but well-known advocates of these views in the Israeli leadership. For them, too, the autonomy plan is merely a tactical manoeuvre. They believe that Palestinians are strangers in the land – and as strangers they should either leave or be driven out in accordance with biblical practice.

From the founding of Israel to 1977, the coalition of Labour parties was in power continuously. Ben-Gurion, Golda Meir, Shimon Peres and Yigal Allon are among the best-known leaders of these parties. The Labour coalition (Ma'arach) is regarded – in the West at least – as 'moderate' and 'pragmatic'. The key passage of its 1980 political programme is abundantly clear: 'The realization of Zionist aims on the basis of the Jewish people's historic right to found and maintain its State in its fatherland . . .'

But there is no denying that this party showed greater flexibility, especially in the eyes of world opinion, than the Likud government. It did not rule out territorial compromises *a priori*. Instead, it described them as possible in vague statements. The area in which compromises might occur were never defined. On the other hand, the Labour party also considered the Israeli army presence in the occupied areas to be essential for security reasons. The Syrian Golan Heights would have to remain in Israeli hands for the same reason. Peres, Rabin and Allon, in their public statements, put the blame for this firmly on the Syrians, who, they argued, were not prepared to seek peace.

Labour differs from the Likud bloc in other areas, too. Labour government policy was always to annex as many areas as possible with as few Palestinians in them as possible – to preserve the 'purely Jewish nature' of Israel. This was the thinking which prompted Shimon Peres' demand for a federation between Israel and the occupied territories. The Labour party rejected and continues to reject the establishment of a Palestinian State. Instead, it wishes to reach agreement with King Hussein on certain areas in the West Bank and Gaza. According to the so-called Allon Plan, 'authorized representatives of the inhabitants' would 'participate' in negotiations on federation with Jordan. The Palestinians would be integrated into an Arab environment – but they would not return. Allon planned a Jewish State in which an Arab minority would have minority rights. The borders of this State would be those of the Palestine mandate.

Yigal Allon declared on 20 March in *Yediot Aharonot* that Israel needed strategic security borders. The borders of 1948–49 could not be defended, and so settlement policy was a necessary part of Israel's security policies. Defensive settlements were to be built in Jerusalem, near Rafah, in the Jordan valley, and near Wadi Bissan. Two new Israeli towns would be built near Hebron and Jericho.

Advocates of this policy regard the Palestinian problem as solved – at least theoretically. They believe that the Palestinians already have their State: Jordan. Ideological and military attacks on the PLO are correspondingly intense. When Israel occupied the Gaza strip, about 40,000 Palestinians were forcibly resettled in Jordan.

Although the Labour government's policies were based on strategic security interests rather than biblical claims, the effects on the Palestinians differed little from those of the present Begin government. Begin has had 80 settlements build in five years – the Labour government's 'score' was 50 in ten years. As Shimon Peres said, the Arabs would have to pay the full price for the defeat of 1967. Peace agreements were to be signed with Arab states only, and would take the form of separate treaties. Jerusalem was indivisible and would therefore remain under full Israeli control. If no agreement were reached with Arab states, Israel would have to retain complete control of the occupied areas.

Since the beginning of the conquest of Palestine, the founding of the State of Israel and – even more emphatically – since the conquest of all Palestine in 1967, successive Israeli governments, regardless of their composition, have moved within an extremely restricted framework. The five essential factors in this framework are as follows: 1) no party disputes or doubts the Jewish right to the land of Eretz Israel, nor do they question the settlement policy or the expulsion of the Palestinian people; 2) the establishment of a Palestinian State on Palestinian land is rejected and actively combated by political and military means; 3) Israel's negotiating partners in the search for a political settlement of the conflict are the Arab states and not the Palestinians; those directly involved are ignored or discounted as political factors; 4) Jerusalem is regarded as indivisible and as the capital of the Jewish state; it is now annexed; 5) the solution of the Palestinian problem is handed over to Jordan. Jordan has quite simply been declared the existing Palestinian State.

All Israeli governments have followed and consistently and successfully implemented these policies. These policies could never lead to a solution of the Palestinian problem – and certainly not to a comprehensive and just peace.

Of course there is opposition within Israel itself to this 'national consensus' of the present and former governments. The political thinking of these dissident groups differs considerably. The Peace Now movement, formed after the Sadat visit to Jerusalem, advocates a 'little' Israel, which would retain its 'Jewish democratic character' and the abandonment of Greater Israel and control over a million Arabs. Peace Now also criticizes the expense of the settlement policies – they cost thousands of millions of dollars – and Israel's increasing international isolation because of its harsh policies in the occupied areas. Occupation, they argue, is sapping the morale of Israeli society. Peace Now does not, however, question the Israeli 'security interests' argument. It is opposed to the PLO, and the majority of its members reject the establishment of a Palestinian State in the West Bank and Gaza. Similar views are propounded by the New Zionism Movement and the religious-pacifist Os we Shalom (Power and Peace) group.[3]

The Shelli party (Peace for Israel), the Israeli Council for Israeli-Palestinian Peace and the newspaper *New Outlook* and its followers advocate partition of Palestine, on the grounds that it is the home of two peoples, equally loved by each. They believe that the best path to peace is to establish two sovereign states, each with its own national identity, which would then live in peace side by side. They do not question Zionism but regard it as the national liberation movement of the Jews. One of their best-known representatives is Uri Avneri, who has held several discussions with PLO representatives.

In the seventies, the Black Panthers movement attracted a certain amount of attention in Israel and abroad. A group of oriental Jews, they protested strongly against their second-class status in Israeli society, arguing that there was a causal connection between discrimination against Sephardic Jews and the Palestinian question.

Nor should we overlook the many and varied forms of individual protest against Israeli expansionism and the occupation of the West Bank and Gaza. An Israeli pupil who refused to do military service in the occupied areas told a press conference in Jerusalem on 22 January 1980: 'If the only alternative is between being a jailer of the Palestinian people

Israel's Ideas on Peace

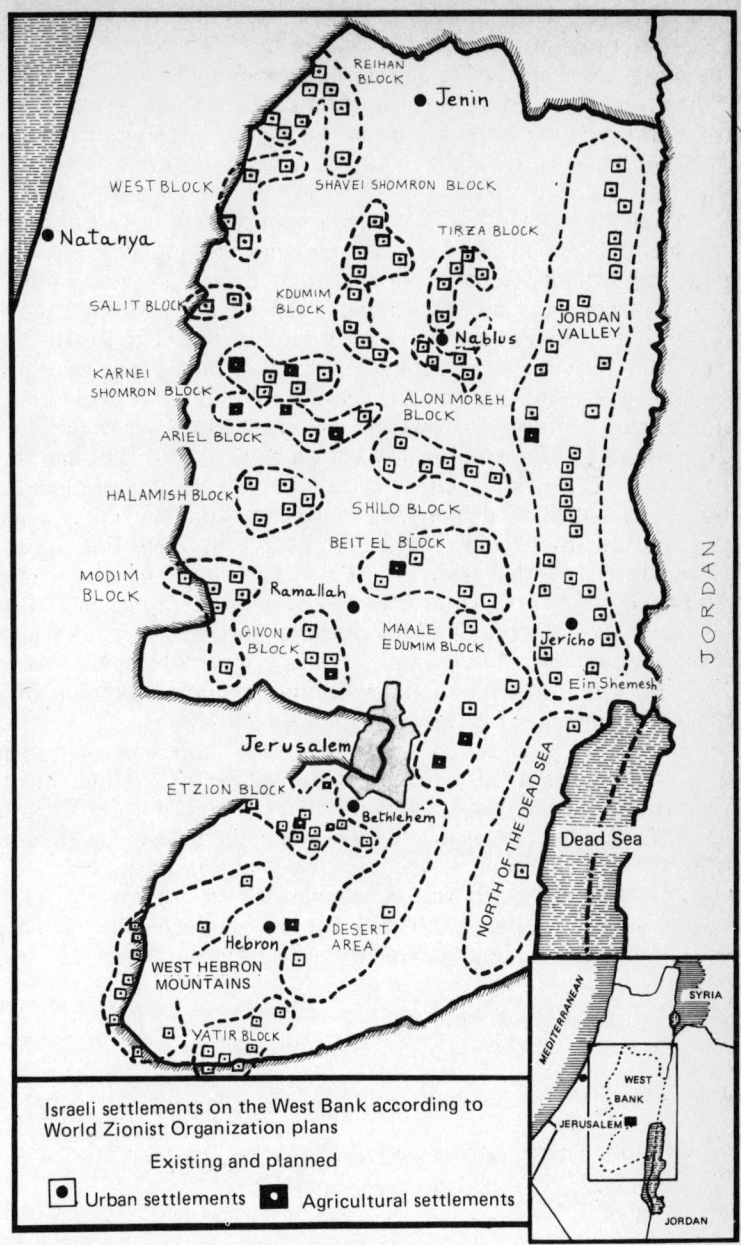

Settlement Blocks Mark the Land the Israeli
Labour Party Plans to Keep

in the occupied areas and prison for conscientious and political reasons – then we prefer prison.'

The pupil was sentenced to one year's imprisonment.

Some strict orthodox Jews reject Zionism on religious grounds. The largest of these anti-Zionist groups is Naturai Karta (Guardians of the Wall), who refuse to take Israeli citizenship, pay taxes or serve in the army.

The Democratic Front for Peace and Equality is also anti-Zionist, but for political reasons. It calls for two sovereign states in Palestine, recognizes the Palestinian people's right to self-determination and regards the PLO as the 'authentic and acknowledged representative of the Palestinian people'. This party has four seats in the Knesset. The Israeli Communist party Rakah is also a member of this front. There have been several discussions and meetings between Rakah and the PLO since 1977.

The severest critic of Zionism in Israel is the Israeli Socialist Organization, founded in 1962 and popularly known by the name of its magazine *Matzpen* (Compass). Matzpen argued that Israel was the product of a Zionist process of colonialization, a fact which has fundamentally shaped the nature of the State. Matzpen, whose long-term conception of peace does not always overlap with the PLO's, has made the most radical demands in Israel to date: complete and unconditional withdrawal of the Israeli army from all occupied territories; defence of Palestinian rights, including the right to self-determination and to return; recognition of the PLO as the representative of the Palestinian people; abolition of all discriminatory laws and institutions within Israel itself.

These proposals and views certainly raise hopes of an Israeli-Palestinian dialogue at least. But the dominant reality in Israel today is utterly different. There can be no doubt that the most influential parties and politicians in Israel see only one solution to the Palestinian problem: the destruction of Palestinian identity, the abolition of the Palestinian people as a factor in history with justifiable claims to self-determination and national independence. And this is the aim of Israeli policies, of their political proposals for a solution and for peace. This in short is the Israeli concept of peace in the region.

Notes

1. Quoted in: John Bunzl, *Israel und die Palästinenser* (Vienna, 1982).
2. *Ma'ariv*, 21 March 1972.
3. See: Bunzl, op. cit.

26. Israel Invades Lebanon

Israel's Longest War against the Palestinians

> 'He believed it would be enough to find a (Lebanese) officer, even a major would do. We should then either win his heart or buy his allegiance and get him to declare himself the saviour of the Maronite population. Then the Israeli army would move into Lebanon, occupy the necessary territory and establish a Christian regime which would form an alliance with Israel. The area south of the Litani river would be completely occupied by Israel and everything would be fine.'[1]

Zionist plans to conquer southern Lebanon go back even further than 1954. At the Versailles Peace Conference in 1919, the World Zionist Organization put forward a plan for the creation of an Israeli State going beyond the borders with present-day Jordan and Lebanon.

This plan was first put into practice when Israel invaded southern Lebanon in March 1978. Israel occupied part of southern Lebanon and then handed it over to the Lebanese Major Sa'ad Haddad, who founded his so-called 'Free Lebanon' on this territory two years later. The major whom Dayan dreamt of had been found and the first steps taken towards the realization of Dayan's plans.

In 1978, the primary goal was to weaken Palestinian resistance by military means. The political motive was to back up and guarantee the 'peace process' with Egypt, including the planned 'autonomy' for Palestinians in the occupied territories. In the following years Israel responded to the growing political strength of the PLO in the occupied areas and its increasing diplomatic recognition by demonstrating its military superiority. For the Israeli government, the threat of a large-scale invasion of Lebanon was more than just a means of exerting pressure. The invasion was prepared and planned as a general staff exercise, with tactics based on the experience gained in the March 1978 invasion.

In 1980 and 1981 the Israeli army carried out a number of commando landing raids and attacks designed to test Palestinian defensive positions, their readiness for battle and their strength.

In the 14-day war against the PLO in July 1981, the Israelis blew up all the strategic bridges in southern Lebanon to interrupt supply routes and test PLO infrastructure. The Israeli air force conducted bombing on an unprecedented scale. All this was incontrovertible evidence of Israel's intentions in Lebanon. The cruel and tragic climax to the war was the bombing of the Fakhani district of Beirut in which 300 people were killed. The Israeli air raids forced the PLO to act. It could not leave Palestinian refugee camps undefended, unprotected and exposed to enemy bombardment.

The attacks on Israeli settlements in North Galilee again provided Israel with propaganda to justify its air attacks on Lebanon.

The escalation of violence which the Israelis were counting on was prevented by international pressure. UN mediation led to the signing of an armistice between Israel and the PLO which was for the most part observed for the following nine months. Israel continued, however, to claim aerial sovereignty over Lebanon and continued its reconnaissance flights unimpeded.

In April 1982, a few days before the return of Sinai to Egypt, the Israelis flagrantly and massively violated the ceasefire agreement. Without any pretext or reason, the Israeli air force bombarded a number of Palestinian refugee camps.

Menachem Begin thought the time had now come to 'get rid of the PLO once and for all', as he put it several times. The first three months of 1982 had given more than just a hint that this threat was to be taken seriously. In this period, Israel massively reinforced its troops along the border with Lebanon, bringing up tanks, troop carriers and élite fighting units.

The Israeli general staff had also carried out several large-scale manoeuvres, including some in Major Haddad's territory.

All the signs pointed to an impending large-scale Israeli attack. The widespread and serious demonstrations against the introduction of so-called 'civilian administration' and the 'autonomy plans' in the occupied territories undoubtedly accelerated Israeli plans to strike at the PLO. Support for the PLO from the West Bank mayors who refused to negotiate in the place of the PLO on the future of the West Bank and Gaza had forced the Israelis to adopt extremely severe repressive policies. Knowing that dismissal of the Palestinian mayors would lead to an intensification rather than a collapse of resistance, the Israeli government resorted to the final means in which it was convinced of its superiority: military force.

'. . . The scene was set. All it needed now was the situation to trigger it off.'[2] The assassination attempt on the Israeli ambassador in London on 2 June 1982 was a threadbare but welcome pretext.

Only a few hours after the assassination attempt, the PLO issued a statement denying responsibility for the attack. Two of the assassins were arrested shortly afterwards and British Prime Minister Thatcher publicly stated that the PLO had nothing whatever to do with the attempt. On the contrary: the name of the PLO representative in London was top of the list of prospective victims. Menachem Begin's reaction showed that the Israeli government was perfectly aware of this. He said he did not care who was responsible for the attempt – he knew that all 'the threads of terrorism' were gathered together in Lebanon.

On 4 June, the Israeli air force conducted heavy bomb attacks on the Lebanese capital, Beirut, and on Palestinian refugee camps in the south of the country. More than 200 civilians were killed in these attacks on 'PLO positions'. The PLO could not simply stand by and watch these arbitrary Israeli bombings. It launched artillery and rocket attacks on Israeli settlements in Galilee. Only one person was killed in these attacks. The PLO was still anxious to prevent the conflict from escalating.

The shots fired at the Israeli ambassador in London were extremely tenuous grounds for justifying the 'retaliatory' bombings of 4 June. Two hundred dead against one man seriously wounded – this awoke memories of punitive mass executions in the Third Reich. The justification for a large-scale invasion was even thinner – and the Israelis realized this. So the Israeli government used the Palestinian reaction to their air raids – i.e. the attacks on settlements in North Galilee – as the pretext and explanation for their invasion of Lebanon.

The operation was codenamed 'Peace for Galilee' and the watchword was '40 kilometres north'.

On 6 June 1981, on a Sunday morning, the largest, most comprehensive and longest war to date against the Palestinians and the PLO began. Seemingly endless columns of tanks and troop lorries rolled into Lebanon. The Israeli air force conducted incessant bombing raids on Beirut: attack after attack. And the ultra-modern, computer-guided death systems of Israel's American fighter bombers seldom missed their targets: towns, villages and refugee camps.

Israel was to have the privilege of being the first state in the world to override United Nations peace-keeping forces, who could only look on and record the extent and brutality of the Israeli invasion. Only a few units actually resisted – but their efforts were doomed in advance. The Israeli war machine was rolling. Israeli cruisers and gunboats shelled the Lebanese coast from the sea. Troops were landed from the sea or by parachute. South Lebanon went up in flames. The towns of Tyre, Saida and Nabatiyeh were enveloped in huge clouds of smoke, evidence of savage and intensive bomb attacks. In the refugee camps, the small, frail huts collapsed like packs of cards under the lethal bombardment of Phantom and F-16 jets, leaving only craters of corrugated iron, dust and stones behind. Columns of tanks tore through the countryside: villages and towns were pounded into the ground by Israeli artillery. Thousands of people were buried under the ruins. Not even bunkers gave protection against the devastatingly destructive force of the bombings. The Palestinian refugee camps in southern Lebanon were almost completely destroyed: Burj El-Shemali, Rashidiyeh, Miya wa Miya, al-Bass, Ain El-Helweh – all either razed to the ground or uninhabitable. Saida and Tyre, two of the oldest towns in history, were 70% destroyed. Hundreds of thousands of people now had to flee for the third or fourth time in their lives from the Israeli army. After only a few days, more than ten thousand had been killed in the war. Artillery shells, grenades and rockets, fragmentation and phosphorus bombs caused terrible maiming and injury among the civilian population. While the official watchword remained '40 kilometres north', Begin, Shamir and Sharon were setting new targets: final 'eradication', the 'liquidation of the PLO'. The language reflected the unbridled brutality of their actions. Within a few days, there were 120,000 Israeli troops in Lebanon. Reinforcements were brought in day and night. In Israel, reservists were called up and sent to the front.

The Israeli government was pursuing three major goals in this invasion: 1) military and political annihilation of the PLO; 2) the establishment of a 'strong' Lebanese government with the aid of Israeli bayonets and the signing of a separate peace treaty with Lebanon; 3) the establishment of Israel as a regional super-power which would have all developments – political and economic – under its control.

To achieve these goals, the Israeli government and the army chiefs of staff hoped for a quick and overwhelming military victory. This was essential if Israel was to avoid political negotiations and discussions. This in turn meant that the timing of the attack was crucial.

No time for the invasion could possibly have been more favourable for the Israeli government than the beginning of June 1982.

The Arab states were at the end of their political tether, more deeply divided than ever before. It soon emerged that, even in the face of Israeli invasion, they were unable to find an area of agreement. They even proved incapable of agreeing on a joint communiqué on the Israeli invasion.

For over a year, Yasser Arafat had been warning his Arab colleagues at various conferences of another impending massacre of the Lebanese and Palestinian people. He had called on the Arab states to take measures to prepare for the expected Israeli attack. The Arab world expressed its solidarity with the Palestinians, but these words of solidarity never got beyond the conference-room doors. At the decisive moment, the Arab states left the Palestinians and the Lebanese in the lurch. The war between Iran and Iraq had weakened the Arab camp further. Thousands of millions of dollars were wasted in this futile war. All the mediation attempts of the PLO and the Non-Aligned States had failed. Israel was the main beneficiary of this war – in its crusade against the Palestinians.

Even when the Israeli invasion had been going on for weeks and the threats and dangers of the war were plain for all to see, the Arab states were still not capable of holding a joint conference, which might at the very least have produced a verbal condemnation of Israeli aggression.

The international as well as the regional situation favoured the Israeli attack. The political and diplomatic attention of the USA and of Europe was distracted by the war in the Malvinas (Falkland Islands). Discussions on economic problems in the West, and in particular the trade conflicts between Europe and the USA, further restricted these countries' room for manoeuvre in foreign policy. Public attention at that time was almost monopolized by the opening of the World Cup, to which the media devoted more time and space than the war in Lebanon.

Israeli Foreign Minister Shamir declared: 'We will smash the terror organizations, their heads, their feet, their land, wherever we find them.' And his Chief of Staff Rafael Eytan echoed: 'We will raze their headquarters to the ground.'

According to a Red Cross spokesman, there were 15,000 dead, twice as many injured and half a million refugees and homeless after two weeks of war in Lebanon.

Israel brought its entire superiority in arms and technology to bear, and its ultra-modern US-Israeli weapons caused appalling destruction and devastation. Israel also used poison gas. It was prepared to run the risk of almost complete international isolation to achieve its goal: the annihilation of the PLO.

After the march on Beirut, the peaceful capture of Falangist-controlled East Beirut and the capture of the government district of Baabda, the Israelis began a siege lasting several weeks of the encircled soldiers of the Palestine Liberation Organization. The PLO fighters were not alone in West Beirut – there were also 500,000 or 600,000 civilians.

As far as Israel was concerned, the civilian population did not exist. In the weeks of the siege, they reduced West Beirut to rubble. For days on end, West Beirut was subjected to a hail of shells, bombs, grenades and rockets of all calibres, from the sea, from the air and from land. Even at night, the Israelis sent up flares so that their fighters could continue their bombings.

The fragmentation and phosphorus bombs hit the civilian population the hardest, causing injuries so terrible that they were often inoperable. The hospitals and clinics of West Beirut were full to bursting – and exposed to Israeli attacks despite Red Cross flags.

Electricity and water were switched off for days. The best-equipped and most modern army in the Middle East resorted to tactics which would have been more appropriate in a medieval siege. The main victims were the civilian population. The supply situation was catastrophic. Typhus and cholera epidemics threatened. The hospitals soon ran out of the most basic necessities for the treatment of the dying and injured. But the Israeli government continued the bombardment of Beirut. Menachem Begin said he was prepared to kill ten Palestinians and five Lebanese if only one 'terrorist' was killed in the process. Israeli history professor Benjamin Cohen remarked that the term 'final solution' became popular in the Israeli media and press at the time.

The Israeli tactics, the siege of Beirut and the bombing of residential areas emphasized the fact that the Israeli government had left the PLO with the simple alternative: capitulation or annihilation.

The Israeli government's hopes that it would be able to force the PLO to its knees in a matter of weeks were soon disappointed. The PLO had been prepared for this confrontation for weeks and had taken measures to counter the attack, storing up stocks of food, arms and ammunition.

Generators were in place and in good working order. Water tanks were full. The PLO had expected to have to rely on itself alone in this confrontation.

Despite the PLO's military inferiority in arms, equipment and numbers, and despite the fact that the PLO was encircled in Beirut, Israeli calculations were proved false. This became the longest war in the history of the Israeli-Arab conflict. The ceasefires, often unilaterally proclaimed by the Israelis, were broken almost as soon as they came into effect and were no more than prolonged breaks in firing. Political discussions and negotiations with the Lebanese government and the US special envoy Habib kept breaking down because of joint Israeli-American pressure. The PLO had no choice but to fight if it was to avoid annihilation. It was a David and Goliath struggle: the Palestinian David against the Israeli Goliath.

This David resisted with courage and skill, striking well-aimed blows and using political cunning to counter the frenzied lunges of the giant Goliath.

The Israeli army did not observe ceasefire agreements. Only the day after the ninth ceasefire, which followed 57 days of destructive bombing of West Beirut, the Israelis launched a major offensive. Israel had shown that it could reduce an entire town to ashes and rubble, that it ruled the skies and controlled the sea. But every day the PLO held out brought it more political recognition – and drove Israel into greater political and moral isolation.

The Israelis' invasion was a calculated venture into the Lebanese quagmire. They wanted to annihilate the PLO and so give themselves a free hand for their annexation plans in the West Bank and Gaza. They wanted to establish a new order in Lebanon in a matter of weeks – with Beshir Gemayel as head of government. The Council of National Salvation which was to help bring this about soon fell apart. The election of Beshir Gemayel as Lebanese president in August 1982 merely confirmed that the Israeli invasion had split the country even more deeply. The vast majority of Muslim deputies boycotted the vote. Gemayel was elected in a military headquarters in East Beirut – at Israeli bayonet-point and with intense political pressure from the United States.

The Israeli army was not just an occupying force – it now arrogated to itself the right to control Lebanon's political destiny. Throughout the country, hate and distrust of the foreign troops intensified.

In southern Lebanon, the Israeli army crammed thousands of Palestinians and Lebanese into internment camps, yet still had to face a guerrilla campaign which inflicted heavy losses. The civilian population went over to passive resistance. In Saida, women and children demonstrated against the arrest and internment of their husbands and fathers. Israeli occupation of Lebanon is foreign rule – and its days are numbered.

The Israeli army, the super-power of the region, could not subdue an enemy which had no regular army, no aeroplanes, warships or modern missiles. The overwhelming superiority of the Israeli forces was not enough to eliminate the PLO.

But the siege went on – and so did its horrors: suffering, hunger, ruins, death.

From the beginning of the siege, various media gave the impression that the surrender of Beirut would take a matter of days. A glaring weakness of the Israeli invasion was that it could be justified only by false propaganda – propaganda which proved to be very poor indeed.

From a reading of newspaper headlines during the early stages of the war, it is easy to pinpoint where the weakness lay. First reports said, for example, that Yasser Arafat, the chairman of the PLO, was in hospital. Then it was claimed that he had sought political asylum in the French embassy. The final fabrication was that he was hiding in the Soviet embassy and would be evacuated in a Soviet warship.

When Yasser Arafat cut the ground from under these rumours and propaganda by giving interviews in Beirut, new propaganda stories were put about. Israeli and other reports rejoiced prematurely at the Israeli army's conquests. A week after reports that the Ain El-Helweh refugee camp had been completely overrun, the Israeli command was forced to admit the deaths of a general and several high-ranking officers – killed in fighting at Ain El-Helweh. The time-lag between the reported and the real capture of Beirut international airport was even greater – a period of several weeks.

Reports that a political solution was in sight shortly after negotiations began were more subtle propaganda and therefore more alarming in their impact.

The issues were no longer the violation of international law and of Lebanese sovereignty by the Israeli army, no longer the appalling extent of the destruction, misery and hardship suffered by hundreds of thousands of refugees and homeless. Nor did the media waste many words on the fate of the 500,000 Palestinians in Israel. All this was simply ignored. The most pressing question for most of the international media was: what was going to happen to the 5,000 or 6,000 Palestinian revolutionary fighters?

One minute, reports said that Egyptian ships had already left to pick up the fedayeen; then there was talk of evacuation to Damascus, sometimes with families, sometimes without families, sometimes with arms, sometimes without. The US 6th Fleet was even brought into this imaginary scenario – it was going to take the PLO fighters to northern Syria. No, now they were going to Sudan, it seemed. Their next destination was neighbouring Arab countries. Finally, Israel put the icing on this rich cake by generously offering to accommodate all the fedayeen in Israeli internment camps.

Readers were given the impression that the crucial problem, the Palestinians' right to return to their home and their right to self-determination, had been solved at a stroke – by the evacuation of a few thousand armed guerrillas.

It became increasingly clear in the course of the war that such a solution would have suited not only Israel. After first voting for UN Security Council resolutions 508 and 509, both passed in the week after the invasion, the US Administration changed tack, believing that there was now a unique opportunity to shift the balance of power in Lebanon, with far-reaching consequences. Incapable of a Middle East policy of its own, the United States eagerly seized the opportunity that the Israeli army had created. Playing the part of the angry but indulgent father who always supports his son when it comes to the crunch, the US government gave its blessing to Israeli aggression and at the same time attempted to play the part of mediator and preserve its mask of neutrality. The United States was determined to be both a player in the game and the referee.

The United States played its part to sub-B movie standards, as the US veto in the Security Council against Israeli withdrawal illustrated. No less a person than General Jones, Chief of the US Joint Staff, publicly admitted that the USA had been informed in advance of Begin's plans and was then kept up to date with new developments.

A further illustration of the US role came in the refusal of Alexander Haig, then US Secretary of State, to travel to Jerusalem to protest against the Israeli invasion. Haig, third man in the triumvirate with Begin and Sharon, later had to pay a high price for his close co-operation with the Israeli leadership. He was the first prominent political victim of this war.

The voting in the UN General Assembly showed that the world had no illusions about US-Israeli co-operation: 127 countries voted for Israeli withdrawal and two voted against. The USA and Israel were right out on a limb. The American government did not once officially condemn Israel for the invasion, and there was no talk of sanctions. On their visit to Washington, Begin and Shamir reached fundamental agreement with Reagan, although great play was made of the 'frosty atmosphere' of their talks.

The USA not only supplied the weapons with which Israel bombed Lebanon to pieces; it also provided the decisive political backing for the implementation of Israel's political goals. It torpedoed every attempt, whether by the UN, France or Egypt, to find a political and diplomatic solution – because none of the proposals would have enabled Israel to achieve its major objectives.

Without this massive political and military support, Israel would never have been able to continue the siege of Beirut, to cut off electricity and water, food and medical supplies.

Militarily, Israel was besieging the PLO – but in political terms Israel was under siege by the PLO. Israel's position – the voting in the UN General Assembly showed this clearly – was no better than South Africa's in world opinion. Despite military successes, the war in Lebanon was a political nightmare for the Israeli government. It was Israel versus Palestine – the confrontation had openly displayed the conflict that Israel had always attempted to conceal. The attempt to liquidate the PLO had backfired – the opposite had been achieved. The PLO was front-page news in all the Israeli newspapers. Never before had Israeli society been so directly affected by and involved with the existence of the Palestinians and the Palestinian nation.

The 'national consensus' which had guaranteed approval and backing for every previous war disintegrated during this confrontation.

In Israel, tens of thousands of people demonstrated against the war, calling for the dismissal of war minister Sharon and peace with the Palestinians.

Many leading Israeli figures publicly spoke out against the war. The 80-year-old Hebrew writer Mordecai Avi Shaul described what was happening in Lebanon as 'deliberate murder of a nation of refugees'.

The Israeli newspapers printed advertisements calling for an end to this murderous war.

Fierce controversies now raged in Jewish communities throughout the world. In Paris and Bonn and many cities all over the world, Jews, often for the first time, demonstrated in front of Israeli embassies, carrying banners saying in Hebrew and Arabic, 'Stop the Israeli liquidation of the Palestinians in Lebanon'.

The Berlin Jewish community drafted the following declaration, and many other Jewish communities elsewhere did likewise:

> As Jews who were once persecuted as such and as the children of persecuted Jews in West Berlin, we protest against Israel's invasion of Lebanon. Yesterday Jews were the victims of German nationalism. Today, Jewish nationalism is inflicting appalling suffering on the Arabs. This must be stopped. We call for Israeli withdrawal. Bomb terror, expulsion and disregard of the United Nations are violations of basic norms of international law. All this conflicts with all the humanistic traditions of Judaism. We are heartened by the increasing numbers of people in Israel who are demonstrating against Begin's war and for peace.

These ordinary members of Jewish communities were joined by some of the highest representatives of international Judaism such as Nahum Goldmann, who issued official statements calling for a fundamental solution of the Palestinian conflict.

Former president of the Jewish Agency Nahum Goldmann and two leading members of the Jewish world organization, former French premier Pierre Mendès-France and Philipp Klutznick signed the following declaration:

> Peace is not signed between friends, but by enemies who have fought and suffered. Our Jewish understanding of history and the dictates of the moment have convinced us that the time has come for mutual recognition by Israel and the Palestinian people. There must be an end to the fruitless battle of words in which the Arab world denies the existence of Israel and Israel denies the Palestinians' right to independence. The real question is not whether or not the Palestinians have this right, but how this right can be realized while at the same time guaranteeing Israel's security and the stability of the region. Plans such as the 'autonomy plan' are no longer adequate, they have led to evasion rather than clarification. What is now required is a compromise between the nationalism of the Israelis and the nationalism of the Palestinians. The war in Lebanon must be ended. Israel must lift the siege of Beirut to pave the way for negotiations with the PLO which will lead to peace.
>
> Negotiations must be conducted with a view to realizing co-existence between the Israeli and the Palestinian people on the basis of self-determination.

Israel had hoped to eliminate the Palestinian problem. Yet every new day of Palestinian resistance brought this problem further into the foreground.

The statements by so many Jews throughout the world showed that they had not only understood the deeper implications of Israeli policies but also that they recognized the existence and the rights of the Palestinians – which had been denied for so long.

Thanks partly to these protesting voices, criticism of the Israeli invasion of Lebanon became louder and clearer in Europe. The European Economic Community condemned the Israeli invasion as 'a flagrant violation of elementary human principles' and called for implementation of UN Security Council resolutions 508 and 509 and the immediate withdrawal of Israeli troops from Lebanon.

Austrian Chancellor Bruno Kreisky and French President François Mitterrand issued a joint statement containing the same demands as the EEC declaration and stressing the 'legitimate rights of the Palestinian people'. Both Mitterrand and Kreisky held talks with Farouk Kaddoumi, leader of the PLO's Political Department.

In view of the 'murder in Lebanon', Kreisky called for the imposition of sanctions on Israel in accordance with the United Nations Charter. Within the Socialist International he also pressed for a condemnation of Israel and a call for an end to the war.

The Non-Aligned States held an extraordinary session on the Lebanese war in Cyprus. They decided to intensify their support of the PLO and the Palestinian people.

The European press was now increasingly critical of Israeli methods. As a Swiss newspaper, *Der Bund* of Berne, put it: 'This time Israel is fighting not against Arab numerical superiority but against people on whose former homes Israel has been built.'³

Leading articles and reports now pointed out that the Palestinian problem could not be solved by military means and that Israel had gone far beyond its 'legitimate security interests'. The destruction of towns, the severity of the Israeli army, the maltreatment of prisoners in south Lebanon and the Israeli refusal to keep them in accordance with the Geneva Convention, its refusal to allow medical aid and food into the camps, the cutting off of water and electricity in West Beirut, the insane bombings: all this was severely criticized in the international press.

Israel's 'scorched earth' and military annihilation policies isolated it even further in world opinion.

Leading figures – professors, writers, deputies and scientists – protested in full-page newspaper advertisements against the Israeli invasion of Lebanon. An advertisement in a German newspaper read:

> Previous invasions of south Lebanon have not brought peace one step nearer. This new invasion has brought death, destruction and the miseries of life as refugees for the civilian population in particular. The longer occupation which the Israelis are planning will lead to repression of the Arab people and possibly also to further annexations. Such an escalation, which goes far beyond the bounds of legitimate self-defence, will not help the peace process but merely exacerbate the violence of the conflict. Three years of futile negotiations on autonomy and the entire policy for the occupied areas to date have shown that a lasting peace solution is not possible without recognition of Palestinian rights and Palestinian political participation. The new war will not remove these requirements for any peace solution.
>
> We acknowledge Germany's special historical responsibility with regard to the Jews. But this must not be taken to mean that we tolerate policies of violence which deny the basic rights of others.

One of the signatories of this declaration was Professor Helmut Gollwitzer, who had hitherto remained silent for reasons of solidarity with Israel. Pastor Heinrich Albertz, former mayor of West Berlin, spoke in a radio broadcast of his horror that the victims of fascism were themselves inflicting such dreadful suffering. He added that it would be a crime not to condemn this.

There was now a radical shift in public opinion in West Germany. The sympathy for the Israelis in the 1967 war now disappeared.

In countless towns in West Germany, Switzerland, Austria, the Netherlands and the Scandinavian countries – indeed throughout Europe – demonstrations were held weekend after weekend in which tens of thousands of people protested against the Israeli invasion and genocide.

Many demonstrations of solidarity with the PLO and the Palestinian people were organized, even in small towns and villages, and PLO representatives were invited to present the arguments of the Palestinian people. In an impressive display of solidarity, many people collected medical supplies or gave donations to show their support for the Palestinian and Lebanese people.

Israel's policies in Lebanon, the continuing devastation of the country, the bombing of towns and the deaths of tens of thousands of innocent people opened the world's eyes to the true nature of the Israeli State. People now realized that the Palestinians are one people with a right to self-determination and to return to their home country. This was a resounding political defeat for Israel.

There was now also a huge flood of solidarity from Palestinians in exile, thousands of whom volunteered to defend the rights and the existence of their people. In occupied Palestine, Palestinians held a general strike lasting several days. Huge demonstrations were held in all the towns of the West Bank and the Gaza strip – and were brutally repressed by the Israeli occupying forces. Five people were killed. The mayors and all the national institutions expressed their loyalty to the PLO and their categorical rejection of the 'autonomy plan' and so-called 'civilian administration' in the occupied territories. Israel responded by dismissing more mayors in Jenin and Gaza. Palestinians in the areas conquered by Israel in 1948 demonstrated, chanting slogans of solidarity with the PLO and condemnation of the Israeli war in Lebanon. Tawfiq Zayyad, mayor of Nazareth, was arrested by the Israeli police.

Israel failed in its objective of muzzling the Palestinians in Palestine. The Palestinian people inside and outside the occupied areas proved that they formed a nation.

Today, 34 years after the first Middle East war, the situation has changed profoundly. In 1948, the Palestinian people were wholly unprepared for the confrontation. They had to go to war without a leadership and without an army of their own. Even then, the Palestinians were left in the lurch by the Arab states. They had no spokesmen and made no impact whatever on the international scene: they were merely victims of the Zionist movement which was backed by the major powers. In 1948 the Palestinians were refugees, without an identity of their own and without a future. In 1982, the Palestinians had their own military organization, their own leadership and their own military units. They are no longer victims, but fighters. Their rights are internationally recognized and in the PLO they have a force which is representing their interests with ever-greater success on the international scene. The world has not only taken notice of Palestinian demands – it has acknowledged that they are just and legitimate. Throughout the world, people demonstrate on behalf of the rights of the Palestinian people. Israel, on the other hand, is largely isolated.

The great historical achievement of the Palestine Liberation Organization (PLO) is the organization of the Palestinian people. It has created the structures and the institutions through which the Palestinian people can realize their social, political and national aspirations.

The PLO has transformed a people of refugees into a nation which today confidently asserts its rights. The Palestinian problem cannot be solved without the Palestinians. It is also certain that there will be no peace in this region without the realization of the Palestinian people's national rights. All these developments in Palestine would have been inconceivable without the PLO, its political and its military struggle. The PLO has started a political process which is irreversible, whatever the setbacks and defeats.

A comment by Erwin Behrens, for many years Middle East correspondent of the *Westdeutscher Rundfunk*, confirms that the views expressed above are gaining credence. It is worth quoting Behrens' text of 21 July 1982 in full:

> For 46 days the Israelis have been fighting against the Palestinians, and the result surprises only those who have learnt nothing from history.
>
> It is becoming increasingly evident that Israel's military triumph in Beirut has turned into a political defeat. The Israelis in Lebanon are in the same situation as the Americans in Vietnam after their major victories. The Americans at that time erred when they succumbed to the illusion that they could bomb the Vietcong into submission. Today the Israelis are learning the same lesson from the Palestinians: superior arms are not a political solution. Prime Minister Begin describes the Palestine Liberation Organization as murderers, yet today for the first time the Israelis are losing a propaganda war because, after ten thousand deaths in Lebanon, they have relinquished all claims to moral superiority. We all know who is the David and who is the Goliath now.
>
> If the Americans want the Palestinians to leave Beirut, they must now negotiate with Yasser Arafat of the PLO.
>
> Direct negotiations will have no purpose unless the future of the Palestinians in their own home country is included on the agenda. If the Americans refuse to take this step, they must reckon with an explosion of anti-American feeling in the Arab world. The new American Secretary of State Shultz is no prisoner of Menachem Begin. Shultz has indicated the USA's willingness to recognize the PLO if the PLO for its part accepts Israel's right to exist.
>
> The PLO is prepared to pay this price. PLO representatives today publicly concede Israel's right to sovereignty within fixed borders – although such recognition would have to be mutual. The Palestine Liberation Organization has never been taken as seriously as a factor in Middle East policy as it is now, after a military defeat which the Palestinians have transformed into a political victory. It is a bitter irony of history that the Israelis, who started this war to liquidate Palestinian nationalism, must now, six weeks later, face the fact that world support for the creation of a Palestinian State is growing.

The PLO Leaves Beirut

> 'Tens of thousands of people lining the three-mile route from the stadium to the port. A deafening staccato as if from an infantry battle. Shots are fired wildly into the air from automatic rifles, heavy machine-guns, anti-tank guns, mortars and flak guns – a bizarre, traditional salute and an expression of grief for the brave fedayeen. "Chin up, we'll meet again in Jerusalem, Jaffa and Haifa" says a banner which a poorly dressed woman is holding in her trembling hands. A little barefooted boy is holding up a banner with the slogan "All roads lead to Palestine".'[4]

After almost three months of war and more than two months' siege of West Beirut, Israel had failed to achieve its objective. West Beirut still held out.

With every means available, the Israeli army had tried to tighten its grip on Beirut: artillery, missiles, tanks, mortars, bombers, fighter jets, gunboats and cruisers. Day and night, the Israeli army fired all its guns at the burning city. The Hamburg news magazine *Der Spiegel* carried the following report on 9 August 1982:

> Towards midnight, loudspeakers around West Beirut began to crackle: 'Attention! Attention! This is the Israeli army speaking. We call on you to leave the town. Our jets will be here soon. Run for your lives. Leave the battle zone.' Before anyone could even think of flight, the inferno broke loose. The people of Beirut had already experienced this during the Israeli siege – but this time it was far more savage than anything before. Before the jets came, 155-millimetre artillery grenades rained down on the area around Burj el-Barajneh camp. Then waves of Israeli Phantoms tore across the sky, dropping bombs on to the smoking and smouldering houses – including the pernicious fragmentation bombs made in the USA, against the use of which Washington protested to Israel. At the same time, Israeli warships off Beirut began shelling the coast.

Three times the Israeli army with its awesome fire power and troop superiority attempted to storm Beirut – and three times the defenders of West Beirut repelled it. Fedayeen emerged from burning ruins and with the simplest of weapons they stopped ultra-modern US-Israeli tanks. All Israeli soldiers wore bullet-proof vests and had air, artillery and tank cover for their attacks. Despite this the Israeli Supreme Command admitted that Israel had never before suffered such losses.

The Israeli army's dilemma was summed up in the Israeli daily *Yediot Aharonot* of 6 August 1982:

It is trained to fight regular armies, not guerrillas prepared to sacrifice their lives. Take for example the destruction of Sam missiles without loss on the one hand and on the other hand the inability of Israeli troops to take effective measures against 12-year-old boys using anti-tank missiles in the narrow streets of Rashidiyeh.

The article continues: 'In conclusion, we can say that Israel should do its utmost to force the terrorists to surrender, and to do so without a fight – to save the lives of civilians and above all of our forces.'

The morale and determination of the fedayeen were far superior to those of the Israeli troops. Their courage alone counter-balanced the Israelis' vastly superior equipment and their 20:1 numerical advantage.

The fedayeen tactics and their effects are described in the *Spiegel* article mentioned above:

> Used to beating the enemy in rapid, clever operations backed by heavy technology, the Israeli army now found itself caught up in a war of attrition with Palestinian 'irregulars'. The initial victors came under increasing pressure, while the losers' chances of gaining a political victory rose. To cope with entire Arab armies, the Israelis needed only seven days in 1956, six days in 1967 and 18 days in 1973. Now, though, against a bunch of 'terrorists' (Begin) and a 'mafia-like group' (opposition leader Peres) they were forced to mount a complicated, prolonged siege involving heavy casualties on their side – and the besieged forces did not surrender.
>
> 'From the strategic point of view, this campaign is the most foolish of all our campaigns' was Peres' verdict.
>
> Even though its ultimate fall was inevitable, Beirut now came to symbolize the possibility of resistance to the most powerful military state in the region, showing that the present Israeli leadership's expansionism and arrogance in its power could be checked.
>
> For the Arabs, Beirut could come to assume the almost mystical proportions which the Alamo took on for the Americans in 1836, when fewer than 200 Texans held out for 12 days against 4,000 Mexicans; or the name of Leningrad for the Russians, because the city held out for 900 days against the Germans and hundreds of thousands died.
>
> But Beirut means even more. For the first time in all Middle East wars, it was not little Israel resisting a seemingly vastly superior Arab force but a small band of Arabs holding out against the frenzied attacks of vastly superior Israeli numbers.
>
> The Israelis were disturbed to find the world condemning them in the moral terms hitherto reserved for their persecutors: war of annihilation, genocide, holocaust.
>
> The French President François Mitterrand spoke of another '*Oradour*', the English *Observer* newspaper wrote of 'indiscriminate slaughter' and the Hamburg weekly *Die Zeit* talked of a 'campaign of annihilation' and an 'oriental Coventry'.

> German sympathies were so obviously on the side of the Palestinian underdogs that the *Süddeutsche Zeitung* felt compelled to warn against the 'moral zeal with which many Germans, particularly young Germans, compare the fate of the Palestinians in Lebanon with that of the Jews in Nazi Germany.' It urged Germans to 'beware of such comparisons'.

The fortress of Beirut under its commander Yasser Arafat remained impregnable for one of the strongest armies in the world. The Israeli army failed to defeat a few thousand poorly equipped fedayeen.

Yet West Beirut remained under Israeli siege. The Israeli government was now looking for some new method to force a capitulation. The new method was: to attack the defenceless civilian population. The Israelis proceeded to cut off water and electricity supplies to West Beirut for longer periods of time.

Meanwhile, Israeli air attacks and artillery and missile bombardment of the besieged city went on relentlessly.

Hardest hit were the poorest of the poor: refugees from the south, inhabitants of Palestinian refugee camps whose little huts had been destroyed and who were now forced to run from cellar to cellar of West Beirut seeking shelter and protection.

Israeli propaganda tried to blame the PLO for this inhuman blockade. But the civilian population of West Beirut was not, as the Israelis suggested, a hostage in the hands of the PLO. It had decided of its own free will to stay on in West Beirut, even though it had the possibility of leaving the besieged part of the town. Israeli loudspeakers were constantly calling on the population to leave – with little success. And the Palestinian inhabitants of West Beirut could not leave even if they wanted to. The Israeli army deliberately prevented them, sending them back to become defenceless victims of Israeli bombings.

After more than two months of siege, with the plight of the civilian population growing more desperate daily – they had no water, no electricity and no bread – the PLO decided it was time to call a halt. It declared its willingness to withdraw its troops from Beirut and, after mediation by the Lebanese government and the US special envoy Philip Habib, an agreement to this effect was signed between Israel and the PLO. Despite this agreement, the Israelis continued their attack, as if trying to punish the population for its steadfastness and resoluteness by reducing the entire city to rubble. Uninterrupted 12-hour bombardments now began. In the Palestinian refugee camps on the southern outskirts of Beirut, not a single house was spared. The Israeli air force now did the work that Israeli bulldozers and tanks had already carried out in south Lebanon. Nor were other parts of the city spared. The Israelis scored a direct hit on an eight-storey block of flats, which collapsed like a pack of cards. More than 150 people were buried under the ruins. Despite all agreements, Israel was sticking to its intention of forcing a military solution in Beirut.

Israel ignored United Nations Security Council resolutions. UN observers sent to Lebanon to check the ceasefire were forcibly prevented by the Israeli army in Damour from getting to West Beirut. The Israeli government rejected the deployment of UN troops to supervise troop withdrawals from the front. Menachem Begin even described the UN as an anti-Semitic organization.

Israel would not allow the multi-national UN force into West Beirut until the PLO had withdrawn. Proposals for an advance party of French troops to ensure safe conduct for the PLO were rejected by the Israelis up to the end. All this underlines the real nature of Israel's intentions.

The PLO withdrawal from Beirut was not a surrender. The Palestinians agreed to withdraw only under certain conditions. While still in West Beirut, Yasser Arafat gave the following interview to *Le Monde*:[5]

> I am surrounded here, and I am speaking to Israeli soldiers and ordinary citizens. And I say to them: Stop now! Military arrogance will not break us. I would also like to greet Colonel Elie Geva. I greatly respect his humane attitude and refusal to take part in the storming of Beirut, despite our other differences of opinion. His noble attitude stems from true Jewish values. Peace will reign in the Holy Land, despite the arrogance of leaders who regard brutal violence as the only maxim for the co-existence of nations. I invite the militants of the Peace Now movement, of *New Outlook* magazine and all those who recognize our right to self-determination to come to Beirut and see the destruction and suffering of the population. The day will come when the Israelis will be ashamed and will be only too glad to forget what their leaders did to the Palestinian people in Lebanon in the summer of 1982.

The military defeat of the PLO in Lebanon and the withdrawal of the fedayeen – grave as they may seem at first sight – were utterly different from the exodus of the Palestinian people in 1948. In 1948, the structures of Palestinian society were destroyed and Palestinian identity was annihilated – and escape was into a dark, uncertain future.

Although the Israelis flung their full military strength at the PLO as the representative of the Palestinian people, they failed to destroy its structures. The identity of the Palestinian nation, dispersed throughout the world, is today stronger than ever before. And during the Lebanon conflict the world was forced to pay greater attention than ever before to the claims of the Palestinians. Wherever the PLO may be evacuated to, it will remain the representative of the Palestinian people and the guarantor of the political and social aspirations of the Palestinian people. It will not lose its international recognition. In this war the PLO proved to world public opinion that its cause is just and that the Palestinians need a State in which to realize their right to self-determination.

Those Palestinians who in 1965 took up the armed struggle against immensely superior Israeli forces were greeted with pitying smiles. Yet after only nine years the national rights of the Palestinian people, their right to self-determination and return, were recognized by the majority of world states – as was the PLO itself. The same leadership which achieved this was besieged by the Israelis in Beirut. Palestinian resistance could not be wiped out 18 years ago, nor can the PLO today be wiped off the map as a political factor in the Middle East. The future development of this region will certainly prove this. The solidarity of the Arab masses with the Palestinians, their admiration for their courage and steadfastness in face of such a superior enemy will bring about important reactions in the Arab world. Support for the PLO will reach hitherto undreamt-of dimensions.

The Israeli army, by marching into Lebanon, has blocked the road to peace. Israeli tanks have injured the pride of the Lebanese people. The opening of Israeli banks and company branches in southern Lebanon, the import of Israeli goods and Israeli economic penetration will lead to new tensions and conflicts. Israel is merely an unloved occupying force in Lebanon.

The military victory in Lebanon has made Israel poorer, politically and morally, and has isolated it further. On the other hand, the Palestinians' military defeat has strengthened them politically and increased support for their cause. The struggle for a home, for a country for the Palestinian people, continues. The Palestinian problem cannot be solved by military means. The Israeli-Palestinian confrontation is not over.

In the *Le Monde* interview quoted above, Arafat proposed that an international conference should be called to find a solution to the Palestinian problem: 'The course of history cannot be stopped. The war has shown that the Palestinians have fought courageously and honourably to achieve their just goal.' Arafat reaffirmed what he had already told US Senator McCloskey:

> We accept all resolutions, I say advisedly all resolutions, of the UN, on the Palestinian problem. Let us not forget that Israel was created by a UN resolution. Besides, Israel has everything, and we have nothing. Yet people call on us to recognize Israel, which for its part categorically refuses to recognize our right to self-determination. I will say what I have to say on the question of recognition, but not under duress, with Sharon's troops besieging us. And I repeat: the question which today is more urgent than ever is that of our right to self-determination.

Questioned about the Palestinian National Charter and the role of the armed struggle, Yasser Arafat replied:

> We have affirmed several times in our National Council that the armed struggle is no longer the only way. Many things have been said about this charter, and people have tried to interpret it tendentiously. To remove all ambiguities, I propose that when the war is over we should call a colloquium in which Palestinian, Israeli and Arab thinkers should take part to study these problems in depth and to reach conclusions. This colloquium could be held somewhere in Europe, possibly under the aegis of a party or an organization. The venue would be chosen with the agreement of all participants.

Notes

1. Diary entry by former Israeli Prime Minister Moshe Sharett on a conversation with the then Chief of Staff Moshe Dayan in May 1954.
2. *Süddeutsche Zeitung*, 8 June 1982.
3. *Der Bund*, 14 June 1982.
4. *Die Zeit*, 27 June 1982.
5. *Le Monde*, 10 August 1982.

27. Palestine: Confrontation or Peace?

'Israel's security interests depend on developments and events outside the area of direct confrontation . . .

We will have to extend the area of strategic requirements and security interests in the 80s; we will have to include states such as Turkey and Pakistan as well as the Persian Gulf and Africa, especially the states of North and Central Africa.'[1]

Many Europeans regard recognition by the PLO of the State of Israel as a fundamental pre-condition for the end of the Palestinian-Israeli confrontation. In political talks, discussions and interviews, Europeans are constantly raising the question of recognition of Israel by the PLO. They do so out of a genuine concern for peace. And many politicians in Europe and the United States make recognition of Israel the condition for talks with the PLO.

This attitude is perfectly understandable from a European point of view. One cannot simply shed the past like a superfluous second skin. Yet at this point it is legitimate to ask why Europeans do not ask Israeli politicians if they recognize the right of Palestinians to self-determination, a return to their country and a state of their own.

The fact that Israel is the only State in the world which has not defined its own frontiers should give Europeans pause for thought. Perhaps they should reflect on the reasons for this.

It is unfortunate that many people in Europe ask this question about the recognition of Israel with the best of intentions but without any real knowledge of the historical facts.

But the Palestinians driven from their homes in Jaffa, Akko or Haifa in 1948, who have lost their families. their homes, their country, who have lived in huts and tents in refugee camps exposed to bombing by the Israeli air force, who cannot return to their families because they are not allowed back to Palestine, who have suffered decades of hardship, misery and constant fear – these Palestinians have a quite different image of Israel, an utterly different experience of Israel from most Europeans. It is the Palestinian who has been driven out and deprived of his rights and who needs security. To demand that a Palestinian should give guarantees for Israel's security is to reverse the relationship between cause and effect, between criminal and victim.

In Europe the ugly rumour and prejudice has been put about that the Palestinians want to drive the Israelis into the sea. On this flimsiest of pretexts, Palestinians living in refugee camps outside their country, without rights, without passports, are asked to give guarantees for a military power, for an army which is reckoned to be stronger than any in Europe. All this despite the fact that Israel has the capacity to produce atomic weapons.

Israel cites the mere existence of the Palestinians to prove that it is permanently under threat. The Palestinians are classified as the enemy, and this gives the Israelis a free hand in their dealings with the Palestinians and with all Arab states.

Any questioning or rejection of this view of the Palestinian as the enemy would not only shake Israel's claim to 'Eretz Israel', i.e. to all Palestine, but also put an end to the even wider ambitions outlined by Ariel Sharon at the beginning of this chapter.

This is why Israel does not want to be recognized by the PLO. Moshe Dayan stated this quite unambiguously in an interview on German television at the end of 1980. Begin, Shamir and Sharon reaffirmed it on several occasions in July 1982.

Recognition of Israel by the PLO would perhaps reassure some concerned and not-so-concerned politicians and journalists in Europe. But it would have no effect on the fate of the Palestinians as long as Israel has the power and the troops to be able to dispense with such recognition. The Palestinians have given plenty of indications that they would be willing to make such a gesture. They have been studiously ignored.

The world has been ravaged by wars since the end of the Second World War. This is by no means the first time that world opinion has been confronted with a war of national liberation. Such wars have been fought in Korea, Cuba, Algeria and Vietnam. They are still being fought in Latin America, Africa and in numerous Third World countries.

All these conflicts are eventually solved, one way or another. Many countries won their national independence in wars of liberation.

The Palestinian conflict has lasted four decades now and is one of the most protracted and complicated in modern history. In fact this confrontation began when the first Zionist Congress in Basle decided to establish a Jewish State in Palestine. Even before 1948, the Zionist movement, through its various organizations, gained considerable influence in Europe and in Palestine in particular. The interests of the European colonial powers, the close ties between Israeli ambitions and these powers (especially Great Britain and later the USA) meant that the Zionist movement could give massive and direct backing – including military support – to its intentions in Palestine. The involvement of the great powers, their influence in the internal affairs of Arab countries and the complexity of the relations between the new Arab states and the Palestinian movement have all helped to make this confrontation the most complicated of our era. It was complicated further by the expulsion of the vast majority of the Palestinian people in 1948–49 and the Israeli conquest of all Palestine in 1967.

The Zionist movement achieved its aim and, in 1948, established the State of Israel on Palestinian territory. It owed this first great success to its military and political superiority. After the dreadful persecution of the Jews in Europe, the Zionist movement had the support and sympathy of world public opinion. The world believed that by supporting the State of Israel it could make up for the wrongs done to the Jews and put an end to their persecution once and for all. From 1948, Israel became increasingly strong. With the support of the United States and West European countries, the State of Israel began to pursue its own policies and its own interests, using its own methods. This policy can be described as one of 'accomplished facts'.

Israel took up the slogan of 'secure borders' and set about solving the problem of the Palestinian refugees by military force. In 1967, the Israelis conquered all Palestine, the Golan Heights and Sinai. The political and ideological justification of this expansion was the biblical claim to 'Eretz Israel'.

The Zionist solution of the Palestine problem since the Basle Congress never allowed any scope for a separate, independent Palestinian nation. Israel claimed all Palestine and tried to shift responsibility for the Palestinian problem on to Jordan. In 1948, for instance, Golda Meir, then director of the Political Department of the Jewish Agency, held secret negotiations with King Abdullah of Jordan. They reached an agreement that the king could annex West Jordan without Israeli demur. So even then attempts to establish a separate Palestinian State were blocked. And since then Israel has done everything in its power to ensure that this status quo is maintained.

In the shadow of Arab defeats, an independent Palestinian resistance movement developed, taking up the tradition of Palestinian struggle against Israeli immigration of the 1920s and 1930s. Although the Palestinians were reduced to a nation of refugees dispersed throughout the world or living under Israeli occupation, the PLO none the less managed to organize the Palestinians and strengthen their resolve to achieve self-determination and national independence.

The PLO's objective was to establish a democratic State in Palestine which, as Yasser Arafat stressed in his speech to the UN General Assembly, would include 'all Jews living in Palestine today and willing to live together with us without discrimination on Palestinian territory.' The Palestine Liberation Organization soon realized that this long-term goal alone, this Palestinian 'utopia', would not make much headway in the international arena.

In 1972, discussions began within the PLO which ended with the passing of the ten-point programme in Cairo in 1974. The Palestinian National Council declared its willingness to establish a Palestinian state authority in all parts of Palestine evacuated by Israel. This was the first clear signal to Israel, the USA and world public opinion to inaugurate the search for a political solution to the confrontation. It was not an easy decision for the expelled and disenfranchised Palestinians to take, but none the less it was carried by the vast majority. By declaring its willingness to take part in international conferences on the solution of the Palestinian problem, the Palestinian leadership showed that it would follow any acceptable path towards a political solution.

In the following years, contacts were established and discussions taken up with Israeli intellectuals and left-wing parties. Said Hammami, the PLO representative in London murdered in January 1978, and Issam Sartawi were among the leading Palestinians who took part in these discussions with the Israeli peace camp. Issam Sartawi and former Israeli General Matti Peled planned to give a joint news conference on 14 June 1982. But the Israeli invasion of Lebanon ruined these plans.

Yet even while Beirut was under siege, these talks continued. Israeli journalist and former Knesset deputy Uri Avneri met Yasser Arafat for several hours of talks in Beirut itself. When he returned, Avneri was threatened with prosecution for 'high treason': a response which is shamefully typical of the Israeli government's attitude. Even under the barrage of bombs from the Israeli air force, Yasser Arafat did not abandon his efforts to find a political solution. In the presence of American congressmen, he signed a paper recognizing all UN resolutions on Palestine.

This paper – like all attempts to find a political solution since the beginning of Israeli-Palestinian confrontation – was buried beneath the bombed ruins of Beirut. The response of the Israeli leadership – and this also applied to the previous governments and present opposition parties – has always been one of violence, continued occupation, intensification of land acquisition and settlement and the bombing of Palestinian refugee camps. The war against the PLO in 1982 was perfectly consistent with these policies.

The Jewish-Moroccan writer Edmond Amran wrote in *Die Zeit* on 6 August 1982:

> The Israeli leadership has transformed the Bible into a handbook of colonial conquest. The paratrooper has become the symbol of Jewish spiritual ambassadorship. The military logic of Begin and Sharon leads to security and peacekeeping operations such as those which have claimed thousands of Palestinian and Lebanese dead and wounded in the past weeks.

The Israelis have deliberately torpedoed all Palestinian signals for a political solution to this complex conflict which has been smouldering for so many years. Israel is still attempting to uphold its claim to all Palestine with military force and violence. As a result, peace recedes into the distance.

Constant confrontation in this permanent trouble spot in the Middle East represents a grave threat to world peace. The conflicting interests of the USA and the USSR in the region contain the makings of a potential world-wide escalation of this confrontation. Every European politician also realizes that developments in the Middle East have a direct impact on Europe and that peace in the Middle East means peace for Europe too. Neither the Arabs in general nor the Palestinians in particular bear any responsibility for the Nazi persecution of the Jews in Europe.

Indirectly, the Palestinians are the victims of the persecution of the Jews in Europe. They too have a right to compensation – not financial, but moral compensation. The very least they expect in terms of moral compensation is the recognition of Palestinian rights and of the PLO. It is legitimate and indeed desirable that the Federal Republic of Germany, in particular, should examine its past treatment of the Jews and make compensation in so far as this is possible. Yet this should not blind people to the indirect consequences of this persecution which have been visited on the Palestinian people. Great Britain and France also bear a heavy burden of responsibility for this conflict.

The division of the Arab world into colonial spheres of interest and influence was the result of European policies. Moreover Great Britain, by assuming the League of Nations mandate over Palestine in 1921, promised to lead Palestine to independence – a promise which still remains unfulfilled. The British should now take their opportunity to help correct their historical error. France, too, as a former colonial power in the Arab world could make a substantial contribution by emulating General de Gaulle's brave initiative on Algeria.

For the past two decades, West Europeans have unquestioningly and uncritically adopted the Israeli point of view. An understanding of Palestinian demands has only emerged in the past few years, and the path to this understanding has often been painful and difficult. Today, West Europe cannot ignore Palestinian demands, and therefore it cannot ignore the PLO.

This also applies to the USA, without doubt the most influential power in the Middle East. For years, the USA has been supporting Israel with thousands of millions of dollars. Today Israel is equipped with the most modern American weapons. It not only enjoys US military support but unqualified political backing for its campaigns of conquest, expansion and annexation. The United States has a moral debt to repay to every single Palestinian family. They are the only power who can exert pressure on Israel to end the confrontation. The USA's present policies will not bring peace – they can only prolong the confrontation for years, perhaps even for decades.

Today the Palestinians are dispersed throughout the world. Yet exile and diaspora have not destroyed their identity as Palestinians. The Palestinians may lose military battles over Palestine; yet the fact remains that the Palestinian problem can only be solved in Palestine itself. Juan Goytisolo, a leading contemporary Spanish writer who has lived in exile in Paris since Franco came to power, said that the Palestinians of today bore the 'most important characteristics and features of the 2,000-year Hebrew diaspora':

> Intellectual mobility, lucid self-confidence in the midst of an indifferent and often hostile mass, refuge in culture and technology, the determination to make themselves indispensable and therefore to guarantee their survival. The Palestinians of today are the modern Jews in an Arab world which is as little inclined to absorb them as they are to be absorbed. The history of the past 15 years has shown them that they can expect nothing from others, that if they are to survive as a people they can count only on themselves.

Israeli-Palestinian confrontation in 1982 is simply a continuation of the confrontation of 1947–48. The conflict has thus been restored to its essential core. Palestinian identity has been re-established. The Palestinian people has gained recognition as a people and established its right to its national home. It has founded a State in exile – and this State is the PLO.

The Palestinians have made great sacrifices and suffered enormously in the past decades to achieve this goal. They are the Jews of our day. Yet their future is no longer uncertain and hopeless. More than a quarter of the Palestinian people still live in Palestine today. And despite expulsion by the Israelis, the vast majority of the Palestinian people have remained near their home.

The refugees of the past are today confident men and women with a clear aim in view: the establishment of a Palestinian State with a Palestinian flag on Palestinian territory.

If this state is founded in the near future, then there are strong grounds for believing that peace in this region can be achieved.

If Israel succeeds in preventing the creation of a Palestinian State, confrontation will continue for many years to come.

Notes

1. Ariel Sharon's *Doctrine* (December 1981).

28. The Massacre of Sabra and Shatila

On 30 August 1982 the commander left the fortress. To the salute of units of the united Palestinian and Lebanese forces and the weeping of Palestinian and Lebanese women, Yasser Arafat made his way to the port of Beirut.

Thousands of people lined his route. The Lebanese government and the leaders of the allied national Lebanese movement were also there to bid farewell to the PLO chairman.

Cheers, lamentations and gun salutes marked the end of an era, the era of Palestinian resistance in Beirut.

After the Lebanese and Palestinian national anthems had been played, Arafat boarded the Greek cruiser *Atlantis*, and, escorted by American, French and Greek warships, the *Atlantis* set sail for Piraeus.

The PLO leader was not heading for the capital of an Arab country. He had accepted the Greek government's invitation to go to Athens – a wordless response to the 'Arab silence' during the war in Lebanon.

The PLO withdrew its troops from Beirut two days before the deadline. In all, more than 11,000 fedayeen and 2,500 Syrian soldiers were evacuated. The Beirut resistance fighters received an enthusiastic reception in all the Arab host countries, greeted on their arrival not only by heads of governments and high-ranking officials but also by huge crowds waving Palestinian flags and pictures of Yasser Arafat. In these crowds were many Palestinians living in exile. In Egypt, the Palestinian flag flew from town council buildings, to salute the Palestinian contingents as they passed through the country on their way to the Sudan and Yemen. Children, given the day off school, waved from the banks of the Nile. Many towns held receptions for the fighters, and everywhere cheering crowds lined their route. The media throughout the Arab world celebrated the battle of Beirut as a symbol of courage and resolution; the PLO had proved that Palestinian resistance could not be crushed by American and Israeli weapons, however modern. This praise and recognition of the Palestinian resistance must be seen as implicit criticism of the attitude of the Arab governments in summer 1982.

It was unclear until the end whether the PLO would evacuate West Beirut at all. As early as 7 August 1982 the PLO leadership had agreed in principle to the proposal of US special envoy Philip Habib, and the Lebanese government, that it should evacuate Beirut. Another two weeks were to pass before this happened. The Israeli Defence Minister, Ariel Sharon, had done everything in his power to prevent the withdrawal, insisting on receiving a list of names of the resistance fighters, on the release of captured Israeli soldiers, and arguing that the PLO should be allowed to withdraw before the multinational troops arrived. Not until 19 August 1982 did the Israeli government give way to intense international pressure and accepted the withdrawal plan. At the request of the Lebanese government the PLO ordered the release of two captured Israeli soldiers, in order to avoid providing the Israeli government with yet another pretext for violating the agreement. On 20 August 1982, after 350 French troops, the first of the multinational force, had taken up their positions, the first PLO units withdrew from West Beirut. The Lebanese chapter of the Palestinian odyssey had now come to an end.

The decisive reason for the PLO's withdrawal from Beirut was the Israeli blockade of water, electricity and food. The effects of this blockade on the civilian population were becoming more catastrophic from day to day. The insane Israeli bombing of West Beirut was also claiming a heavy toll of lives among the civilian population; 84% of the victims of the Israeli extermination campaign of summer 1982 were civilians.

The Habib plan stated that the multinational force would remain in Lebanon for at least one month after the PLO withdrawal, in order to protect the civilian population of West Beirut. If necessary its mandate could be extended at the request of the Lebanese government. Point five of the evacuation plan stated categorically that the international force would be deployed from the day of the evacuation to guarantee the safety of Palestinians and Lebanese living in West Beirut and to support the Lebanese state. Palestinian refugees in Lebanon, according to the agreement, now came under Lebanese jurisdiction.

On 23 August, while the PLO was still withdrawing from Beirut, Beshir Gemayel was elected as the new Lebanese President in a military academy on the far east side of the city. Of the 92 deputies – none of whom had stood for re-election since the Lebanese civil war of 1975/76 – 30 boycotted the election in protest at the candidate.

The first congratulatory telegram came from Israel, signed 'Your friend Menachem Begin'. An Israeli Foreign Ministry spokesman commented: 'We are pleased that the Lebanese people has succeeded in electing a new president in democratic elections.'[1] For more than the past six years Gemayel's militias had been trained and equipped by the Israelis, so Israel had every reason to expect allegiance and pliancy from him. The Israeli government also stated its price: a peace treaty with Lebanon and normalization of political and economic relations.

On 1 September 1982, at a secret meeting in the Israeli town of Nahariya, Begin, Sharon and Shamir insisted that Beshir Gemayel should now honour his debt. Press reports from Tel Aviv and Beirut were unanimous in their accounts of serious disagreements between the two allies. Gemayel, it was said, wished first to establish a kind of national consensus, or at least to consolidate his power with the aid of the Kataeb militias. The Israeli leadership was not prepared to wait.

Beshir Gemayel was to be sworn in on 23 September 1982. But he was never to take up office.

On 13 September 1982 the last units of the multinational force left West Beirut, eight days before their mandate officially expired.

At about 15.00 hours on 14 September 1982 all Israeli soldiers were withdrawn from the Kataeb headquarters in the Ashrafiyeh district of East Beirut. The weekly meeting of the Kataeb was due to take place in the headquarters building, which was always heavily guarded. About 400 people were present, including, as always, leader Beshir Gemayel.

At 16.15 hours a 200 kg TNT bomb exploded in Kataeb headquarters, killing more than 30 people. For some time the fate of the President-elect was not known. In the evening, the Lebanese state radio and the Kataeb radio station changed their programme to taped music. By this time Israeli troops had advanced into the district of West Beirut, which, according to the Habib agreement, they were on no account to enter. Shortly before midnight the news of Beshir Gemayel's death was officially confirmed.

Sharon now enjoyed a belated triumph, the capture of an Arab capital. He was unperturbed by the fact that his enemy had withdrawn from the city more than a fortnight before. One hundred civilians were now killed and 300 injured; West Beirut was occupied by the Israelis; thousands were arrested and imprisoned.

On 16 September 1982 the Israeli government issued an official statement that its intervention was a measure to prevent general chaos and restore law and order in the city after the death of Beshir Gemayel. There were indignant protests throughout the world, with the notable exception of the USA. West European governments expressed their grave concern at Israel's flagrant violation of the Habib agreement. Lebanese politicians, such as Saeb Salam and Prime Minister Shafiq al-Wazzan, both of whom played key roles in the evacuation negotiations, made no secret of their anger and disappointment at the Israeli action and sharply criticized the violation of the Habib agreement.

Farouk Kaddoumi, chairman of the PLO Political Department, said: 'They gave us their word of honour that Israel would not march into West Beirut; this word has now been broken'. In Rome, where Arafat was visiting the Pope, the PLO called for multinational forces to be sent immediately to West Beirut to guarantee the life and safety of the civilian population.

On 17 September 1982 the Security Council of the United Nations unanimously condemned Israel's occupation of West Beirut.

Early in the afternoon of 15 September 1982 the Israeli army used tanks and mortars to cordon off the Palestinian refugee camps of Sabra and Shatila in the south of Beirut. A Lebanese who tried to go to his job in the port that afternoon was turned back at the Israeli checkpoint. *No one could get into or out of the camps without the permission of the Israelis.*

On the evening of 15 September, the Akka and Gaza hospitals were full of injured people. The Israeli army continued to fire sporadically on the surrounded camps. The following morning, local people were awoken by low-flying Israeli bombers screaming over the camps. It was 16 September 1982. No one had any idea of the barbarity and cruelty that was to take place in the huts and ruins of this Beirut suburb in the next 48 hours.

At three o'clock that afternoon there was a meeting between Amos Yaron, commander of Israeli troops in Beirut, Fadi Ephram, supreme commander of the 'Lebanese Armed Forces' and Elias Hobeika, Ephram's secret police chief.

They decided to carry out a 'mopping-up operation in the camp', a move that had been planned for some time. The operation was to begin when darkness fell. Sharon gave his blessing over the telephone: 'My congratulations. The operation of our friends is approved.'[2]

As agreed in the plan, the Israeli army gave covering fire, and throughout the day artillery fire rained down on the camp. Many refugees fled to shelters and bunkers.

According to the unanimous accounts of survivors, the militias, about 250 men at first, entered the camp from the south and south-west at around five o'clock on the afternoon of 16 September. The bloody massacre began in the Arsal district opposite Israeli headquarters. Kataeb militia, Kataeb military and secret police, the 'Guardians of the Cedars', members of the former 'Tiger' militias of the National Liberal Party and units of Sa'ad Haddad were involved. Various eye-witnesses have also said that some of the murderers spoke Hebrew.

The military correspondent of *Yediot Aharonot*, the Israeli daily with the highest circulation, described these units thus:

> The authorities in the army have long known that the Falangist fighters (if they can be called fighters at all) . . . have a rather poor military and an even more dubious moral standard. Basically they are nothing more than organised riff-raff with uniforms, motorised vehicles and training camps who have been responsible for abominable atrocities.[3]

The Israeli political and military leadership was undoubtedly aware of the 'fighting strength' and 'discipline' of their allies, especially as these fighters had been equipped and trained – militarily and politically – by the Israelis since the Lebanese civil war in 1975–76.

A number of Israeli newspapers published detailed articles on their allies' plans weeks before the massacres. *Bahamaneh*, the Israeli Labour Party weekly, carried the following report on 1 September 1982:

> An Israeli staff officer heard a Falangist officer say: 'What shall we do, rape them or kill them first? . . . If the Palestinians had any sense, they should try and get out of Beirut. You've no idea of the massacre the Palestinians are going to suffer. The swords and rifles of the Christian militia will pursue them everywhere and exterminate them'.

There is clear evidence that other officers and officials were also aware of the Falangists' intentions. Despite this, Ariel Sharon told the Knesset on 22 September:

> As soon as we began to have doubts about what was happening in these camps, the supreme commander of the north front (General Drori) immediately took measures to stop Falangist operations in Shatila . . . From midday Friday on, Tsahal* ended Falangist activities and we finally evacuated them from there on Saturday.[4]

In the late afternoon of 16 September a five-man Palestinian delegation headed for the sports stadium; its mission: to ask the Israelis to stop firing on the camp and to tell them that they could enter and search it without resistance. The five men, aged between 55 and 65, were never seen alive again. The bodies of three of them were found two days later near the sports stadium.

The first victims that afternoon were either stabbed or axed to death. The militias operated with stealth to prevent the alarm being raised.

At half-past seven that evening the Israeli cabinet met. It 'approved' the militia operation to 'clean up' the camp.

By then, the massacre was already well under way:

> They shot anything that moved in the small streets. They smashed down doors and exterminated entire families who were eating their evening meal. People were killed in bed, in their pyjamas. In many huts, three and four-year-old children were found dead, in their pyjamas or wrapped in blankets. Often the murderers were not satisfied with killing. In many cases, they cut off their victims' limbs before killing them. They smashed the heads of young children and babies against the walls. Women and even young girls were raped before being axed to death. Sometimes people were pulled out of the houses and summarily executed in groups on the street. With axes and knives the militias spread terror, indiscriminately slaughtering men, women, children and old people. Sometimes they deliberately spared one member of a family so that the unfortunate one could later tell what they had seen and experienced. A Shi'ite girl said that her parents had gone down on their knees to beg the executioners to spare them, swearing that

---

*Israeli troops.

they were Lebanese. The only answer they got was: 'You lived with these Palestinian pigs, you're going to meet the same fate'. The entire family was then killed, with the exception of the witness. Later it was found that the dead included nine Jewish women who had married Palestinians at the time of the British mandate and accompanied their husbands to Lebanon in the exodus of 1948. The names of four of these women were published in the Israeli press. In the Horch Tabet district of Shatila camp, the entire Mikdad family was murdered at the beginning of the massacre: 39 people, men, women and children, all massacred. This Lebanese family, originally from Kesseruane, had owned a garage in Shatila for over 30 years. Some had their throats cut, others had their bodies slit open, among them a 29-year-old woman called Zeinab. Her belly was cut open and the foetus put in the arms of the dead mother. One of her relatives, 26-year-old Wafa Hamud, seven months pregnant, was murdered with her four children. In the same district several other women were raped and then killed. After that they were undressed and their bodies laid out crossways. One of the girls in the Mikdad family who was raped was only seven. Milad Farouk, aged 11, was brought to Gaza hospital with arm and leg injuries. He said his mother and his little brother had been killed while watching television. The militias broke into the house and shot at them all point blank, without saying a word. Then they went off, saying nothing.

Some had the presence of mind to escape as soon as they heard the first shots and screams of the victims. Mrs Hashem was one who tried to flee, alarmed by these noises coming from the south. Along with her husband and children, she ran out of her hut in Shatila camp and ran north to seek shelter. She did not know that this was a planned, organized massacre. Having found a shelter, she asked her husband to go back to the house to get food from the refrigerator and milk for the children. She never saw her husband alive again. His bullet-ridden body was found in his house on Saturday.

The militias were not content to torture and kill. They also plundered. The severed hands of women were found in the camp, cut off at the wrists to get at their jewellery. An Israeli journalist quoted a Shatila survivor:

> The Falangists broke into my brother's house on Thursday night. They demanded all his money. He gave them 40,000 Lebanese pounds and two kilos of gold. But this was not enough. They told him to write them a cheque for 500,000 pounds (about £68,000). My brother agreed. When he had signed, they said: 'Now you're worth nothing' and shot him down, along with his father and two other brothers. Only his wife and his two daughters managed to escape from the house and survived.

A 13-year-old Palestinian girl, the sole survivor in her family (her father, her mother, her grandfather and all her brothers and sisters were killed) gave the following account, in the presence of a Lebanese officer:

> We stayed in a shelter until late on Thursday night. Then my girl-friend and I decided to go out. We couldn't breathe in there any more. Suddenly we saw Falangists coming. We ran back to the shelter and warned the others. Some people came out waving a white flag and went up to the militias, shouting out 'We want peace'. They were immediately shot. The women screamed and begged for mercy, I ran away and hid in the bath in our house. All the others were killed. Then I saw them bring people near to our house and shoot them. I wanted to look out of the window, but a militiaman saw me and shot at me. I got back into the bath and hid there for five hours. When I came out, they caught me and put me with the others. They asked me if I was a Palestinian and I said yes. They said: 'Well, do you want to conquer Lebanon?' I said 'No, we are willing to leave here.' Beside me was my nephew, a nine-month-old baby. He was crying all the time. This annoyed one of the soldiers and after a while he said: 'I'm fed up of all this whinging' and shot him in the shoulder. I started to cry and told him it was the only child left in my family. This made the soldier even angrier and he took hold of the baby and tore it in two. Just then my uncle Faisal came along. He is a bit simple. They wanted to kill him too, but I begged them not to kill him. We stayed out all night, beneath the flares that were being fired over the camp. Early in the morning, they took my uncle with them to help them clear away the bodies. When he saw his mother's body, he broke down and cried. Then they took us to the stadium and told us to stay there. I ran away with my girl-friend. I'm living with my aunt now. There's no point in going back to Shatila, what can I do there? I won't be able to work, because they won't give me a work permit. Wherever my aunt goes, I'll go with her. I don't know what to do or what will happen to me.[5]

Umm Hussein was another woman who witnessed and survived the massacre. She said:

> Artillery fire was thundering around us until the evening. We took our children and stayed put. Then, about 6 o'clock, they came and took us from the house and led us at rifle point to a cellar on the way to the stadium. It was bright as day on the streets, from the flares. They ordered us to stand up against a wall. We wept and they told us: 'Count yourselves lucky it's us and not the Jews. We're better than the Jews' and then they shot the men down right in front of us – my husband and two of my sons and four of our neighbour's children. Their blood ran down the wall. A friend ran after us to bring nappies for my baby. They shot him along with my sons. Then they tried to bury the dead but it was too much for them in the narrow streets. They threw mattresses over the corpses. Outside they were working with bulldozers, throwing hand grenades into houses. Then they put us into a room, maybe 15 women and 30 children altogether. They tied up most of the girls there, even an old woman, and did what they wanted with them. They had rifles, big knives and pistols. There were already about 20 dead in the room. One woman, they'd blasted a hole right through the middle of

her. There was a nine month old child, they'd already killed its family, one of the pigs shot it in the stomach and then strangled it. Others were dragged out of the room and shot. We sat next to the corpses, they were searching them for money and jewellery. If they wanted a bracelet, they just chopped off the dead person's hand. We were guarded all this time, there were soldiers coming and going constantly. On some uniforms I recognized the cedar (of the Falangists), others had things on I couldn't read. Most of them spoke Arabic, with an East Beirut accent. I know their accent, I lived in Bourj Hammozud for five years. But there were also some tall blond men with them, they didn't speak Arabic. Lorries kept arriving, unloading food, fruit and mineral water and ammunition. And then they even cracked jokes about it: 'Do you want pork?' one of them asked his mate. 'I'll shoot you the best pig I can find'.[6]

Sharon, Begin and Eytan, the Israeli ministers responsible, insisted in their evidence to the Commission of Enquiry that they stopped the massacre as soon as they found out about it. Two Israeli paratroopers, belonging to an advance guard near Shatila said: 'We could have stopped the massacre on Thursday evening if anyone had taken any notice of what we told our officers.'[7]

Many Israeli soldiers realized what was happening in the camps and informed their superiors. They received the same stereotyped reply: 'Everything is fine, don't worry'.

At 23.00 hours on 16 September the leader of the militias in the camps telephoned the Israeli general in command to tell him that so far '300 civilians and terrorists had been killed'. The report was passed on to the staff in Tel Aviv, going through the hands of more than 20 staff officers.

The massacre continued unimpeded throughout the night; Israeli army flares provided the floodlighting. The manhunts and barbaric killings were intensified, taking an appalling toll. Survivors and those who managed to escape are so shaken by fear and hysteria that they cannot talk about what has happened.

On the Friday morning Akka hospital, where many had fled in the hope of finding help and protection, was attacked. Patients were slaughtered in their beds. Two Palestinian doctors and an Egyptian clerical worker were shot down in cold blood. Intisar Ismail, a 19-year-old Palestinian nurse, was raped several times and then murdered and mutilated. She could be identified only because of a ring on her finger.

The 'Christian' militias in their frenzy made no distinction between Palestinians and Lebanese.

Women and children who were not killed immediately were taken to the sports stadium, which was under Israeli control. But here nothing was done to stop rapes, killings and the looting of the victims. Captured boys and men were herded into lorries and driven off towards the south. Some bodies were later found along the road leading south. Most of them have not been seen since and are presumed dead.

On Friday afternoon a second militia group entered the camp. Eyewitnesses reported that these murderers, including numerous Israeli soldiers and officers, entered Shatila from Beirut airport, the south and the east. They brought Israeli bulldozers with them – and these bulldozers completed the work of destruction, demolishing huts and houses, shovelling all the corpses into heaps and burying them beneath piles of rubble.

Friday was a day of unspeakable horror. The extent of the savagery and brutality cannot be described in words. This inferno stunned even the survivors into shocked silence.

Yet the massacre continued with undiminished ferocity until late Saturday afternoon. Only then did the murderers withdraw, as agreed with Eytan and Sharon. No Israeli soldier attempted to prevent them.

Their gruesome trademarks remained on the walls of the ruins: 'Tony was here. God, fatherland, family, the Kataeb.' Or: 'The troops of Babdaat.' Or simply: 'Sa'ad Haddad.'

They left behind them thousands of murdered, mutilated and tortured women, children, men, rubble and ruins, despair and helplessness; silent immeasurable horror. The stench of decaying bodies filled the air.

The toll of victims soon became a major political factor. All too often, attempts were made to play down the extent of the massacre and the responsibility of those involved. Lebanese government sources spoke of 762 bodies found and buried. The Red Cross and the Lebanese government estimated that about 1,200 of the victims were buried in private graves by their families. To open the mass graves dug by the bulldozers was expressly forbidden. It is reckoned that several hundred people were buried in these mass graves. The number of those buried beneath the ruins is also estimated at several hundred. Attempts to identify these bodies were soon abandoned because the corpses putrefied so quickly in the heat. The final category of victims is that of the missing, those who were driven off in lorries to the south and never been seen since. The number of missing is unknown, perhaps it was impossible to find out; reliable news agencies, basing their reports on eye-witness accounts, estimate them to be around 2,000. This means that 3,500 people were massacred in the space of 42 hours.

'Following the murder of Beshir Gemayel, Tsahal has taken up positions in West Beirut to avoid the risk of violence, bloodbaths and chaos.' This official Israeli communiqué was issued on the night of Thursday 16 September.

From Thursday evening on, Israeli soldiers reported what was happening in the camps to their superiors. Lieutenant Abi Grabowski later told the Israeli Commission of Enquiry: 'I saw Falangists killing civilians ... one of them told me that the pregnant women would give birth to children who would become terrorists.'[8]

Shatila camp is overlooked by a seven-storey building which provides an unimpeded view over the whole camp; this is where the Israeli army command centre is located. The view from here, according to one Israeli officer, is like 'the front row in the theatre'. No need, then, for the Israelis to use their binoculars and ultra-modern night-sight equipment. The evidence of an ordinary Israeli soldier to an Israeli journalist shows how well-informed the Israelis were about what was going on in the camps. Weeping bitterly he said at the end of the massacre: 'I cannot tell the truth now. I have to keep my mouth shut. But one day I will speak.'[9]

One of the first journalists to receive information about what was going on in the camps was Zeev Schiff, the military correspondent of *Ha'aretz*. On Friday morning, he phoned the Israeli Communications Minister, Mordechai Zippori, who then informed Foreign Minister Shamir and asked him to speak to the Minister of Defence.

Amos Yaron and Amir Drori, the Israeli commanders in Beirut, called on the Falangists to end their operations on Friday morning. The Commission of Enquiry later found that in fact they did nothing to prevent the Falangists' operations although they were well aware of what was happening.

According to General Yaron's evidence to the Israeli Commission of Enquiry, Chief of Staff General Eytan, who arrived in Beirut on Friday afternoon, expressly congratulated the Falangists on their 'work' to date. That evening, a number of staff officers, and Ron Ben Yishai, military correspondent of the Israeli army, were together in Baabda, the Lebanese government headquarters. In view of the alarming 'horror stories' from the camps, Yishai decided to phone Defence Minister Sharon at 11.30 at night. Ben Yishai told Sharon what he knew and confirmed in answer to Sharon's questions that Israeli soldiers had witnessed summary executions in Shatila. Speaking of this conversation later, Ben Yishai said: 'The minister did not react. He thanked me and wished me a Happy New Year. I have the impression that he knew what was going on in the camps.'[10]

On the eve of the Jewish New Year, the Israeli newspapers *Yediot Aharonot* and *Ma'ariv* brought out special New Year issues. Their headlines read: 'Our invasion of West Beirut prevented a catastrophe.'

There is no doubt that, by the Friday morning at the latest, Israel's political and military leadership was fully aware of the appalling atrocities at Sabra and Shatila. Nor is there any doubt that the Israeli army leadership expressly approved the operations of further military units on the Friday afternoon. Clearly, the Israeli politicians responsible were fully aware of what the Falangist troops were doing. They had never made, nor could they ever make a secret of their peculiar 'fighting morale'.

But their responsibility does not stop there. The 'cleaning-up operation' in the camp to 'flush out' terrorists had long been prepared down to the finest detail by the Israeli leadership. This view is supported not only by the surrounding of the camp, the rapid availability and deployment of bulldozers, the firing of flares or statements by Israeli officers to ordinary soldiers, but Sharon himself categorically confirmed in evidence to the Commission of Enquiry that he ordered and approved the operations by Falangists in Sabra and Shatila.

The fate of the Ain El-Helweh refugee camp in south Lebanon illustrates what 'cleaning-up a camp' means in plain Hebrew. This camp was razed to the ground; its inhabitants were killed and buried – even in their shelters and bunkers.

The Israeli troops in West Beirut bombarded the refugees with artillery fire for no apparent reason at all. On the nights of the massacre, they fired flares over the camp so that the killers could carry out their murderous deeds in the dark. They threatened violence to Lebanese and Palestinian women and children trying to flee from the camps – thus sending them back to a certain death. They provided the bulldozers which dug the mass graves and demolished houses. The Israelis monitored radio contact between the militias. The plan to use militias in the camps had been expressly agreed with the Israeli army command in Beirut and with Defence Minister Sharon; the militias were provided with aerial photographs and maps of the camps. This massacre was no spontaneous outbreak of rage or revenge for the death of Beshir Gemayel, it had been premeditated, planned and prepared down to the tiniest detail.

This is not simply the Palestinian view, but one shared by experts such as military correspondent Zeev Schiff, Ehud Yaari, Israeli television expert on Arab affairs and the well-known Israeli journalist Amnon Kapeliouk – none of whom can be suspected of pro-Palestinian bias.

> Without homes the Palestinian refugees would have no choice but to leave. Despite claims to the contrary, the bulldozers were not there to pull down possible barriers. Besides, the Israelis knew quite well, thanks to their aerial photographs, that there were neither barriers nor barricades in the camps. So the bulldozers could only be used to demolish houses or to push corpses into a mass grave. On 7 November General Yaron told the Commission of Enquiry: 'We knew that they wanted to destroy the camps.' Since the beginning of the war in June 1982 the Israelis had several times tried out the tactic of demolishing homes with bulldozers to drive out their inhabitants. Refugee camps in south Lebanon were bombarded and then destroyed by dynamite and bulldozers. In Israel this operation was described as 'the destruction of terrorist infrastructure'. Its purpose was to prevent the Palestinians organising themselves as a national community in Lebanon. This meant that not only houses but also the various Palestinian institutions (schools, hospitals, buildings housing social institutions) had to be destroyed and the population had to be 'rid' of its adult males – several thousand men were arrested, thousands of others had to flee.[11]

This tactic was nothing new to the Palestinians. Begin used it with devastating success in Deir Yassin in 1948 and Sharon used it – as a deterrent – in the village of Qibya in 1953.

The savage terror perpetrated by the militias was intended not only to force the people of Sabra and Shatila camps to flee, but also to cause panic and shock among the entire Palestinian population. The aim of this massacre was to drastically reduce the number of Palestinian refugees in Lebanon to an insignificant, easily controllable minority.

The first news of the massacre was broadcast on Saturday 18 September 1982 – from the Israeli press centre in Baabda. All other telephone and telex communication was cut because of the power blackout. Prime Minister Begin later claimed that he first heard of the massacre at 17.00 hours on 18 September 1982, from a BBC news broadcast.

Israeli Chief of Staff Eytan later told the Commission of Enquiry that at 9.00 hours on the same day Begin personally asked him for a report on the incidents in Gaza hospital. Eytan's assistant, Lieutenant-Colonel Zacharin, in evidence to the Commission confirmed that Eytan had given him instructions emphasizing that the Prime Minister himself had asked for the report. By his own account the pious Begin was at this time in the synagogue.

By midday, newspaper correspondents from all over the world were going into the camps. Several journalists began counting the corpses but soon gave up, appalled by the hopelessness of the task. Their photographs and reports led to storms of indignation and protest throughout the world. Officially, Israel was still washing its hands of the matter.

On the afternoon of 18 September, a military spokesman told journalists in Tel Aviv: 'We know nothing of these alleged massacres. There is no Israeli presence in the camps.'[12] The Israeli radio broadcast that evening was also a cover-up. 'Authorized military sources' had reported that 'heavy fighting had taken place, with casualties on both sides.' The Israeli army had ended the hostilities. Towards midnight, the Israeli Foreign Ministry finally put out the statement that 'Israel condemns the massacre'. It said there had been an exchange of fire between the Israeli army and Falangist extremists. The Israeli army, it appeared, had prevented the worst by its bold intervention. But all these versions were too late.

That evening the entire world knew that the massacres had taken place with the Israeli army looking on. Even Israel's most loyal ally, the USA, who approved and supported the invasion of West Beirut, blamed Israel for the massacre, saying it would have been surprised if Israel knew nothing of what was happening in the camps. 'The Israeli forces were in complete control of the sector in which the massacres took place.'[13] American diplomats in Beirut openly admitted that they had been misled by the Israelis and that they in turn had misled the Palestinians. The promise given by Philip Habib and Morris Draper, to protect the civilian population in the camps from massacres, had not been kept.

On the Sunday morning (19 September) the Security Council of the United Nations unanimously condemned the bloodbath in Beirut as a 'criminal massacre of civilians'. The Israeli ambassador to the United Nations, Blum, described the criticisms of Israeli behaviour as 'a procession of liars'. French President Mitterrand said of the massacres: 'The news from Beirut is shocking. Those who are responsible for such excesses are betraying the goals they think they are pursuing.'[14] The Bonn

Ministry of Foreign Affairs spoke of a crime that could not be justified. Minister of State for Foreign Affairs Corterier took up official contacts with the PLO to express the Bonn government's consternation at the massacre.

In protest at the massacre and the continuing occupation of Lebanon by Israeli troops the Egyptian government recalled its ambassador, Dr Sa'ad Murtada, from Israel.

The Soviet news agency Tass blamed Israel directly and the United States indirectly for the massacre. Newspapers throughout the world condemned Israel as being at least 'partly responsible' for what happened in Sabra and Shatila in the 42 hours between Thursday evening and Saturday morning.

Huge protest demonstrations were held throughout the world. In the two weeks following the massacre the world press continually published new revelations about the massacre. Israeli responsibility emerged more and more clearly, in greater detail. The American magazine *Time* published details of close co-operation between Fady Frem, head of the 'Lebanese Armed Forces', his secret service officer Elias Hobeika and the highest echelons of the Israeli army leadership. According to *Time*, Elias Hobeika, whom the Israelis entrusted with the camp 'cleaning-up' operation, was a graduate of the Israeli military academy. 'They [the Israelis] knew that he had taken part in the Tel Al-Zaatar massacre, that he was brutal and unscrupulous and that the forces under his command were anything but disciplined.'[15] *Time* also reported that Fady Frem told of a meeting between Israeli and Falangist commanders on 16 September 1982, and that Hobeika was going to lead his men to a 'kasach' (massacre, slaughter). The same source reported that Israel flew Sa'ad Haddad's militias into Beirut in helicopters to take part in the massacre.

As soon as the massacre became known, the political and military leadership of Israel attempted to explain the discrepancy between their promise to prevent bloodshed and the actual course of events at Sabra and Shatila. On the Sunday after the massacre, General Eytan told a press conference:

> We did not know what was really happening there. It was night-time. We assumed it was just normal fighting. When day broke and we saw what had happened and what could still happen, we stepped in quickly and they left the camp.[16]

But all attempts at self-justification were vain. The Israeli newspapers frustrated government efforts to clear themselves. *Yediot Aharonot*, for example, pointed out that Israeli ministers and high-ranking military had known the facts since Thursday night-Friday-morning (16–17 September 1982). 'Although they knew exactly what was happening, they did not lift a finger to prevent the massacre until Saturday.'[17] The first protest demonstrations outside Begin's house were held on the Saturday evening.

Demonstrators called Begin and Sharon murderers and demanded their resignation. The past now caught up with the Israeli leaders. Chants of 'Begin, terrorist', 'Beirut-Deir-Yassin' and 'Down with Sharon, the butcher of Qibya' resounded outside the Prime Minister's private house. Finally the police drove the demonstrators away with tear-gas and batons. Hundreds of people demonstrated in Tel Aviv, chanting the same slogans. On Sunday evening the cabinet met. Begin said: 'Goys killing goys, what's that to us?'

The Israeli government put full-page advertisements in all the West European and American national newspapers, and Israeli embassies were instructed to act according to the message. The advertisement read:

> During the New Year a bloodthirsty conspiracy against the Jewish state and government and the Israeli army took place. At a place far from Tsahal positions a Lebanese unit entered a refugee camp where terrorists were hiding. Their aim was to arrest them. This unit attacked the population of the camps and killed many people, a fact which deeply saddens us and which we deeply regret. As soon as the Israeli army found out what had happened in Shatila camp, it put a stop to the murder of innocent civilians and forced the Lebanese unit to leave the camp.
>
> The civilian population openly showed its gratitude for the rescue operation by the Tsahal forces. All accusations, whether open or tacit, that Tsahal was in any way involved in this human tragedy are groundless. The government rejects them with contempt. The fact is that the number of victims would have been even higher if the Israeli army had not intervened. Tsahal was engaged for two whole days against terrorists in West Beirut and not a single complaint about maltreatment of civilians was made in this time.[18]

Even observers with many years' experience of Israeli politics were shocked by the cynical arrogance of this advertisement. The Israeli government pulled out all the stops to exculpate itself, to cover up its knowledge of the events and the involvement of the Israeli army. But the excuses, prevarications and lies burst like bubbles as soon as they were launched.

The Israeli newspapers, in the first issues to appear after the New Year's feast on 20 September, unanimously concluded, on the basis of their own researches, that Israel bore 'indirect if not direct responsibility for the deaths of hundreds of defenceless people'. In an article headlined 'The Shame of Beirut', *Davar* wrote: 'The acts of the author of Deir Yassin, the commandant of Qibya and the man who commuted Daniel Pinto's sentence[19] are a stain on the honour of the entire nation.'[20]

Many newspapers called for the resignation of Sharon and Eytan and the setting up of an independent commission of enquiry. Israeli journalists reported that their offices were flooded with letters from readers expressing horror and disgust at the massacres and the undeniable Israeli involvement in them. Some Israelis compared the massacres with the crimes of the Nazis and anti-Semitic pogroms.

On 21 September the Knesset debated the massacres. The Opposition called for the withdrawal of Israeli troops from Beirut and the setting up of a commission of enquiry. Begin denied any Israeli responsibility and threatened to resign if a commission was set up.

Defence Minister Sharon's reply to the accusations and demands of Shimon Peres is curiously revealing: 'Mr Peres, you were Minister of Defence at the time, where were the officers of the Israeli army during the Tel Al-Zaatar massacre? I challenge you to tell us.'[21]

The Israeli army stated a few days later that its 'liaison officers' had returned to Israel a few days before the massacre. These denials cannot disguise the fact that the Israeli army was actively involved in the Lebanese civil war and also played a part in the Tel Al-Zaatar massacre. Sharon's allusion made this abundantly clear.

The emotional turmoil in Israeli society was intense, never before had it experienced such a trauma. Even in Israel, the moral, political and legal responsibility for the massacre was placed on the shoulders of the Israeli government. Novelist Itzhak Orpaz summed up the feelings of many Israelis when he wrote: 'My mother and father, whom I lost in the holocaust, were murdered again in Sabra and Shatila.'[22]

Protest marches and demonstrations against the Israeli government went on for a week. The demonstrators' main demands were: withdrawal of the Israeli army from Beirut and the setting up of an independent commission of enquiry. The more details about the massacre emerged, the more pressing were international demands for a commission of enquiry.

A week after the end of the massacre in Beirut, the greatest demonstration in the history of Israel was held. Five hundred thousand people – one Israeli in eight – demonstrated against the government, calling for an end to massacres and wars, the dismissal of Sharon, the resignation of the entire government and the setting up of a commission of enquiry.

'We don't want a future built on the graves of Palestinians' – this slogan encapsulated the feeling that had brought these people on to the streets of Tel Aviv.

The Israeli cabinet, facing a government crisis, finally bowed to the pressure from the demonstrators, revised its previous decision and, on 27 September, decided to set up a commission of enquiry to be chaired by Supreme Court judge Kahan. The Commission was given wide-ranging powers.

In view of the size of the demonstrations on 25 September, a planned pro-government counter-demonstration was called off. An opinion poll in Israel revealed that 60% of the population believed the government to be responsible for the massacre; 80% thought that the Lebanon war had harmed Israel.

Meanwhile, international public opinion was also being mobilized. An international commission of enquiry consisting of famous scholars and lawyers was formed, with Sean MacBride, the Irish Nobel Prize winner and former UN Deputy-Secretary, as its chairman. Over a period of more than three months, this commission heard evidence from Israelis, Falangists and survivors. In February 1983, after carefully weighing up all the facts, the commission published its findings. The report concluded that Israeli troops had given the militias 'vital assistance and logistical support'. It found the political and military leaders of Israel to be 'personally responsible'.[23]

A few days later, the Israeli Commission of Enquiry report was published, and its findings also apportion serious blame to Israel's political and military leadership. The report called on the Prime Minister – whose own behaviour it criticized – to dismiss Sharon from his post as Minister of Defence, on the grounds that he 'bears personal responsibility'. Army chief Eytan was accused of 'breach of duty'. As Eytan was due to retire the following month, the commission refrained from making any recommendation in his case. The Kahan report called for the immediate dismissal of Jehoshua Sagui, head of military counter-intelligence; it recommended three years suspension from service for Brigadier-General Amos Yaron. Israeli Foreign Minister Shamir, the head of the Israeli secret service, Mossad, whose name cannot be made public in Israel, and Major-General Drori, commander of the north front, were all found to have been indirectly responsible for the massacre.

The Kahan report left no doubt that Israel, as the occupying military force, bore full legal responsibility for the bloodbath in Sabra and Shatila.

The world's press welcomed the commission's report as evidence of the 'rule of law' and democracy in Israel. It was expected that Sharon would now be dismissed, the government would resign and general elections would be called. But apparently ethics and a sense of responsibility are not the strengths of the Begin government. To keep up appearances of 'moral purification', Sharon, after tough and lengthy discussions in cabinet, resigned his post as Minister of Defence. But he remains in the cabinet as a minister without portfolio, keeping his influential positions on the foreign policy and defence committees. He was succeeded as Minister of Defence by Israel's ambassador in the USA, Moshe Arens, a tough advocate of Israeli settlement and annexation policies. To sum up: the Israeli government has 'amnestied' itself.

The purely cosmetic nature of this reshuffle in the Israeli cabinet can be read only as confirmation of Israeli policy to date towards the Palestinians – including the massacres.

The Lebanon war and the massacres in Beirut had already opened up deep rifts in Israeli society. The Begin government's response only served to intensify the divisions. Pro- and anti-Sharon demonstrations kept public opinion on tenterhooks in the following weeks. A 'Peace Now' demonstrator was killed by a hand-grenade outside the Prime Minister's office; nine people were injured. The hand-grenade came from a group of pro-Sharon demonstrators. No one was arrested. The funeral of the victim, 33-year-old Emil Grünzweig, was a powerful demonstration against the government.

The rift in Israeli society affected even the families of ministers and high-ranking government officials. Among those injured by the hand-grenade attack was Abraham Burg, son of the Israeli Minister of the Interior, Josef Burg.

The reaction of the Jewish community throughout the world was similar to that in Israel. Many official representatives spoke out against Sharon and Begin. The Israeli peace movement won many supporters and sympathizers, not only among the Jewish communities in the USA and West Europe.

Two responses by European authors to the massacres are especially worth mentioning: one is the epic 'After the Mass Murders in Sabra and Shatila Refugee Camps' by the London-based Jewish writer, Erich Fried, the other is French novelist and playwright Jean Genet's 'Four Hours in Shatila'.

Erich Fried first read his poem at a demonstration of 10,000 people in Bonn on 25 September 1982. Fried unmasked the official web of hypocritical phraseology, exposing the real nature of Israel's interests.

> Just as the debris and rubble had to be swept away from the murdered Palestinians, so the debris and rubble will have to be swept away from the minds and hearts of people in Europe and America, the debris and rubble of old lies and prejudices which have now been shattered by the unbearable truth – so that at last the murderers too can be swept away, the murderers and their instigators, wherever they are and whatever their names may be, whether Christians or Jews, and also the Muslims who helped these murderers. (Author's manuscript.)

Jean Genet's essay is a hymn to the Palestinian fedayeen, their moral and aesthetic values – freedom and beauty – contrasted with the real, visible and tangible horrors of the human remains in Shatila.

> How are they to tell their relatives, who left with Arafat, trusting the promises of Reagan, Mitterrand and Pertini, who assured them that the civilian population of the camps would be unharmed? How can we tell them that children, old people and women were butchered and their bodies left unprayed-for? How can we break the news that we do not know where they are buried?
>
> The massacres did not take place in darkness at dead of night. They were lit up by Israeli flares, and from Thursday evening onwards Israeli ears heard what was happening in Shatila. What feasts and pleasures of the soldiers, drunk with wine, hate and joy to be of service to the Israeli army. And they listened, watched, encouraged, blamed. I did not see the Israeli army that listened and watched. But I saw what it did.[24]

At the end, Genet writes:

> On the way back from Beirut I met young fedayeen at Damascus airport who had just escaped from the Israeli inferno. They were sixteen or seventeen years old: they laughed and were like those of Ajlun.
>
> Fighting for one's country can make life very rich, but short. This is the choice, let us remember, that Achilles made in the Iliad.[25]

> Within the army the reaction was silence. On the morning of 21.9.82, the General Staff met. According to one of those present who passed the information on to the *Davar* correspondent, the Chief of Staff spent only five minutes talking about the 'events of Sabra and Shatila'. No one made the least remark, not a single question was asked. No one asked to speak.
>
> At the same time, a woman in the camp went on searching frantically at a mass grave. Thirteen members of her family were killed, including her four month old baby. She stopped, sat down, shook ashes on her head and screamed: 'Where shall I go now?'[26]

The honourable withdrawal of the fedayeen from West Beirut was followed by the treacherous revenge of the humiliated victors: the massacre of Sabra and Shatila.

This massacre was not only the cruel consequence of the Israeli campaign of extermination in summer 1982. It also reflected the immanent logic of Israeli policies since the Palestinians were first expelled from their land. Flee or be massacred – that is the only choice the Zionist movement and the state of Israel give the Palestinian people. The massacre of Sabra and Shatila bears chilling similarities to the massacre of Deir Yassin in 1948.

The purpose of Deir Yassin, the purpose of Sabra and Shatila was to show the survivors the fate that awaited them if they did not flee, disappear, if they did not of their own free will decide to give up their independence as a people, as a nation, and merge with the community in which they were living.

Sabra and Shatila are a warning to the peoples of the world to resist Israeli deeds and plans. The Palestinian problem cannot be solved by expulsion, nor by war or massacres. This, too, is a lesson to be learnt from Sabra and Shatila.

Notes

1. *Süddeutsche Zeitung*, 24 August 1982.
2. *Time* magazine, quoted in *Le Monde*, 29 September 1982.
3. A. Kapeliouk, *Sabra et Chatila: Enquete sur un massacre*, Paris, 1982, pp. 40–1.
4. Ibid., p. 58.

5. Ibid., pp. 47–51.
6. *Tageszeitung*, 8 October 1982.
7. Kapeliouk, op. cit., p. 52.
8. Ibid., p. 60.
9. Ibid., p. 86.
10. Ibid., p. 75.
11. Ibid., p. 71.
12. Ibid., p. 87.
13. Ibid., p. 89.
14. *Süddeutsche Zeitung*, 20 September 1982.
15. *Time* magazine, quoted in *Le Monde*, 29 September 1982.
16. AFP, 19 September 1982.
17. The *Guardian*, 21 September 1982.
18. Kapeliouk, op. cit., pp. 102–3.
19. Pinto murdered two civilians during the invasion of Lebanon in March 1978. Chief of Staff Eytan was responsible for considerably reducing his sentence.
20. Kapeliouk, op. cit., p. 106.
21. Ibid., p. 115.
22. Ibid., p. 112.
23. *Süddeutsche Zeitung*, 5/6 February 1983.
24. *Revue d'etudes palestiniennes*, Beirut, No. 6, Winter 1983, p. 13.
25. Ibid., p. 19.
26. Kapeliouk, op. cit., p. 116.

29. The 16th Palestinian National Council

The Salweh Hotel, Tunis. This was the new address of PLO Headquarters in the late summer of 1982. Tunis as the headquarters of the Arab League guaranteed neutrality and independence. At the same time, the choice of Tunis emphasized the strong interweaving of the Palestinian cause with the national Arab context.

The new situation was difficult for the Palestinians in many respects. Important political and social structures of Palestinian society in exile had been destroyed. The PLO now faced new, unknown challenges. But Arafat, and the leadership of the Palestinian resistance, had no time for downheartedness. A race with time began. The task now was to brave all the difficulties, rebuild the PLO's structures, resume activities and prove that the Palestinian resistance, far from being crushed, was capable of surviving even the most terrible ordeals. Immediately after a reception in their honour given by the Tunisian government, the Central Committee of Al-Fatah under Yasser Arafat's leadership began its first discussions. These were followed by sessions of the PLO Executive Committee and the Al-Fatah Revolutionary Council, and discussions with PLO representatives from all over the world. New facts had now, and were to be faced. The time of heroic resistance in Beirut was not forgotten, but everyone realized that the glories of the past alone could not overcome the challenges of the future.

New political activities, diplomatic offensives and many organizational and contentious decisions had to be made to ensure that the PLO retained the standing it had gained in world opinion during the battle of Beirut.

There was certainly no shortage of readiness and determination to reorganize the PLO, its institutions and units. But the auspices for such reorganization at this time could hardly have been less favourable. The PLO's military units were dispersed throughout many countries. Often they were housed in isolated camps in the desert and thereby condemned to reservist status. The Palestinian resistance organizations in the PLO had also dispersed to various Arab host countries. This made informal discussions and official meetings of the leaders of the Palestinian resistance difficult. The headquarters of the Palestinian news agency Wafa was in Cyprus, as was *Falestin al-Thaura*, the PLO central organ which now appeared weekly. Reconstruction was a severe drain on finances and soon huge inroads were being made into the funds of the Palestinian National Fund. New accommodation was needed for resistance cadres, equipment to train new cadres; expensive new purchases had to be made in the information services. The Palestinian professional associations and trades unions also needed new homes. The Palestinian Red Crescent had lost its hospitals, out-patients' departments, ambulances, medical equipment and, above all, many doctors and nurses. Here, too, expensive appointments and purchases had to be made. It soon became clear that the PLO would be unable to solve all these problems at a stroke. The destruction of its institutions and the dispersal of its resistance organizations also put a severe strain on Palestinian national unity. The different political positions of the Arab host countries, without whose toleration or approval the PLO could operate only on a restricted scale, inevitably had an impact on discussions within the PLO on its future course. Yet there was now a counterbalance to these political restrictions: the growing recognition of the PLO since Beirut, both in the Arab and in the international arena.

Impressive evidence of this came at the second phase of the 12th Arab Summit meeting in Fez, from 6–9 September 1982. The first phase of this conference, in November 1981, had broken down because the Arab states could not agree on the Fahd plan. Some delegations also demonstratively boycotted the November 1981 summit. Nineteen Arab delegations took part in the second phase of the conference in September 1982 in Fez, Morocco. Only Egypt and Libya were absent.

Last to arrive at the Fez summit were the PLO chairman Yasser Arafat and his delegation. All the Arab heads of state and kings attending the conference gathered at the airport to welcome the PLO leader with full honours. Only the Syrian President, Hafez al-Assad, was absent. When he arrived, Arafat said that the PLO in Beirut had fought for the 'defence not only of Palestine and the Lebanon but of the entire Arab nation'.[1] In saying this, Arafat struck a responsive chord, and so the PLO had an important part to play at the discussions and resolutions of this 12th Arab Summit conference. Newspaper reports stressed that Arafat himself had played a decisive role in the drafting of the 'Fez Charter'. The discussions revolved around a reworked version of the Fahd plan. For the first time in the history of the Palestine conflict this conference was to put forward a united Arab peace plan.

> The summit paid tribute to the resistance of the forces of the Palestinian revolution, of the Lebanese and Palestinian people and of the Syrian Arab forces and reaffirmed its support for the Palestinian people in its struggle to regain its inalienable national rights.[2]

These were the opening words of the peace proposals in the summit conference's final communiqué. The main points of the 'Fez Charter' are:

'the establishment of a Palestinian state with Jerusalem as capital' (point 6); 'the withdrawal of Israel from all Arab territories occupied in 1967' (point 1); the 'dismantling of settlements established by Israel . . . after 1967'; and 'the reaffirmation of the Palestinian people's right to self-determination and the exercise of its imprescriptible and inalienable national rights under the leadership of the Palestine Liberation Organization (PLO), its sole and legitimate representative' (point 4). The Gaza Strip and the West Bank were to come under United Nations control for a transitional period. The UN Security Council was to guarantee 'peace between all nations in the region' and the 'respect of these principles'.[3]

The Fez Summit was a political victory for the PLO, which was able to make considerable improvements on the Fahd plan. Admittedly, the Fahd plan had called for an independent Palestinian state with Jerusalem as its capital. The 'Fez Charter', however, made it absolutely clear that this state would be established under the leadership of the PLO; and once again it expressly recognized the PLO as the sole legitimate representative of the Palestinian people.

In its Fez peace proposals, the Arab world put forward a serious peace plan in accordance with international law and international treaties. The will to solve the Palestinian conflict by political and not by military means was acknowledged and met with a positive response throughout the world.

West European politicians stated that after the breakdown of Camp David, the Fez decisions represented a genuine basis for peace negotiations. Editorials in the international press stressed that in the 'Fez Charter' the Arab states and the PLO had paved the way for negotiations.

The Israeli government 'completely rejected' the Fez proposals. An Israeli Foreign Ministry statement said that the strike against the PLO in Lebanon had been undertaken to enable the population of the West Bank to take part in an autonomy solution à la Camp David. Begin said, in an interview, that Israel would not hesitate to extend its sovereignty to West Jordan and Gaza when the time was appropriate.

Given the power-political constellation in the world, the Fez proposals were addressed primarily to the United States government. The Fez resolutions were the Arab answer to the 'Reagan plan'. On 1 September 1982 (the PLO had only just withdrawn from Beirut) in a television address, President Reagan called for a 'fresh start' in the Middle East. Reagan affirmed that this fresh start would 'on the whole, follow the guidelines laid down by my predecessors'.[4] He added: 'The Camp David accord remains the basis of our policy.' Reagan then went on to call for an immediate end to Israeli settlement policies and the 'transfer of domestic authority from Israel to the Palestinian inhabitants.'

Reagan continued:

> The final status of these lands must of course be reached through the give-and-take of negotiations. But it is the firm view of the United States

that self-government by the Palestinians of the West Bank and Gaza in association with Jordan offers the best chance for a durable, just and lasting peace.[5]

Peace, he said, could not be guaranteed by permanent Israeli control of the occupied territories. Nevertheless, he explicitly rejected the formation of an independent Palestinian state, and made no mention of the PLO. Nor did he say how Israel could be persuaded or forced to withdraw from the occupied areas.

Reagan also rejected Arab demands on Jerusalem. He conceded that the 'final status should be decided through negotiations' yet 'remained convinced that Jerusalem must remain undivided.'

The annexation of Jerusalem by Israel and the preservation of the status quo were, thereby, de facto legalized.

The Arab reaction to the Reagan plan was similar to Reagan's reaction to the Fez resolutions. Immediate statements were avoided, a wait and see policy was adopted.

The Israeli government, however, responded with a loud and clear 'no'. Prime Minister Begin was particularly annoyed by the proposal to stop the Israeli settlement policy. This would have ruled out any possibility of future Israeli sovereignty over the occupied areas – a right which Israel had expressly reserved to itself in the Camp David accords. Deputy Israeli Prime Minister Levy described Reagan's proposals simply as 'one-sided and anti-Israeli'. Several Knesset MPs proposed a large-scale settlement offensive in response to Reagan's proposals – a suggestion which was taken up by the Israeli government six months later.

The US Administration had carefully considered the timing and the content of the Reagan plan. In his television address, Reagan had stressed that the war in Lebanon had created a 'new opportunity' for peace in the Middle East. The US Administration was undoubtedly working on the assumption that the PLO had been crushed in Beirut and that PLO representation of the Palestinian people could now be ruled out. The timing of Reagan's speech – before the Arab summit meeting and before any political reorganization of the Palestine Liberation Organization was possible – confirms this supposition. The 'fresh start' in the Middle East was to take place without the PLO.

These US hopes were soon dashed – not only by the Arab summit in Fez. On 15 September 1982 the Soviet Union re-entered the Middle East negotiating arena. During a state visit to Moscow by the President of the People's Democratic Republic of Yemen, Leonid Brezhnev presented a six-point peace plan. This plan gained further importance in January 1983 when it was formally approved by the East Bloc heads of state at a meeting of the Warsaw Pact Council in Prague.

The Brezhnev plan opened by stressing the 'unacceptability of the acquisition of foreign territory by aggression.'[6] From this it concluded that Israel must give back all territories conquered since 1967. The

Palestinian people had the right to 'self-determination and the establishment of its own, independent state in Palestinian territories.' Israel would also have to give back East Jerusalem. The state of war should be ended, with all states in the region 'including Israel and the Palestinian State' committing themselves to 'mutual respect of sovereignty, independence and territorial integrity.'[7]

International guarantees for these agreements would be given by the Permanent Members of the UN Security Council. The Brezhnev plan concluded:

> Such a comprehensive, truly just and really lasting agreement can only be worked out and translated into action by the collective efforts and participation of all interested parties, which must, of course, include the PLO as the sole legitimate representative of the Arab people of Palestine.[8]

The Brezhnev plan now meant that the PLO had clear and substantial support from outside the Arab world. The Soviet proposal not only called for the creation of a Palestinian state but expressly recognized the legitimacy of the PLO and called for its participation in all Middle East peace negotiations.

In diplomatic circles in Europe and the USA, in commentaries by many journalists and observers the Brezhnev plan was seen as a support and affirmation of the Fez resolutions. It was also regarded as an unmistakable Soviet answer to the Reagan plan.

This meant that in September 1982 there were three plans for a solution to the Palestinian conflict on the negotiating table. The only party which refused to sit at that table and rejected all three sets of proposals was Israel. It was generally expected that the US Administration would best be able to persuade Israel to relent and negotiate. The USA alone had the necessary means of bringing pressure to bear: in the form of financial, economic and military aid. But these hopes were soon disappointed. Only a few days after the publication of the Reagan plan, Israel emphasized its refusal to take part in peace negotiations by building five new settlements on the West Bank. In response, the White House issued a statement describing the five new settlements as a 'highly unwelcome' threat to the American peace plan; a docile response. And the American Administration left it at that. A reaction which, especially after American promises in Beirut, could hardly be expected to inspire confidence among the Arab states and the PLO.

The Reagan Administration was undoubtedly hoping to involve King Hussein of Jordan in the Camp David process. According to the Reagan plan, Hussein's sphere of influence was to be extended to the West Bank and the Gaza Strip. King Hussein, though not ill-disposed to the American plans, was tied by his commitment to the Fez proposals. He could not leave the Arab camp merely for the sake of dubious promises.

For the PLO the situation was grave. Reagan was now calling for an end to Israeli occupation of the West Bank and the Gaza Strip in return for denial of the national rights of the Palestinian people and de facto elimination of the PLO. Clearly, this was a development the PLO had to resist, having already made all the compromises it could at the Fez summit. The minimum demand was an independent Palestinian state. The PLO decided that such a state would have to be established first and could then discuss confederation with Jordan. Jordanian-Palestinian negotiations now began. Yasser Arafat and King Hussein of Jordan met for discussions several times. The negotiations broke down in the spring of 1983. King Hussein, under American pressure, insisted that the PLO should recognize UN Security Council Resolutions 242 and 338. In neither of these 1967 Resolutions does the word Palestinian occur, nor do they contain any mention of the Palestinian people's national rights. The American government had also insisted that no member of the PLO should be allowed to participate in any joint Palestinian-Jordanian delegation. These demands amounted to a call for the abolition of the PLO.

Robert Neumann, former US ambassador in Saudi Arabia and an expert on American Middle East policy, blamed Washington for the failure of these negotiations. 'It's not good enough for the President to make a speech and then do nothing for the next eight months,' said Neumann, adding that Washington had failed to take any steps to increase Arab states' confidence in American policies.[9]

Meanwhile, the PLO had successfully completed the reorganization of its structures in many areas. Its political power to act had now been fully restored and preparations were going ahead for the 16th session of the Palestinian National Council, which as the highest decision-making organ of the PLO, would determine its future political course. Above all, decisions were expected on the Reagan plan and on negotiations with King Hussein of Jordan.

Yet the PLO still faced other almost insoluble problems. The persecution of Palestinians in Lebanon had not ended with the massacres of Sabra and Shatila. The Lebanese army and the Falangist militias continued their arbitrary arrests and murders of Palestinians. According to figures provided by the churches, more than 1,600 people disappeared in this way, of whom several hundred were killed. In the refugee camps in south Lebanon, thousands of Palestinians had no roof over their heads. The tug-of-war between the Israeli occupying forces and the Lebanese authorities meant that several weeks passed in which nothing at all happened. Palestinian families had to seek refuge in tents or makeshift huts. It was not rare for women, children and grandmothers to be forced to seek shelter under trees or in orange groves. With Israeli approval, Sa'ad Haddad's militias now extended their control as far as Sidon. Threats of murder drove many Palestinian families out of their homes in Tyre and Sidon and forced their return to the misery of the destroyed camps. A UNWRA report said that Palestinians who had refused to leave their homes had been murdered by militias. In the spring of 1983, in the space of three days, the bodies of 12 murdered Palestinians were found.

In the Israeli internment camp of Al-Ansar near Nabatiyeh, in south Lebanon, 9,000 people were imprisoned under atrocious conditions; even children and old people were among those interned. Israeli guards and foreign journalists were to compare Al-Ansar with Nazi concentration camps. Prisoners were continually being taken away for 'special treatment' in Israeli prisons, where they were maltreated, and in many cases tortured. Food in the prison was utterly inadequate, medical services virtually non-existent. Below zero temperatures, rain and biting winds weakened the emaciated prisoners still further.

Those who were released had all their identity papers confiscated. In return they were given a document in Hebrew only, by means of which they could be easily identified as former internees in any control. Many who failed to escape from south Lebanon soon after their release were murdered by Falangist militias; on flimsy pretexts the Israeli authorities sent others back to Al-Ansar.

The Palestinian families lacked the barest necessities of life; militias frequently prevented attempts to rebuild houses in the refugee camps. The Palestinian women in the camps had no means of earning a living. Indeed, women were often arrested and tortured.

Death threats, fear, insecurity and hunger were daily commonplaces for Palestinians in south Lebanon. Those responsible for the massacres of Sabra and Shatila, along with their henchmen, were in absolute control of that part of Lebanon where the Palestinian refugee camps – what was now left of them – were located.

In the West Bank and the Gaza Strip it soon became clear that the Israeli government intended to annex every square inch of ground. The Lebanon war had not achieved its objective – the total elimination of the PLO – in compensation, the Israeli government now pursued its settlement policies with even greater rigour and determination. Their aim was to bring about accomplished facts and thus permanently nullify the Palestinians' claim to their own land. Expropriation of land and building of settlements reached hitherto unheard of proportions in the months following the Lebanon war. Protests, strikes and demonstrations were crushed with brutal force. Attacks by Zionist settlers on Palestinians, even those living in larger towns, became more frequent. In a number of incidents several Palestinians were killed. Arrests and curfews were the most frequent methods of Israeli repression. Gangs of Zionist settlers attacked Palestinian villages at night, maltreating their inhabitants and smashing furniture.

In April 1983, over 1,000 Palestinian schoolgirls in the West Bank went down with a form of poisoning. Israel refused to allow an independent commission to study the causes of this mysterious epidemic.

The Israeli settlements were all concentrated close to Palestinian towns, especially Nablus, Tulkarem, Al-Bireh, Jenin, Hebron and

Jerusalem. The Israeli government encouraged would-be settlers with advertisements promising 'cheap accommodation and good air'. Palestinian towns and villages were surrounded and effectively strangled by Israeli settlements. Like fire, Israeli land appropriation spread uncontrollably, and fears grew among Palestinians that soon they would lose the last bit of land they possessed.

In occupied Lebanon and occupied Palestine, the Palestinian people were trapped in a bitter and bloody net of expropriation and expulsion, persecution and murder, massacres and extermination.

The Palestinian National Council faced a difficult task. Fully aware of the daily persecution to which the Palestinian people were subjected, it yet had to make wide-ranging decisions on the political course and the continuation of the struggle.

The 16th session of the Palestinian National Council was not held until 14 to 22 February 1983 in Algiers. Numerous obstacles and difficulties had been placed in the way of this meeting of the National Council. Initially, it had been due to take place immediately after the conference of Palestinian resistance leaders in the first week of December 1982 in Aden. However, subsequent events seemed to prove those who said that the session could not be held at this time right. Two conferences cast their shadows over the forthcoming National Council sessions. In January 1983 five Palestinian organizations, including Dr George Habbash's Popular Front and the Democratic Front under Nayef Hawatmeh, formulated a communiqué criticizing PLO chairman Arafat's negotiations with King Hussein of Jordan.

They called for outright rejection of the Reagan plan by the PLO and an end to discussions with King Hussein. It was difficult to avoid the impression that there were serious and deep differences of opinion within the PLO about its future course. Reports of divisions from the Tripoli conference, at which the same five Palestinian organizations held discussions with representatives of the Libyan government, augmented this impression. The communiqué, signed by Major Abdul Salam Jalloud and the five Palestinian organizations, condemned the resolutions of the Arab summit at Fez and violently attacked any proposed contacts with Zionist Israelis. Some of the organizations later dissociated themselves from the form and content of the communiqué, but this could not disguise the fact that serious differences of opinion and in-fighting were taking place between various wings about the PLO's future course.

Those critics who had predicted that after the withdrawal from Beirut the PLO would disintegrate now seemed to have been proven right. The atmosphere was extremely tense. Quite a few observers believed that a split within the PLO was likely, if not inevitable.

Before the session proper, the leaders of the Palestinian resistance organizations met for discussions in Algiers. The main subject of these discussions, which lasted for 70 hours, was the agenda for the National Council session. The discussions were frank and tough. The key questions were how the Palestinians and the PLO should respond to: a) the Reagan plan, the 'Fez Charter' and the Brezhnev plan; b) the negotiations with King Hussein; c) to Egypt; d) contacts with the Israeli peace camp; e) the Rejection Front (Front of Steadfastness and Confrontation), and to Syria.

No agreement on the points at issue was reached in these marathon discussions either. Nonetheless, an important and crucial decision was made. All Palestinian resistance organizations expressed their will to preserve Palestinian national unity whatever the circumstances. They all agreed not to enter any pact outside the framework of the PLO. This meant that the Palestinian National Council could now start under somewhat more favourable circumstances.

The opening ceremony of the 16th Palestinian National Council on 14 February 1983 in Algiers was attended by the Algerian President Shadli Ben Jedid (as host), Shadli Qlibi, Secretary-General of the Arab League, and Habib Shattli, Secretary-General of the Islamic Conference.

Also present were the chairman of the PLO, the members of the PLO Executive Committee, the 355 members of the National Council, more than 600 journalists from all over the world and 120 delegations and representatives of friendly states, parties and organizations, as well as observers and guests. The number of people going to Algiers had been estimated at 1,000 to 1,200, but, in fact, there were more than 6,000, which exceeded all expectations. These included thousands of Palestinians who had come from all over the world. Algiers was a demonstration of Arab and international solidarity – and even more so of the survival of the Palestinian cause. The 16th Palestinian National Council was a direct and clear answer to American and Israeli hopes that after Beirut the PLO would split and disappear from the political and military scene. The exuberant Palestinian way of life, culture and national identity – all these things had their place in Algiers in addition to the political discussions. Mahmud Darwish read a long epic on Beirut which stirred memories and strengthened the determination to remain steadfast. A Palestinian living in the USA made a speech to the National Council in his local dialect to demonstrate that he would never forget his language. Even the prisoners in the Israeli internment camp at Al-Ansar were represented at this National Council. They had smuggled drawings about Palestine and the PLO out of the camp. These drawings were exhibited in the foyer of the conference hall. A Palestinian state may still lie far in the future, but Algiers demonstrated beyond all doubt that the Palestinian nation lives. Many delegations acknowledged this in their messages of welcome, expressing their admiration for PLO resistance in Beirut and underlining the need for independent Palestinian decisions and resolutions.

This right was fully asserted by all members of the National Council in the open plenary sessions and in the closed committee meetings. The discussions – as journalists and observers later agreed – were held in a matter-of-fact, extremely democratic atmosphere. Everyone had the chance to express his or her opinion on the conflict or on problems of detail. The crucial discussions were those that took place in the committees where every single phrase was carefully weighed and debated. As previously agreed, the concluding statements to the plenary session were made by the general-secretaries on behalf of their organizations. Among the outstanding speeches at this National Conference were those of Yasser Arafat, Dr George Habbash and Abu Iyyad. Habbash's speech was a political signal that was greeted with applause and appreciation by all delegates. In it, he analysed the dangers of the present phase of Palestinian resistance and stressed the vital need for national unity.

Abu Iyyad's speech – several times interrupted by applause – dealt once again with the crucial questions of a change of direction within the resistance – questions first discussed in the preparatory session in Algiers. With great persuasiveness he put the arguments of Al-Fatah to the conference.

Ahmed Jibril, leader of the Popular Front/General Command, had a rather less happy day. Many delegates left the conference hall in protest at his speech.

Yet the will for unity clearly dominated the speeches and contributions of many other delegates – an attitude which paved the way for the final political communiqué of the Palestinian National Council – which was approved by all organizations.

The Political Declaration of the 16th Conference of the Palestinian National Council stressed, above all, Palestinian national unity, Palestinian independence of decision-making and – after the experience of Beirut – the need to continue the armed struggle in the framework of a united national liberation army.

Also eagerly awaited were the Council's resolutions on the three peace plans and, in particular, on the Reagan plan.

The National Council's statement on the Fez peace plan read:

> The Palestinian National Council regards the Fez resolutions as the minimum for political action by the Arab countries. This should be complemented by military action to alter the balance of power in favour of the Palestinian and Arab rights and struggle. The Council affirms that its understanding of these resolutions does not contradict its commitment to the PLO political programme and resolutions.[10]

Just as it supported the Fez resolutions, so the National Council wholeheartedly backed the Brezhnev plan:

> The Palestinian National Council expresses its appreciation and support for the proposals included in President Brezhnev's plan of September 1981, which affirmed the inalienable national rights of our people, including the right to repatriation, self-determination and the establishment of an independent state under the leadership of the PLO, its sole legitimate representative. The Palestinian National Council also appreciates the stands of the socialist bloc countries towards our people's just cause. These stands

were affirmed in the Prague Communiqué on the Middle East issued on January 3 1983.[11]

The drafting of the resolution on the Reagan plan had been preceded by vehement discussions. The question was whether this plan should be condemned outright or whether a more cautious formulation should be adopted, welcoming its positive aspects. After long discussions a kind of compromise formula was reached.

> The Reagan plan in its procedure and contents does not respond to the Palestinian people's inalienable national rights. The Reagan plan negates the Palestinian rights to repatriation, self-determination and the establishment of a Palestinian state. It also ignores the PLO as the Palestinian people's sole legitimate representative and contradicts its international legitimacy. The Palestinian National Council declares its refusal to consider the plan as a sound basis for a just and permanent settlement to the Palestinian question and the Arab-Zionist conflict.[12]

This formula succeeded in reconciling the various differing opinions and demands. The entire plan had not been rejected as such, only consideration of the 'plan as a sound basis for a just and permanent solution'. By this means the PLO could keep all its options open.

The Reagan plan envisaged that Jordan would play a key role in future peace negotiations. Discussions between Arafat and Hussein on a joint negotiating position and possible confederation between Jordan and a Palestinian state had been taken up even before the National Council. Various Palestinian organizations had spoken out strongly against these discussions. The National Council made it clear that only the PLO could speak and negotiate on behalf of the Palestinian people. The National Council spoke of 'special and distinctive relations that link the Palestinian and Jordanian people.'[13] It said that these relations should be developed further in the interests of both parties, 'to achieve the Palestinian people's inalienable rights'. The statement continues:

> Adherence to the PNC's resolutions relating to relations with Jordan and on the basis that the PLO is the sole legitimate representative of the Palestinian people inside and outside the occupied territories. The Palestinian National Council considers that future relations with Jordan may be established on the basis of a confederation between two independent states.[14]

This was an unequivocal declaration that the PLO would not delegate its right to represent the Palestinian people to anyone, and that its goal remained the establishment of an independent state – and not some form of autonomy.

The PLO's relations with other Arab states also needed clarification. After the experiences of the Lebanon war, these relations could hardly be described as ideal. The most serious strain lay in the PLO's relations with Syria. Syria was dissatisfied with the PLO because Arafat had not taken his troops to Damascus after the withdrawal from Beirut. The Syrian government also disapproved of the contacts and discussions between Arafat and King Hussein. At the National Council conference the PLO reaffirmed its determination to be recognized as an equal partner with Syria.

'The PLO and Syria are on the front line facing the common danger.' Hence the importance of strategic relations between the PLO and Syria. The Council applied the same criticism to Syria as to the Steadfastness and Confrontation Front, namely that they 'did not live up to the standard of required duties during the Zionist invasion of Lebanon'. The Palestinian National Council entrusted the Executive Committee with the conduct of talks with the parties of the Steadfastness and Confrontation Front 'on the means to revive it on a new, effective and clear basis.'

Relations with Egypt were also to be put on a clear basis; the Egyptian delegation was the largest at this National Council. It included almost all the leading figures in the Egyptian opposition. The National Council called for relations with the national democratic forces in Egypt to be reinforced, 'in order that Egypt could return to its militant position in the heart of our Arab nation'. The National Council was also anxious to bring about a rapprochement with the Egyptian government. It reiterated its rejection of the Camp David accords, the autonomy plan and civilian administration. But it also found a formula which did not rule out the possibility of future relations with the Egyptian government.

> The Palestinian National Council calls on the Executive Committee to define relations with the Egyptian regime on the basis of the latter's abandonment of the Camp David policy because this [abandonment] takes into account the fundamental interests of the Arab nation and the Palestinian people's struggle for its national rights.[15]

Another crucial and fiercely-debated item on the Council's agenda was the question of contacts with the peace camp in Israel. For the first time an Israeli journalist, Amnon Kapeliouk, took part in a National Council conference. In previous Council sessions in 1979 and 1981, Arafat's adviser, Issam Sartawi, a firm advocate of such contacts, had been regarded as an outsider. This National Council, far from treating the subject as taboo, called for an open discussion to clarify the issue. In his speech, Abu Iyyad also stressed the need for such contacts.

> On the basis of point 14 of the Political Declaration of the 13th session of the Palestinian National Council of 12.3.1977 the Palestinian National Council calls on the Executive Committee to study activities within this framework in accordance with the interests of the Palestinian question and the Palestinian national struggle.[16]

Behind this somewhat dry formulation lay the determination to pursue the debate, and to pursue such contacts further in an organized framework.

The National Council also called for the 'strengthening of relations with the non-aligned, Islamic and African states' and the 'consolidation of relations with friendly countries in South America' as well as the 'stepping up of political action with West European nations and Japan'.

The National Council expressed its solidarity with the liberation struggles of the peoples of South Africa and of Latin America.

It was undoubtedly a successful achievement that the 16th session of the Palestinian National Council could be held at all, in view of all the difficulties. But this was by no means the most important success. Despite all the predictions, not all of them malicious, the PLO with its Algiers resolutions preserved Palestinian national unity. Algiers guaranteed the democratic nature and the unity of Palestinian decision-making. The PLO, and in particular its leadership under Yasser Arafat, who was unanimously re-elected chairman, emerged even stronger than before. The Fez resolutions remained 'minimal' demands. No doors were unnecessarily closed, either in the political or the military sphere. The 'partial state solution' had been affirmed by all PLO organizations as a viable basis for the present phase of the Palestinian struggle, In Algiers, the PLO demonstrated that it is capable of making policies and of fruitfully integrating political options into its strategic calculations. The PLO rebuilt its political, military, cultural, social and medical institutions. Algiers underlined the political maturity of the Palestinian liberation movement and its legitimacy as the representative of the Palestinian people.

The Algiers consensus pinned its hopes on a political solution of the Palestine conflict.

Notes

1. *Süddeutsche Zeitung*, 7 September 1982.
2. *Le Monde*, 11 September 1982.
3. Ibid.
4. Amerika Dienst. Dokumentation, Bonn. No. 35, 8 September 1982.
5. Ibid.
6. *Pravda*, 16 September 1982.
7. Ibid.
8. Ibid.
9. *Stern*, No. 8/83, 28 April 1983.
10. *Palästina Bulletin*, No. 8/83, 25 February 1983.
11. Ibid.
12. Ibid.
13. Ibid.
14. Ibid.
15. Ibid.
16. Ibid.

A Guide to Further Reading

Abu Iyad, *Palestinien Sans Patrie*. Fayolle, Paris 1978.
Abu Lughod, Ibrahim (ed), *The Transformation of Palestine*. North Western University Press, Evanston 1971.
Adams, Michael, *More Honoured in the Breach than the Observance: Human Rights and the Israeli Occupation*. International Committee for Palestinian Human Rights, Paris 1979.
Ainzstein, Reuben, *They Fought Back: Jewish Resistance in Nazi Europe*. Shocken, NY 1976.
Albright, W F, *The Archaeology of Palestine*. Penguin, Harmondsworth 1949.
Amnesty International, Annual Reports 1978–80.
Antonius, George, *The Arab Awakening*. G P Putnam's Sons, NY 1946.
Arafat, Yasir, 'Speech before the United Nations', November 13 1974. *Journal of Palestine Studies*, Issue No. 14, 1974.
Baron, Ari-Yonah, *Geschichte der Juden im Zeitalter des Talmuds*. 1962.
Begin, Menachem, *The Revolt*. Dell, NY 1978.
Ben Elissar, E, *La Diplomatie du IIIième Reich et les Juifs*. Paris 1969.
Bendt, I and Downing J, *We Shall Return: Women of Palestine*. Zed Press, London 1982.
Ben Gurion, David, *Rebirth and Destiny of Israel*. Yoseloff, London 1959.
Bober, A (ed), *The Other Israel, the Radical Case against Zionism*. Doubleday 1972.
Bottero, J, Cassin, E and Vercoutter, J, *The Near East: The Early Civilizations*. Weidenfeld and Nicolson, London 1967.
Budeiri, Musa, *The Palestine Communist Party 1919–1948*. Ithaca, London 1979.
Caplan, Neil, *Palestine Jewry and the Arab Question 1917–25*. Frank Cass, London 1978.
Cattan, Henry, *Palestine and International Law*. Longman, London 1973.
Collins, L and Lapierre, D, *O Jerusalem!* Weidenfeld and Nicolson, London 1972.
Davis, U, Mack, A and Yuval-Davis, N (eds), *Israel and the Palestinians*. Ithaca, London 1975.
Dayan, Moshe, *The Story of My Life*. Weidenfeld and Nicolson, London 1976.
Dimbleby, J, *The Palestinians*, Quartet, London 1979.
Divine, R, *American Emigration Policy 1924–52*. New Haven, Conn. 1957.
El-Asmar, Fouzi, *To be an Arab in Israel*. Frances Pinter, London 1975.
Ernst, Morris, *So Far So Good*. NY 1948.
Flappan, Simha, *Zionism and the Palestinians*. Croom Helm, London 1979.
Gauthier, Paul, *Jérusalem et le Sang des Pauvres*. Paris 1967.

A Guide to Further Reading

Gilmour, David, *Dispossessed: The Ordeal of the Palestinians*. Sedgwick and Jackson, London 1980.
Goldmann, Nahum, *Mein Leben*, Parts 1 & 2. Munich 1981.
Graham-Brown, Sarah, *Palestinians and their Society 1880–1946*. Quartet, London 1980.
Gray, John, *The Canaanites*. Thames and Hudson, London 1964.
Hadawi, Sami, *Bitter Harvest*. New World Press, NY 1967.
────── *Crime and No Punishment, Zionist-Israeli Terrorism 1939–1972*. Beirut, 1972.
Hammami, Said and Machover, Moshe, 'Vivre Ensemble'. *Hamsin*, No. 3, Maspero, Paris 1976.
Harden, D, *The Phoenicians*. Penguin, London 1980.
Herzl, Theodor, *The Jewish State*. Pordes 1972.
────── *Altneuland*. Kronberg 1978.
────── *Wenn ihr wollt, ist es kein Märchen*. Königstein 1978.
Hirst, David, *The Gun and the Olive Branch*. Faber and Faber, London 1977.
Horn, Carl Von, *Soldiering for Peace*. Cassell, London 1966.
Hütteroth, W D and Abdulfattah, K, *Historical Geography of Palestine, Transjordan and Southern Syria in the late 16th Century*. Erlangen 1977.
Irabi, Abdulkader, *Jerusalem – A collection of UN documents*. IPS, Beirut 1970.
Jansen, Michael, *The Battle of Beirut*. Zed Press, London 1982.
Jingis, Sabri, *The Arabs in Israel*. Monthly Review Press, NY 1976.
Khader, Bichara, *Histoire de la Palestine I–III*. Algiers.
Khalidi, Walid, *From Haven to Conquest*. IPS, Beirut 1971.
Kimche, John and David, *Secret Roads*. Secker and Warburg, London 1955.
Langer, Felicia, *With My Own Eyes*. Ithaca, London 1975.
Leon, Abraham, *The Jewish Question*. Pathfinder.
MacBride, Sean et al, *Israel in Lebanon*, Report of the International Commission. Ithaca, London 1983.
Mathiot, Elisabeth, *L'oppression culturelle dans les territoires occupées*. France – Pays Arabes. France 1979.
Metzger, J, Orth, M and Sterzing, C, *This Land is Our Land*. Zed Press, London 1983.
Moscati, S, *Ancient Semitic Civilisations*. London 1957.
────── *The World of the Phoenicians*. Weidenfeld and Nicolson, London 1968.
────── *The Semites in Ancient History*. Cardiff 1959.
Ott, David, *Palestine in Perspective*. Quartet, London 1980.
Palestine Research Centre, *Black September*. Beirut 1971.
Rodinson, Maxime, *Israel and the Arabs*. Penguin, Harmondsworth 1982.
────── *Israel: A Colonial Settler State?* Monad Press, NY 1973.
Rokach, Livia, *Israel's Sacred Terrorism*. Association of American Arab Graduates, Inc., Belmont, Mass. 1980.
Roy, Raoul, *Jesus, guerrier de l'independence*. Montreal & Paris 1975.
Said, Edward, *The Question of Palestine*. Routledge and Kegan Paul, London 1980.
Sayegh, A, *La confrontation israelo-arabe*. Paris 1969.
Sayegh, Fayez A, *Le Zionisme*. Le Mont.
────── 'The UN and the question of Palestine'. *Journal of Palestine Studies*, 1968.

Sayigh, Rosemary, *Palestinians: From Peasants to Revolutionaries*. Zed Press, London 1979.
Schechtmann, J, *Fighter and Prophet: The Jabotinsky Story*. NY 1961.
Shahak, Israel, *The Non-Jew in the Jewish State*. Jerusalem.
Sharif, Regina, *Non-Jewish Zionism: Its Roots in Western History*. Zed Press, London 1983.
Shehadeh, Raja, *The West Bank and the Rule of Law*. International Commission of Jurists, Geneva 1980.
—————— *The Third Way*. Quartet, London 1982.
Sid-Ahmed, Muhammed, *After the Guns Fall Silent*. Croom Helm, London 1977.
Stevens, Richard P, *American Zionism and US Foreign Policy 1942–47*. IPS, 1962.
Stevens, R and Elmesseri, A, *Israel and South Africa*. New World Press, NY 1976.
Tawil, Raymonda, *My Home, My Prison*. Zed Press, London 1983.
Turki, Fawaz, *The Disinherited*. Monthly Review Press, NY 1972.
UN Documents, *The International Status of the Palestinian People*. NY 1979.
—————— *The Status of Jerusalem*. NY 1979.
Van Arkadie, Brian, *Benefits and Burdens*. Carnegie 1977.
Weinstock, Nathan, *Zionism: False Messiah*. Ink Links, London 1979.
Wild, Stefan, *Ghassan Kanafani*. Wiesbaden 1975.
Yahya, Faris, *Zionist Relations with Nazi Germany*. Palestine Research Centre, Beirut 1979.
Zureik, Elias, *The Palestinians in Israel, A Study in Internal Colonialism*. Routledge and Kegan Paul, London 1978.

MIDDLE EAST TITLES FROM ZED PRESS

POLITICAL ECONOMY

SAMIR AMIN
The Arab Economy Today
(with a comprehensive bibliography of Amin's works)
Hb

B. BERBEROGLU
Turkey in Crisis:
From State Capitalism to Neo-Colonialism
Hb and Pb

SAMIR AMIN
The Arab Nation:
Nationalism and Class Struggles
Hb and Pb

MAXIME RODINSON
Marxism and the Muslim World
Pb

GHALI SHOUKRI
Egypt: Portrait of a President
Sadat's Road to Jerusalem
Hb and Pb

CONTEMPORARY HISTORY/REVOLUTIONARY STRUGGLES

KAMAL JOUMBLATT
I Speak for Lebanon
Hb and Pb

GERARD CHALIAND (EDITOR), A.R. GHASSEMLOU, KENDAL, M. NAZDAR, A. ROOSEVELT AND I.S. VANLY
People Without a Country: The Kurds and Kurdistan
Hb and Pb

ROSEMARY SAYIGH
Palestinians: From Peasants to Revolutionaries
Hb and Pb

BIZHAN JAZANI
Capitalism and Revolution in Iran
Hb and Pb

ABDALLAH FRANJI
The PLO and Palestine
Hb and Pb

SUROOSH IRFANI
Revolutionary Islam in Iran:
Popular Liberation or Religious Dictatorship?
Hb and Pb

PEOPLE'S PRESS
Our Roots are Still Alive
Pb

ANOUAR ABDEL-MALEK (EDITOR)
Contemporary Arab Political Thought
Hb

MICHAEL JANSEN
The Battle of Beirut:
Why Israel Invaded Lebanon
Hb and Pb

REGINA SHARIF
Non-Jewish Zionism:
Its Roots in Western History
Hb and Pb

HUMAN RIGHTS

JAN METZGER, MARTIN ORTH AND CHRISTIAN STERZING
This Land is Our Land:
The West Bank Under Israeli Occupation
Hb and Pb

GERARD CHALIAND AND YVES TERNON
The Armenians: From Genocide to Terrorism
Hb and Pb

WOMEN

ASMA EL DAREER
Woman, Why do you Weep?
Circumcision and Its Consequences
Hb and Pb

AZAR TABARI AND NAHID YEGANEH
In the Shadow of Islam:
The Women's Movement in Iran
Hb and Pb

RAQIYA HAJI DUALEH ABDALLA
Sisters in Affliction:
Circumcision and Infibulation of Women in Africa
Hb and Pb

RAYMONDA TAWIL
My Home, My Prison
Pb

INGELA BENDT AND JAMES DOWNING
We Shall Return:
Women of Palestine
Hb and Pb

MIRANDA DAVIES (EDITOR)
Third World — Second Sex:
Women's Struggles and National Liberation
Hb and Pb

NAWAL EL SAADAWI
The Hidden Face of Eve:
Women in the Arab World
Hb and Pb

NAWAL EL SAADAWI
Woman at Zero Point
Hb and Pb

JULIETTE MINCES
The House of Obedience:
Women in Arab Society
Hb and Pb

Zed press titles cover Africa, Asia, Latin America and the Middle East, as well as general issues affecting the Third World's relations with the rest of the world. Our Series embrace: Imperialism, Women, Political Economy, History, Labour, Voices of Struggle, Human Rights and other areas pertinent to the Third World.

You can order Zed titles direct from Zed Press, 57 Caledonian Road, London, N1 9DN, U.K.

/956.94F814P>C1/